Dukakis
and the Reform Impulse

Dukakis
and the Reform Impulse

by
Richard Gaines and Michael Segal

QUINLAN PRESS
Boston

Published by Quinlan Press
131 Beverly Street, Boston, MA 02114

Printed in the United States of America, 1987.

Library of Congress Cataloging-in-Publication Data

Gaines, Richard.
    Dukakis and the reform impulse.
    Includes index.
    1. Dukakis, Michael. 2. Massachusetts—Governors—
Biography. 3. Massachusetts—Politics and government—
1951-   4. Presidential candidates—United
States—Biography. I. Segal, Michael. II. Title.
F71.3.D85G35 1987   974.4'043'0924   87-43137
ISBN 1-55770-025-7

Acknowledgements

This book, our first, required special measures of love, tolerance and understanding from our families, from whom we, for all intents and purposes, took leaves of absence during the summer and early fall of 1987, when this volume was researched and written. Thank you Lynne, Ben and Rachel Gaines, and Cathy Dunham and Konrad Schlater for putting up with two harried and phantom husbands and fathers for far too many months. Next summer will be different, we promise.

The summer was especially trying for Cathy, who, as a senior policy advisor on Michael Dukakis's State House staff, could not bring herself to read any of our many drafts. Not to worry: the next one, hopefully, will be a cookbook.

Our agent, Helen Rees—who in 1970 came within a few votes of succeeding Michael Dukakis as a state representative in the Massachusetts House of Representatives—responded enthusiastically to our call, and we are grateful.

When we told Michael Dukakis's mother, Euterpe Dukakis, that we were writing a book about her son, she reacted by saying, "What's to write about?" It is an assessment that many people in Massachusetts share of a man of whom it is often said, "What you see is what you get." Our publisher, Henry Quinlan, a student of Massachusetts politics, understood that there had to be depths of complexity to a political leader who set out to transform and uplift politics and government in Massachusetts, and who, over an unrelenting quarter-century effort, achieved his goal. Our many thanks to him for recognizing the potential for a biography of this man.

Sandy Bielawa, our editor at Quinlan Press, brought good humor to this hurry-up project, and Kevin Stevens, also of Quinlan Press, deserves thanks for his efforts.

A special debt of gratitude is owed to Stephen Mindich, the founder, owner and publisher of the *Boston Phoenix*, and *Phoenix* president H. Barry Morris. They were extraordinarily generous and supportive in allowing their editor, Richard Gaines, to divert so much time and effort from his day-to-day responsibilities to work on this book. The editor adds his acknowledgement for the support and understanding of the entire *Phoenix* staff, which compensated for his hardly having been a leader during the four months it took to produce this book.

A special expression of appreciation goes to Eric Selinger, assistant to the editor at the *Phoenix*, who spent countless hours in the clip files of the *Phoenix*, and at the State House, Boston Public and *Brookline Chronicle Citizen* libraries pouring over microfiche of old newspaper stories until he was bleary-eyed. His tireless dedication to this project allowed us to get it done on time. Scott Lehigh and Francis J. Connolly, staff writers at the *Phoenix*, provided invaluable research and conducted helpful interviews, especially on Michael Dukakis's Kennedy School years and second-term chapters. Their assistance permitted us to spend the time we needed to look into the Dukakis's formative years, the ones we knew the least.

Thanks also to John Cronin, chief librarian of the *Boston Herald*, for making time for us to browse through his extensive clip and photo files.

To Dennis Duffin and his always cooperative staff at the Massachusetts Office of Campaign and Political Finance, our thanks for being patient as we thumbed through the contributor reports you have on file—and especially for locating the pages that we were convinced were missing. The staff at the Elections Division of the Massachusetts Office of the Secretary of State was also most helpful in responding to our many requests for election results.

Sandy Bakalar, one of Michael Dukakis's oldest friends, was extraordinarily gracious in taking the time to talk us through the first thirty years of his life, and in providing us with valuable information on Michael and Kitty Dukakis's life together.

Fran Meaney spent many helpful hours with us, and provided considerable amounts of insight and information on the early years of Michael Dukakis's political career, years in which the two former friends were virtually inseparable. We are indeed grateful for his willingness to devote so much time and interest to our project.

Michael Widmer, Michael Dukakis's communications director during most of his first term in office, reviewed the chapters on the seventies, when he worked in the Frank Sargent and Dukakis administrations; predictably, his comments were full of insight and wisdom. Bill Geary, Dick Giesser and Andy Sutcliffe were invaluable resources for this period and for the years after Dukakis was defeated in 1978.

Al Raine, who has served Michael Dukakis in each of his terms in the economic development area, and John DeVillars, Dukakis's chief of operations during the second and third terms, helped us to better understand the evolution of Dukakis into a national figure, and as an activist governor who became dedicated to economic development as his first priority.

We had the pleasure of spending many hours with a few people who have been at the political barricades with Michael Dukakis at various stages of his career. They were our guides as we attempted to reconstruct the life of their friend and colleague. We couldn't have done it without Herb Gleason, Tom Glynn, Beryl Cohen, Joe Grandmaison, Lanny Johnson, Phil Johnston, Steve Kinzer, Dave Liederman, Dolores Mitchell, Dan Payne, Carl Sapers, John Sasso and Frank Sieverts.

And for their assistance as we attempted to fill in the gaps in the life and career of Michael Dukakis, our thanks go out to Marty Abramowitz, Ben Alper, Barbara

Anderson, Peter Anderson, Rick Anderson, Michael Ansara, Chuck Atkins, Joe Baerlein, David Bartley, Frank Bellotti, Dick Bigos, Steve Bing, John Bok, Ben Bradlee, Jr., Kingsbury Brown, Jr., John R. Buckley, Marty Burke, Dick Cauchi, Naomi Feigelson Chase, Jack Cole, Peter Cove, Kristin Demong, Ned Dever, Lou DiNatale, Jim Dorsey, Ray Dougan, Kate Downing, Kitty Dukakis, Susan Estrich, Alice Esty, Bob Farmer, Tom Ferrick, John Finnegan, Jack Flannary, Howard Foley, U.S. Representative Barney Frank, Dan Friedman, Dick Gavone, Kay Gibbs, K. Dun Gifford, Michael Goldman and Jerry Grossman.

Also: Fran Halpern, Betsy Hamrah, Greg Harney, Ken Hartnett, Joan Hertzmark, Bill Homans, Jr., John Isaacson, Ira Jackson, Paul Kantrowitz, Barry Kaplovitz, George Kariotis, Hackie Kassler, Frank Keefe, Robert Keeton, Jim Kerasiotes, Al Kramer, David Kuhn, Joan Lamphier, Ed Lashman, U.S. Senator Carl Levin, Jay Levine, Michael Lipsky, Alan Lupo, Laurence Lynn, Jr., Dick Manley, Bill Masiello, Paul Menton, Mark Moore, Ed Moscovitz, Laurie Nason, Rita Nason, John Petropulos, Tony Podesta, Lincoln Potter, Betsy Reveal, Allan Rodgers, Barbara Salisbury, Fred Salvucci, Jerome Schiller, Jim Segel, Shirley Sidd, Bunny Solomon, Edith Stokey, Jim Stone, Barbara Tanzer, Bob Weinberg, Dan White, Kevin White, Ralph Whitehead, Bob Wool, Leonard Zakim, Richard Zeckhauser and Nick Zervas.

In a very real sense, this book is their book. They are, however, not responsible for the judgments and opinions expressed herein, or for any errors that were made.

Contents

Dukakis
and the Reform Impulse

Preface

What kind of a president of the United States would Michael Stanley Dukakis be?

Prospectively, no one can know how an individual will behave and perform under the pressures of the office, but it is possible to suggest the probabilities. That is what we have attempted to do in this book.

When it became clear in the first months of 1987 that Dukakis, the three-term governor of Massachusetts, would run for the Democratic nomination for president, we began to write a biography that attempted to lay out his formative experiences—the cultural, intellectual, political and familial forces—in his career in politics.

No one seeking the presidency is a simple study. We found Dukakis to embody a remarkable set of contradictions. Lean, at five-foot, eight inches tall, most comfortable in corduroys and a crew-neck sweater, puttering around the house making pancakes or muffins on a weekend morning before heading off to do the supermarket shopping—he is truly an Everyman, the practical, earnest, unpretentious Mr. Rogers of politics, the son of a family physician and a schoolteacher turned homemaker, whose grandfathers in the old country were a shopkeeper and clerk, respectively.

We found an idealistic reformer and an iconoclast who forged a political transformation in Massachusetts that came to comport closely with the democracy he had imagined. This unpretentious man drove himself relentlessly until he had obtained a power and influence over his state that is unmatched in the long history of Massachusetts.

The Michael Dukakis we came to know combines a standard of moral rectitude worthy of Cotton Mather with a prideful ambition worthy of John F. Kennedy. In Dukakis coexists a strain of modernity, the practice of secular humanism with its respect for human and civil rights and privacy, and an old-world dedication to the family as the building block of social stability.

To begin to understand him, one must think of Dukakis as a seventeen-year-old runner in the Boston Marathon, who, to this day, has, as his only known vice, a preference for too much coffee. A man of remarkable discipline, Dukakis loves structure, and structure requires discipline. Day in and day out, routinely at 6:00

p.m., Michael Dukakis goes home to be with his family for dinner. It does not matter what contretemps may be embroiling his administration. He will deal with it in the morning. After dinner, Dukakis reviews the approximately six inches of paperwork brought home from the office, scans the nightly TV news, and then walks the sidewalks of his suburban neighborhood, clutching his "heavy hands."

In Dukakis, we found a political hybrid. He was formed politically in the fifties in response to the frightening prospect of Wisconsin Senator Joseph McCarthy's brand of anti-communism bordering on paranoia, when even the most modest expression of international cooperation and political dissent was fraught with danger. He came of age in the sixties, when progressive politics was organized, vocal and decidedly anti-establishment.

In writing this book, we repeatedly were forced to choose incidences and events from a vast pool of material to develop a portrait that fairly reflects the life and times of Michael Dukakis. In this endeavor, we were not aided by the subject, who did not make himself available for interview.

The portrait of Dukakis that follows emerged from hundreds of hours of conversations with Michael Dukakis's closest friends, political allies and adversaries, whom we know from covering Michael Dukakis and the Massachusetts political scene for many years. In addition, we reviewed scores of books, newspaper, magazine and political journal articles, and government documents.

In the process, we came to see post-war Massachusetts transformed by economic and cultural forces, and Michael Dukakis as the catalytic element in the political transformation that followed. This book, the first extended look into the transformation and the transformer, is a starting point, not the final word.

Richard Gaines
Michael Segal
November 1987

Introduction

Michael Dukakis began his quest in 1960, twenty-seven years before he set out on his run for the White House. It was a remarkably ambitious quest, one to cleanse the Massachusetts political system of its legendary corruption and lethargy, its cynicism and cynics; a quest for reform which would invigorate the government and give it new, honorable and able leaders.

This vision, in the mind of the 27-year-old honors graduate from Swarthmore College, was no mere wistful daydream of a young romantic. To be sure, Dukakis was both a romantic and an idealist. He was imbued by his parents—proper, educated and strong-willed Greek immigrants—with a deep-seated need to serve society and, in the process, to get ahead, but his picture of a reform government was hardly a daydream.

In 1960, at Harvard Law School, Dukakis was bursting with self-confidence. He had succeeded at almost everything he had tried, and he believed he could lead a movement that would transform the Democratic party of Massachusetts to reflect the energy and idealism he so admired in John F. Kennedy. When Kennedy, who was born in Dukakis's hometown of Brookline—on the opposite side of town from where Mike Dukakis grew up—won the 1960 presidential election, setting off orgies of chauvinistic celebration, Dukakis dwelt on the concurrent demise of the state Democratic ticket, and felt the need and the desire to bring the state Democratic party back to life.

In college Dukakis dedicated himself to public service and elective office. He had a brilliant mind, was highly disciplined and was gifted with a near-photographic memory. But Dukakis was not an introspective sort. He used his intellectual skills, together with moral righteousness—another trait of both parents—to determine his life's work, which he pursued with a boundless physical energy that seemed to exude from his athlete's body.

The mental, moral and physical expressions of Mike Dukakis were of an intensity that set him apart and made him a natural leader. He was constantly thinking, constantly lecturing—like the teacher his mother had been—and constantly on the go. The organization that carried Dukakis's ambition in 1960 was the Commonwealth Organization of Democrats (COD); a group founded by Dukakis and a handful of his friends, COD was aimed at attracting new blood to the dissolute Democratic party of Massachusetts. Their goal was simple: to elect more and more honest, energetic and talented young Democrats to ward and town party commit- tees and to the state legislature up on Beacon Hill in Boston until the government was reformed to comport with the values which they held.

Dukakis and his friends were reformers, spiritual descendants of the Puritans, who had worked to create a new heaven on earth, as surely as they were inspired by the Progressives around the turn of the century, who spoke in moral terms, set impossible standards, attacked concentrations of wealth and political power, and proposed the nation's first anti-trust laws, regulatory commissions and consumer protection statutes, wanting nothing less than to transform governments into voices of truth.

In 1909 the historian Herbert Croly wrote that reform is "a moral protest and awakening, which seeks to enforce the violated laws and to restore the American political and economic system to its pristine purity and vigor.... Reform means at bottom no more than moral and political purification." Fifty-one years later, in 1960, Michael Dukakis began working systematically on the moral and political purification of the Democratic party of Massachusetts and the government of his state.

The *Boston Globe* devoted half a page to the nascent reform movement on November 27, 1960. Under the headline "Young Democrats Plotting To Give Party New Blood," columnist James H. Hammond explained that COD was committed to reforming the government from the inside. "They pledge their allegiance to the party now and in the future," he wrote. "They disavow any label such as liberal or conservative." Hammond quoted a spokesman for COD as saying, "Our im- mediate goal is to get young blood out in the '62 election and put some of them into office. We are not rebels. We just want people with ability."

To be sure, the young Mike Dukakis and his co-founders of COD were people of ability: well-bred, well-educated professionals or soon-to-be professionals. But they were also rebels of a sort; not radicals in a philosophical sense, but rebels in their restlessness to take over their party and, one day, hopefully, their state govern- ment. In the process they wanted to revitalize democracy itself by making it work as it was intended. In 1962 COD succeeded in electing a handful of reformers, including Dukakis, to the Massachusetts House.

The trap set for Dukakis and COD, as Professor Samuel P. Huntington of Har- vard University points out in *American Politics: The Promise of Disharmony,* is that the "intense moral fervor that gives reformers and the reform movement their political power cannot be sustained for any length of time." An additional prob- lem noted by Huntington is that those reforms with the broadest appeal, which are therefore most easily achieved, are, paradoxically, those that are least likely to be supported by a well-organized constituency. Thus, they are those most easily corrupted and eroded. As a result, reform eras in American politics—the Jacksonian reforms of 1820-1840, the Progressive period of 1890-1920, and the political party participation reforms of the 1970s—while passionate and powerful, were relatively short-lived.

But the effect on the politics and government of Massachusetts that Dukakis and his crusade achieved has proved an exception to the historical pattern. In the fall of 1987, in the first year of his third term as governor of Massachusetts—while running for president—Dukakis removed doubt about his capacity to sustain moral fervor and the spirit of reform by taking personal charge of a stalled effort to craft the greatest reform of his career: an intricate piece of legislation designed to provide health insurance to the six hundred thousand residents of Massachusetts who have none, meanwhile containing the cost of hospital care.

As for the conundrum of how reform government is sustained, the answer for Dukakis was electoral. If reformers ran the government, the reform spirit would be safe. Dukakis took his reform spirit into electoral politics and encouraged other people from one corner of the state to the other to do so as well. From 1960 until he ran for statewide office in 1970, he routinely spent as many as three or four nights each week on the road, recruiting young professionals like himself to run and serve on local ward and town Democratic party committees, and he encouraged them to serve as delegates to semi-annual state party endorsing conventions so that they could help elect young reformers to serve on Beacon Hill.

After winning a seat in the state legislature in 1962, Dukakis achieved reform after reform throughout the decade. His terms as a legislator climaxed with the success of a three-year effort to reform the state's auto insurance system, which was charging Massachusetts drivers the highest rates in the nation. The springboard of auto insurance reform lifted Dukakis onto the statewide Democratic ticket as the nominee for lieutenant governor in 1970. After his ticket was defeated, Dukakis set about getting himself elected governor at the next election. When he won in 1974, he went forth with messianic zeal systematically to reform the government without the slightest concern for the political toll he would pay. His term in office climaxed in 1978 with a reform of the entire state court system which dwarfed the auto insurance reform in its technical and political complexity.

After a coalition of interests whose arrangements he had challenged and whose special advantages he had attacked drove him from office in 1978, the analytical Dukakis examined how and why he had failed, in the process providing new evidence, or so it seemed, that reform movements "cannot be sustained for any length of time." He determined how it might be possible to fuse the reform impulse to a realpolitik in a way that would allow him to stay around until Massachusetts was habituated to reform values.

In the most bitter and costly election in memory, Dukakis roared back to the governorship in the 1982 elections, triumphing over the conservative businessman who had beaten him four years earlier, and proceeded to institute reforms in how the state collects taxes and spends money on welfare recipients, reforms that were so creative and appealing across the ideological spectrum that they lifted Dukakis to prominence in the national Democratic party.

Deeply traumatized by his loss in 1978 and conscious of the futility of transient reform efforts, Dukakis took nothing for granted when he ran for reelection in 1986. For his efforts, he got 69 percent of the vote in November. He was the reformer entrenched. His power unchallenged, he had become the unquestioned boss of Massachusetts politics. And a clean, honest, intellectual, zealous and family-oriented boss at that.

He was, by then, the reformer who was running for president.

Chapter 1
Panagis Doukakis and Euterpe Boukis

As Panos Doukakis rode the train through the Maine woods on a sunny Saturday morning in the spring of 1920, traveling back to Bates College, he could not stop thinking about the beautiful high school girl who had said hello to him back at the station in Haverhill.

Doukakis had gone to Haverhill, on the banks of the Merrimack River just across the New Hampshire border in Massachusetts, as a member of Professor George Chase's Philhellenic Club to perform Euripides' *Hippolytus* for the large Greek community of the factory city. A noted scholar of ancient Greek, Professor Chase each year directed a different classical Greek play, which was performed for campus audiences; the production for 1920 had been so good that he wanted to see it performed off campus. Nick Boukis, a leader of the Greek community of Haverhill, had heard of Professor Chase and his troupe. Thinking that his friends and neighbors would enjoy the play, he invited the professor to bring his play to their town. Chase agreed, and a single performance was given on a Friday night.

One of Nick Boukis's four younger sisters, Euterpe, could not attend. A serious student with a love for learning, especially literature and history, the seventeen-year-old high school junior had responsibilities at school that night from which she could not be excused; she had to dance at a gym exhibition. Since she was still considering what college to attend, she was determined at least to meet the Bates professor, his wife and the troup, before they left town. To this end, Euterpe made it down to the railroad station just in time on Saturday morning; there she talked briefly with the crew from Bates, including Panos Doukakis, a pre-medical student, before they headed north.

Doukakis lived in Lowell, a larger city than Haverhill with many woolen mills not fifteen miles down river. Even though he and Euterpe Boukis had spoken for only a few moments, he was smitten. She was the girl for him, he knew it immediately.

His instincts were good; the two had much in common beyond their Greek heritage. Both were ambitious, sober and mannered, with simple tastes, and they were loyal, serious, determined and intellectually curious. He tended to be impulsive, she was analytical. Once set in mind, they could be headstrong and stubborn. They liked balanced, patterned lives.

Panos Doukakis (he was given the name Panagis at birth but was always called Panos) had come to the United States in 1912, at the age of fifteen, to live with his older brother, Arthur. The boys, members of a large family of Greek nationals originally from the island of Lesbos, grew up in Asia Minor in the commercial center of Edremite. The Doukakis family owned and ran a successful general merchandise store and, as part of a large and prosperous Greek community, lived quietly and peaceably among the quiescent Turkish majority in the years around the turn of the century, as the Ottoman Empire faded.

In 1908 a group of army officers, disgusted at the decline of Turkish fortunes, took control of the government. These "Young Turks," as they were known, were determined to modernize and revitalize Turkey, and give the nation first-rank standing. Whispers of nationalism, encouraged by the Young Turks, began to be heard across the country. As the nationalism turned xenophobic, many foreign nationals fled. The Doukakises' business began to fail. Arthur decided, much against his father's wishes, to emigrate to America, which he did in 1910.

He settled in Manchester, New Hampshire, one of the region's largest industrial cities, where row after row of brick factories lined the Merrimack River. In Manchester Arthur Doukakis changed his name to Arthur Duke, and when his younger brother Panos arrived four years later, he was told his name in the new country would be Peter Duke; he went to work in the mills sweeping floors. Soon after Panos arrived, the Dukes moved down the Merrimack just over the Massachusetts border to the factory city of Lawrence.

Frequently displaced by war and social upheavals, the Greeks long had valued education as the irrevocable key to economic security, and Peter Duke, a short, broad-shouldered, very serious boy, came to the United States determined to get educated. In Lawrence, that meant working at a Greek lunchroom during the day so that he could afford to attend night school at the YMCA, where he learned English. He enrolled at American International College, a school in Springfield, in western Massachusetts, dedicated to educating foreign-born students—and he did so as Panos Dukakis—his original name minus the unnecessary "o" of the diphthong. He was in America, but he was proud of his Greek heritage. Alternating between work and school, Dukakis took more than four years to get through AIC, but finally he graduated.

After AIC Dukakis decided to become a physician, and he entered a pre-medical program at Boston University. After a year, however, he decided that he missed the kind of campus life he had had at AIC, so, in 1921, he transferred to rustic Bates, a small, co-educational liberal arts school with a reputation for academic excellence.

Like the Doukakises, during the last years of the nineteenth century and the first years of the twentieth, tens of thousands of Greeks came to the United States to escape from the seemingly endless dislocations brought on by the deep-rooted Greek-Turkish conflict and because of the desire of the generation growing up in the new century to try the land of opportunity. The Boukises originally came from Epirus and settled in Larissa, the capital of Thessaly province, in northern Greece.

The Larissa of Euterpe Boukis's youth, population twenty-five thousand, was a center of radical political activity. In 1906 seventeen thousand refugees streamed into Larissa fleeing political disturbances nearby, and it took the Greek government two years to build villages for them to live in. Bands of propertyless anarchists were beginning to make their presence felt. Finally, in 1910, fighting broke out in Larissa aimed primarily at the remaining Moslem property holders. The Turkish army, which fought a debilitating war with Greece in 1897, was once again amassing troops on the Thessaly border. Within three years, another ninety thousand refugees would seek a safe haven in Thessaly province as the Balkan Wars erupted, adding further stress to an already fragile, agrarian economy and encouraging increasing numbers of Greeks to seek a more secure future elsewhere.

Michael Boukis, Euterpe's father, was a clerk and an intellectual. It was a learned household in Larissa, though one of decidedly modest means. Nick, "a young man of adventurous spirit," said Euterpe of her older brother, left for the United States with high hopes to live with an uncle in Manchester, New Hampshire, in 1907, but soon moved, first to Brockton, Massachusetts, and then to Haverhill, where he worked in a shoe factory and became a community political leader. A couple of years later he brought his younger brother Adam over, and by 1913 the brothers had saved enough money to bring over their parents and four sisters, reuniting the family. The industrial revolution, hungry for unskilled labor, and the steamship firms, which were often owned by industrialists, were making it easy to afford passage to America. It cost Nick and Adam Boukis a total of eighty dollars to bring their six family members across the Atlantic. The Boukis girls and their parents made the difficult journey from the port of Patras to New York City on a converted coal freighter.

Clearing immigration on Ellis Island was a traumatic experience for Euterpe. "It was the physical exam; you didn't know if you were going to be sent back," she said. "I, as a child, understood that. I remember very well the doctor roughly turning up my eyelids. I had the pain for days." Afterward, the Boukises took a steamship on an overnight journey through Long Island Sound to Fall River, Massachusetts. From there, the family traveled by train to Haverhill, a shoe and textile manufacturing city about twice the size as Larissa, not ten miles northeast of Lawrence on the Merrimack River, where the Dukakises had settled.

Nine-year-old Euterpe had gone to school in Larissa, and though she knew not a word of English when she arrived, she had already mastered the basics of reading, writing and arithmetic. She and her younger sister Efti spent the first six months in Haverhill unable to communicate in English, except to say "hello, goodbye and that sort of thing," she said. "And after six months, both my sister and I spoke English fluently, as if we had always spoken it. We just absorbed English because we were very young."

Her elementary school principal, Stanley Grey, took Euterpe and a small number of the most intelligent students under his wing. He worked with them for years before and after classes "on our algebra, and in English, in literature," she said. "We read Shakespeare. My goodness, how many of them we read in eighth grade." With a remarkable memory, a serene disposition and dauntless dedication, Euterpe flew through elementary school, skipped the ninth grade and earned good marks in high school. She found she had a special propensity for languages, but was not strong in the sciences.

It was her meeting with Professor Chase and the rest of the troupe that started Euterpe Boukis thinking about Bates. With the encouragement of Stanley Grey, a native of Maine who knew of the small, well-respected liberal arts college, she became the first Greek woman from Haverhill to go off to college and the first Greek woman ever to matriculate at Bates.

By the time Euterpe entered Bates, Panos was off to Boston to work his way through Harvard Medical School, but he continued to think about Euterpe as his girl. Quietly but effectively, he managed to keep track of her through family connections and common acquaintances. Euterpe's sisters were wed through arranged marriages, and one sister who was living in Lowell was acquainted with members of the Dukakis family, who were also living there. On a couple of occasions Panos and Euterpe crossed paths and spoke briefly with one another. But Panos gave no hint of his feelings for Euterpe.

At Bates, majoring in English and history, Euterpe Boukis maintained her academic excellence. "She was definitely the kind of person who has everything under control," said Alice Esty, her roommate for her final two years at Bates. "She had a kind of pragmatism. She wasn't inclined to do visionary things. Life was acceptable. Her parents expected her to bring home A's. She brought home A's. She had an extraordinarily good memory; it was part of her extraordinarily good mind.

"She wasn't in the socializing part of college," Esty said. "She wasn't playing cards. She was totally dedicated to her work. She was curious about everything."

"I was not so serious [a student]," said Euterpe. "I was consistent. I did my work. I did my studies. I did my preparations every day. I did not let go of anything." And she never had to cram for an exam. For fun and to break up the tedium of studies, Euterpe and Alice would go for long walks and sing, in perfect harmony, romantic ballads of the day like "Beautiful Ohio."

To pay for her studies at Bates, Euterpe worked in a shoe factory during the summer. She was able to save about two hundred and fifty dollars each summer, half of what was needed to cover the next year's tuition, room and board; Nick and Adam helped out with what her scholarship did not cover.

In the spring of 1925, after thirteen years in the United States, Euterpe Boukis, age twenty-one, was honored for her academic excellence by election to the Phi Beta Kappa honors society and was graduated from Bates College. Because of her Greek nationality, she had some trouble finding a teaching job. She nonetheless kept looking until she got a job teaching in the little New Hampshire town of Ashland, where she stayed for two years, living in a house with a family and another teacher. Then in 1927, Euterpe found a teaching job in Amesbury, Massachusetts, a small city on the Merrimack closer to the mouth of the river and not far from her family in Haverhill. There, in the junior high school, she taught French, Latin, English, history—everything but the sciences.

After Panos Dukakis was graduated from Harvard Medical School, he interned at Boston City Hospital and Boston Lying-in Hospital. He did his residency at Providence City Hospital before setting up a medical practice of his own. Always severe, hard-driving and self-motivated, Panos worked tirelessly, often seven days a week, learning surgery, obstetrics and gynecology. After nearly five years of hospital training, Dr. Panos Dukakis opened his office for the general practice of medicine in a brownstone building opposite the Boston Museum of Fine Arts on Huntington Avenue, a few blocks from Symphony Hall. He continued to work seven days a week, and soon he had developed a respectable practice.

With his professional standing now established, the exceedingly proper physician decided it was time to announce his intentions. "I think he wrote or called me when I was in Amesbury," Euterpe said. "Could he come to see me? I said, 'Fine.' " Though the Boukises had married off Euterpe's sisters, they had not ever considered the same treatment for their fiercely proud, willful and independent Phi Beta Kappa daughter. "The family knew that could not be with me," she said.

"I always said that Pan was so Greek that he had to be completely well established before he would go and get himself a wife," she said. "So, when he was ready to marry, he came after me. But, of course, we had known each other, but not very much. We had never dated, or corresponded, or anything like that." On their second date, Dr. Dukakis proposed marriage. "He was talking about our life together; how much he cared for me. And I said, 'Well, just wait a minute! We don't know each other.' He said, 'What do you mean, we don't know each other? We've known each other for ten years.' "

In the spring of 1929, Euterpe Boukis became engaged to Dr. Panos Dukakis, a decade after the fleeting handshake and hellos on the railroad station platform in Haverhill with Professor Chase and the cast of Euripides' *Hippolytus*. They were married September 4, 1929, on the eve of the Great Depression. "He'd always told me that, from the first time he saw me, he decided that this was the girl for him," she said.

Chapter 2
The All-American Boy

At the time of the American Revolution, Brookline was a farming town of 350 inhabitants; by the middle of the nineteenth century, merchants, artisans, tradesmen, commercial farmers and farm laborers had swelled the population. With mass transportation at mid-century came middle-class commuters and some blue-collar workers, but Brookline was still a wealthy Yankee town, and after the Civil War it became a bastion of Republicanism.

Frederick Law Olmstead, who created Boston's famous Emerald Necklace of parks, helped produce a true suburban-style development form in Brookline beginning around 1880. Olmstead, who laid out subdivisions into the twentieth century, favored curved rather than straight streets, and irregular-shaped lots with houses set back from the road, often screened by trees and shrubs, or concealed by the contours of the land. His goal was to maximize the rural illusion and the symbolic associations of nature. The rolling topography of Brookline was perfectly suited to Olmstead's vision of the ideal suburban town.

It was at the end of the last century that Brookline became substantially wealthier and even more of an elite enclave, when the old monied aristocracy of Boston, much of it anyway, moved out to Brookline. The old line Brahmins fled their luxurious townhouses in Boston as the city they had built and had pretty much had to themselves since their ancestors first settled there in the early seventeenth century was overwhelmed, so they felt, by the Irish hordes. The Irish were escaping famine in the old country, beginning at mid-century, and after huddling in hated ghettos near Boston's waterfront for a generation, were now, by sheer dint of number and a dawning understanding of the ways of the land of opportunity—especially the way the politics of this democracy worked—taking over.

Brookline offered the wealthy Yankees a perfect escape, and compelling inducements. There were fine homes on large lots convenient to the downtown centers of finance and commerce, in a well-run community unthreatened by the great mass of Irish Democrats but connected to Boston by clean and efficient streetcar and subway lines.

The same trollies that carried the corporate and financial leaders of Boston into the city from Brookline in the mornings were packed on the return trips with Irish women from the ghettos. They were heading out to Brookline to work as domestics or, if they were fortunate, as nannies. According to the 1895 census of Massachusetts, on average a full seven out of every ten households in Brookline employed female servants. No other community could come close to competing with that kind of gentility. In fact, in no other community did even half the households enjoy the luxury of "help." In Boston, overall, there was a servant in not quite two out of every ten households.

Not only was Brookline extraordinarily rich, it was exceedingly well run, through the town meeting system of government, a legacy of seventeenth-century New England. In town meeting government, residents elected town meeting members from precincts; the town meeting served as the legislative and appropriating body. Executive duties and the administration of the town's affairs were conducted by a board of selectmen, which was elected townwide.

Town meeting government, which was a model for the Founding Fathers, tended to be quite a direct form of democracy, especially when practiced in small communities. Brookline, as towns go, was unusually large—it had the largest population of all Massachusetts towns throughout much of its modern history—but, because of its educated and professional populace, it managed over the years to conduct its political affairs with tolerable efficiency and laudable effectiveness. Here was Democratic government that worked beautifully; of course, it was democratic government of, by and for the elite of Massachusetts, for the most part.

By the time Dr. Panos and Euterpe Dukakis settled in Brookline to raise a family, the town had long been legendary. At a time when urban life was losing its appeal to the middle class, Brookline became a veritable model of suburbanization, and an inspiration for it. Newspapers from as far away as Baltimore had published glowing accounts of the miracle in Massachusetts. In 1898 an article, "Brookline: A Model Town Under the Referendum," was published in *Arena* magazine. In 1904 the same publication gave its readers another piece on Brookline, "Democracy and Municipal Government; or How the Richest Town in the World Is Governed by the Referendum." And in 1908 *New England Magazine* reported on Brookline with an article entitled: "The Wealthiest Town in the World and the Best Governed."

Pre-war Brookline was still then a Republican stronghold, surrounded by Democratic Boston, but now the town was more developed. Into the stately apartments along tree-lined Beacon Street and into the handsome suburban homes in South Brookline came many Jews, who had settled in Boston after emigrating from Europe, and third- and fourth-generation Irish, the middle-class "Lace Curtain Irish," as they were called. What the new middle class of young lawyers, merchants and other professionals sought from Brookline, for the most part, was peace and quiet close to the city, and access to what had been for a long time one of the finest public school systems in the nation. When the Dukakises settled in Brookline, the ratio of Yankees to Irish to Jews was two to one to one.

By all accounts, the Dukakis family was happy, stable, dedicated to one another, exceptionally disciplined and hard-working. A Spartan quality, strongly present in both Dr. Dukakis and Euterpe, was transmitted to the boys. Responsibilities to the family were assigned and carried out, no questions asked. Every Sunday Euterpe would take out the old steam iron and go from Panos's closet to Stelian's to Michael's, pressing their suits, slacks and shirts. Along with the rigorous discipline the Greek immigrants demanded of their children was instilled a parsimony. To the Dukakis household, material possessions did not bring happiness; nor were they the measure of success.

The boys learned Greek and English at home; they used Greek to communicate with Grandmother Dukakis, who lived with the family on Rangely Road. Michael's first word was "*yaka* (grandma)" and his first phrase was "*monos mou* (by myself)." Stelian and his little brother were both extremely bright, and Michael seemed to have something of a photographic memory, a gift passed down from Euterpe. As a child, Michael would go off by himself, to stand before a mirror to work on his pronounciations of new words. Like his mother, Michael was gifted in languages.

Like many immigrants, Dr. and Mrs. Dukakis pushed their children to take advantage of the "land of opportunity," a phrase that was repeated time and again at 210 Rangely Road. Yet, although they were determined that their children would benefit from the opportunities America—and Brookline—had to offer that could only be dreamed of back in Greece, the couple initially was not active in American politics.

The Great Depression had knocked much of the rest of the nation off its feet, but so long ago had Brookline become filled with old money that it was spared the extremes of economic hardship; the town continued to support its fine municipal golf course throughout the thirties. Republican Brookline, untraumatized by the Depression, was not a bastion of New Deal ferment. Likewise, the family physician and the simple life he and his family led were generally unaffected in any dramatic way. The Dukakises were not New Dealers; in fact, they were not even registered voters in the thirties, but they did care about civics and current events, gathering together around the radio to listen to the six o'clock news each night.

Dr. Dukakis ("Panagis Doukakis," as his name is recorded on town voter and residence lists) first registered to vote, as an "unenrolled" (Independent) voter, in 1940, the year Democrat Franklin Delano Roosevelt won an unprecedented third term. In the Dukakis household, interest in the presidential election of 1940 was high. Stelian, ten, and Michael, seven, kept tabs on the convention balloting in the Republican party on a scorecard while listening to the states one by one announce in dramatic fashion whether their delegations favored Thomas Dewey, Wendell Wilkie or Robert Taft.

With Roosevelt running for a fourth term in 1944, Dr. Dukakis reregistered as a Republican, presumably to vote for FDR's opponent, Dewey. The next year, Dr. Dukakis returned to the unenrolled designation, which he maintained until 1953. After that, and until 1962, when Michael began his political career as a Democrat, Dr. Dukakis shifted back and forth between Republican party affiliation and no party affiliation.

Euterpe, like her husband, moved back and forth between Republican and unenrolled registration, but she was already registered in 1934, the year after Michael was born and six years before her husband. These Dukakises took their independence seriously. While her husband was a Republican or an unenrolled voter for the seven years, 1956 to 1962, Euterpe became a Democrat, beginning in 1956, the year Democratic Illinois Governor Adlai Stevenson made his second campaign against Dwight Eisenhower, the incumbent Republican, and remains one to this day.

Michael's political career began on a modest, if encouraging note, when he was elected president of his third-grade class at the Baker School. He was a self-motivated, conscientious and serious child who devoted himself to both his schoolwork and sports; baseball was an early passion. Typically, he practiced long and hard, until he was satisfied he could play up to the standards he had set for himself; he made himself into a pretty good right-handed contact hitter and catcher—he called the signals. Stelian hardly took a back seat to his younger brother. Three years ahead of Mike in school, Stelian was brilliant, handsome and an impressive athlete.

Mike Dukakis excelled at almost everything he tried, and seemed to find time for just about everything; it was when he got to Brookline High School that hints of his vast potential began to emerge. Throughout his four years at B.H.S., a school with a long-standing reputation as one of the finest high schools in the nation, Mike Dukakis was acknowledged as the smartest and most dedicated student. And he found time to become an Eagle Scout. But Dukakis was not a bookworm. Bookworms do not letter in baseball, basketball, cross country and tennis, as Michael did, meanwhile picking up enough trumpet to play in the band. He was, even then, recognized as an extraordinarily energetic and honorable young man, precisely the kind of fellow who emerges as the natural leader, not by dint of compelling personality or charm, but because his peers acknowledge his superior capabilities and willingness and desire to lead.

So it was that Mike Dukakis, the president of his third-grade class, an exceedingly serious student leader with little time for idle chatter, a handsome young man but hardly a hunk, was elected vice president of the class of '51 in his freshman, sophomore and junior years. His life then was steeped in the values of his family; he was a zealous idealist, dedicated to taking full advantage of every iota of opportunity Brookline High School could offer him—and remembering almost everything along the way. In return, he served B.H.S. with the same dedication and commitment. In these ways, he was very much the classic All-American Boy.

But in other ways, he did not quite fit the mold. For one thing, Mike Dukakis was so serious, so idealistic and so honorable that the fun component in the All-American Boy image was seriously lacking. He was even something of a scold. While Dukakis was a student, Brookline High switched from glass milk bottles to the newfangled, disposable waxed paper containers for the lunchroom. Kids being kids, the containers soon presented a new litter problem. Mike Dukakis being Mike Dukakis, he went around informing the litterbugs of their civic and school responsibilities. "It's not right to make other people pick up after you," he never tired of repeating to his classmates. It wasn't that he wanted to preach the gospel of responsibility to his schoolmates; it was just that Mike Dukakis did not know any better than to hold his peers to the same standards he was trained to hold himself to by his stern and demanding, yet loving and supportive parents. If there was a bit of a goody-two-shoes in this All-American Boy, there was also a bit less litter around B.H.S. while the class of '51 was still in school.

Dukakis's senior year at Brookline High was one of extraordinary personal achievement. He played varsity baseball and basketball, ran cross country, was captain of the tennis team, and continued to blow trumpet for the band. He was chosen president of Alpha Pi, the school's honor society, a distinction given to the student who had accumulated the greatest number of A grades. About the only honor and achievement that still eluded him was the class presidency.

While he had been serving as vice president for the past three years, a friend and back-court mate on the basketball team, Bobby Wool (who went on to serve as political editor for the *Sunday New York Times Magazine*, and who now writes books and publishes a newsletter on tax planning), had been elected president of the class three times. Dukakis might have been the best student and one of the best athletes in the class, but as long as Bobby Wool was around, he would have to concede that he was no better than the second-best politician in the school. Bobby Wool was as good looking as Dukakis—not an insignificant factor in the ways of high school politics, even in Brookline—and he was charming, outgoing and gregarious, distinct advantages when measured against Dukakis's cerebral personality.

In his senior year, Mike Dukakis challenged Bobby Wool for the one prize that had eluded him, the presidency of the class. The Dukakis insurgency failed; the student body had no reason to change presidents, and they decided not to. Dukakis was hardly deterred by his defeat. The next available political prize he could seek, the student council presidency, he ran for and won.

Yet another imperfection in the All-American Boy image of Mike Dukakis was the almost complete lack of a social life. Not that he didn't want one: it was just that socializing was a pleasure, the payoff for achievement, indulged in only when time allowed. For the hard-driving Dukakis, time, it seemed, never allowed. Rather than give up any opportunity for scholastic, athletic or political advancement, the fun stuff just got put on hold. It was a matter of priorities. And Mike Dukakis was nothing if not disciplined.

In April Dukakis, still seventeen, lied about his age to enter the 1951 Boston Marathon, a grueling race from the western suburb of Hopkinton to Boston's Back Bay. Mike strategically positioned Sandy Cohen, a classmate he had begun dating, near the end of the course, in Brookline, holding an orange with the top sliced off so that the underaged runner might get a final burst of energy. Dukakis finished fifty-seventh in a field of 191.

Bright and pretty, Sandy Cohen was Mike's first romantic interest. They had been friends for some time, but he started getting serious about her at the end of their junior year, even though Cohen had been dating Bobby Wool pretty steadily for three years and, in fact, had promised to go with Wool to the senior prom a year ahead of time. ''Nobody would go to the symphony with me,'' she recalls, "just Mike." Along with classical music, Dukakis also loved jazz, and the friends frequently went into Boston to one of its many jazz clubs. And occasionally Sandy and Mike would forego culture for an afternoon at Fenway Park rooting for the Red Sox.

One night Cohen went home with Mike to have dinner with his family. Dr. Dukakis was in his place at the dinner table, the embodiment of stern authority in his tie and vest, as he began to interrogate the somewhat shaken young guest about her grades and her interests. Another night Euterpe tried to show Cohen how to make authentic Greek phyllo dough. The quite proper teacher instructed the pupil: "Now, my dear, you take the corner and fold it along the hypotenuse of the right triangle." Though Mike's friend was very bright, she seemed confused at that. "My dear Sandy," Euterpe asked, "You do recall your geometry from school, don't you?"

Despite his inexperience in courtship, once he set his mind to it, Dukakis swept Cohen off her feet. She found herself becoming romantically involved with him. With the senior prom looming, something had to give. Ever assertive, Dukakis decided it ought to be his friend and rival, and he asked Sandy if she would get Bobby Wool to release her from her commitment of the previous fall to go to the prom with him.

It was clear where Sandy's heart was. While these teenage plans, dreams and negotiations were taking place, before anything was resolved, in the remote possibility that she could somehow show up at the prom arm in arm with Mike, Sandy spent a few weeks teaching the socially inept, bookish jock how to dance the fox trot. So austere was his family background and makeup that he had never gone out with a girl before, and he had no idea how to dance.

But Wool would not give in, not even when Sandy pleaded, in the awkward way of teen love, that it was not fair to deny the student council president the opportunity to attend his senior prom. Bobby Wool had won out over Mike Dukakis again. Sandy ended up going with the class president while the student council president, dateless for his senior prom, checked hats and coats.

Despite his social setback, young Michael Dukakis was clearly the star among his peers at Brookline High. He was selected the "Most Brilliant" male in his class, or "Big Chief Brain in Face," as his class yearbook nicknamed him in the naive and insulting American Indian vernacular used back then. Sandy Cohen, the object of desire of the two big political heavies in her class, was designated "Most Popular." "Mike was the one we always went to when we had problems," says Cohen (now Bakalar). "He was the one who could figure out how a decision would affect everyone else, and the best solution." This sentiment was echoed by many classmates who knew Mike Dukakis well.

But skilled as he was, the solution to some problems was beyond his grasp. It was during Mike's senior year of achievement, first romance and high school politics that Stelian, his big brother, a junior at Bates College, became very depressed and tried to commit suicide. It was a dark and sad turn for the close-knit family. The thought that his big brother, a success story in his own right, was so depressed

that he would try to take his own life weighed heavily on the constitutionally optimistic Dukakis. Stelian came home from Bates and began psychiatric treatment
that would continue for years.

Dukakis had entered Brookline High School imbued with the faith, imparted
by his parents, that he could achieve anything so long as he set his mind to the
task and spared no effort in the process. Now he left Brookline High School for
college at prestigious Swarthmore, a liberal arts school run by the Quakers, armed
with the empirical evidence that his parents had been correct. He hadn't won every
election, aced every exam or won every race. But he had won enough elections and
done well enough in school and on the playing fields to know that he really could
write his own ticket.

Chapter 3
College Days

The best student from the best high school in the Boston area was expected to take his undergraduate education at what was considered to be the best college, which meant Harvard, in Cambridge, Massachusetts, a short commute from Brookline. However, the seventeen-year-old scholar/athlete and pol yearned to leave the nest for the first time and try flying "monos mou," but Harvard was not going to get Mike Dukakis. Sandy Cohen saw her dear friend's decision not to attend the school as an act of rebellion. "The smartest kids always went to Harvard," she recalled. Mike had always been without pretense. It was a sin against which his father vociferously preached and which his mother more quietly avoided. Mike Dukakis would not follow the well-worn course across the Charles River to Harvard Square.

Instead, in September 1951, two months before his eighteenth birthday, Mike Dukakis set up residence outside quiet, secure Brookline for the first time. He unpacked in Wharton Hall on the campus of Swarthmore College, one of only about two hundred members of the class of '55. Dukakis had left the nest, but the environment at Swarthmore was remarkably similar to the one he had left behind.

Located eight miles west of Philadelphia, Swarthmore was a prosperous town of 4,800, with large, gracious Victorian and Tudor-style homes. Its households were headed for the most part by moderate, comfortable Republicans: successful businessmen, lawyers and executives who commuted daily into the city. The region's claim to fame was the presence of Swarthmore College, an institution founded by the Quakers and known for its liberal arts curriculum, high academic standards and its capacity to attract intelligent and well-to-do students. Entering Swarthmore with Dukakis and the class of '55 were a child of U.S. Supreme Court Justice Hugo Black and one of Supreme Court Justice William O. Douglas's children. Swarthmore long had been the most expensive school in the area. Because of its Quaker roots, it was also a school that tolerated, indeed encouraged, social activism and political dissent, even in the bland fifties. Like Brookline, Swarthmore was but a short train ride away from the big city.

Away from home for the first time, Michael relied on Sandy Cohen to keep him informed about Stelian's struggle with his emotional demons. Cohen had gone to college at Wellesley, less than thirty minutes from Brookline, and was solicitous of Stelian, bringing him out to Wellesley for day visits, and at night calling Michael in Pennsylvania to fill him on how his brother was doing. Michael himself remained too busy for dating, treating college as he had treated high school. He was all but oblivious to the existence nearby of Bryn Mawr, a prestigious women's college.

For Dukakis, the proximity to Philadelphia was fortuitous, as was the timing of his arrival. Imbued as he was with the sense of adventure—footloose for the first time—Dukakis was just settling in at Swarthmore, getting his bearings, when his imagination was fired by news of an exciting election campaign that was roaring in the city. After the small-time politics of Brookline High School, here was the real thing, an opportunity for Dukakis to put into practice the ideals he had been taught at home and had practiced with his chums at school.

Unlike most of the cities of the Eastern Seaboard, which had fallen into the hands of the Democrats under the seemingly inexorable forces of European immigration during the early half of the century, the Republicans of Philadelphia had kept their clutches on the city of Brotherly Love, even through the Depression and the New Deal. But by 1948 the GOP was beginning to lose its grip. The bosses were getting old, the corruption was getting more obvious, and a new generation of young leaders, back from the war and determined to make a break with the kind of nineteenth-century politics that had moved Lincoln Steffins to condemn Philadelphia as "the worst governed city in the country," was elbowing into power. Philadelphia was beginning to shake off the cobwebs.

A team of reform-minded Democrats, Joe Clark and Richardson Dilworth, led the insurgency. In 1947 Dilworth ran for mayor and lost, but the race marked the end of the GOP hegemony. Dilworth named names, and the corruption charges against the Republican machine started to stick in people's minds. The next year Clark won the post of city comptroller. Now the reformers had access to the books, and there was hell to pay. Clark, a righteous, wealthy Brahmin who owed nothing to anyone in politics and made no effort to hide the disdain he felt for pols, spent two years exposing graft and corruption. All in all, nine Republicans committed suicide while the Democratic reformer cleaned house.

In 1951 Clark, running for mayor this time, was trying to turn the Republicans out of city hall for the first time in sixty-seven years, and he looked like he just might make history. The symbol of the campaign was a broom; his slogan: "Sweep out corruption." Educated, righteous and aloof, Joseph Sill Clark, at fifty, was a slight and thin-lipped patrician, a liberal advocate of reform politics who saw righting wrongs as his principle duty. Clark's family long had lived in a section of Philadelphia very much like the Dukakises' South Brookline neighborhood. In fact, each was known as Chestnut Hill.

Even as he was trying to orient himself to campus life at Swarthmore, Dukakis threw himself into the Clark campaign for mayor. Though he would not be eligible to vote for more than three years (twenty-one was then the voting age across the United States), Dukakis organized the Swarthmore campus for Clark and took his workers on the twenty-minute train link into downtown Philadelphia to serve as poll-watchers for his first political hero. Dukakis brought his brigade to some of the toughest neighborhoods in the city. On November 6, 1951, Clark won his historic victory, by 124,000 votes.

Joe Clark became Dukakis's political role model. Clark was a pol whose values of honesty, integrity and reform, and whose impatient intolerance for corruption and waste, closely mirrored Dukakis's own.

Dukakis went to Swarthmore assuming that he would follow his father into medicine, but the thrill of the Clark campaign was an assumption-shattering experience. In addition, he was not thrilled with the science curriculum, and he could not stand physics, nor could he understand it no matter hard he tried. Freshman physics defied Mike Dukakis, and he was spared his first failure when the professor, out of the goodness of his heart, as Dukakis well knew, gave him a D for the course. The practice of medicine, as Dr. Dukakis demonstrated, was personally rewarding, but politics, enlightened leadership, reform of the very democratic structure by which we govern ourselves—therein lay contributions, not to mention extreme pleasures, that were transcendent. Dukakis decided to major in political science as his brother had done at Bates, and he began to plan his future.

Students routinely settle on professions and proceed along the appropriate paths, but when Dukakis planned, he planned: for a career of public service in politics. He could hardly expect to follow Joe Clark's inspiration and become mayor; Brookline town meeting government precluded that. But Dukakis could become governor, and, as he told his roommate, he would someday. He and Frank Sieverts, his roommate for four years, discussed his plan frequently. Sieverts (who went on to become a foreign service officer and is now employed to the Senate Foreign Relations Committee), took Dukakis quite seriously. "Other people talked that way, too," Sieverts said, "but it was casual, and in almost every instance, they spoke of being a senator or house member. Michael saw right through the mystique of power; he saw that, administratively, one could do more." Dukakis was a sophisticated observer. He was aware, as many were not, that some of the most influential Democratic and Republican political figures of the era—such as Franklin Roosevelt and Thomas Dewey, governors of New York, and Adlai Stevenson, governor of Illinois—were first chief executives before they became national party leaders.

It wasn't just a hope or a desire to be governor; Dukakis really had a completely logical plan, which, if pursued with total dedication and energy, was designed to leave the young pol on the doorstep to the governor's office, in the position to determine how he would ascend past, over or around the final impediments to the summit. First there would be further academic success and the continued development of political skills as opportunity allowed at Swarthmore. Then, after graduation, rather than applying to a graduate or a professional school and prolonging his selective service deferment, as many students from the prestige schools were doing at the time, Dukakis would enlist in the army immediately to fulfill his military obligation. When his tour of duty ended, he would go on to law school. "It was the best way to advance a political career," he told Sieverts at the time.

Of course, even someone as logical as Dukakis would, at such a young age, slip from concrete planning from time to time. Lincoln Potter, another classmate of

Dukakis's, remembered his saying that one day he would be president of the United States.

As in high school, Dukakis proved to be an exemplary student and a valuable addition to the athletic program. Yet of his three passions—academics, politics and athletics—clearly his talents lay in the first two. With the competition a notch better than it had been in high school, Dukakis was no longer a super jock, though that did not stop him from lettering in three sports at Swarthmore: cross country in the fall, basketball in the winter, and tennis in the spring. The big difference was, instead of being a starting basketball guard as he had been at Brookline High, Dukakis was second or third off the bench at Swarthmore, and instead of being the captain of the tennis team, he was the sixth man on a six-man team. "He was not a superstar, but he was good," said Sieverts. "He could hold his own."

More and more, Dukakis found himself drawn toward political activism, sometimes in response to issues he confronted on campus and sometimes as an extension of his involvement in the Clark campaign. It was becoming obvious that Dukakis would leave his mark at Swarthmore not on the athletic field but in the political arena. What was also becoming obvious were the rough outlines of a political philosophy, patched together from campus and real world concerns, growing out of his family values of personal integrity, equality of opportunity and service to society, and catalyzed into active expression by honest Democrat Joe Clark's triumph over the entrenched, crooked enemy.

Early in his days at Swarthmore, during pledge week, Dukakis was struck by the revelation that college fraternities refused to admit blacks or Jews. He had not known many blacks back in Republican Brookline, but there were plenty of Jews—such as Sandy Cohen—in town. In liberal circles, it was a time of growing impatience with racism. The previous year the Supreme Court had struck down segregation on interstate railroads, and in sports Jackie Robinson's integration of baseball, with the Brooklyn Dodgers in 1947, and the falling of the color barrier on other teams, stirred a sense of the possible.

Swarthmore's local fraternities did not discriminate, but they were members of national fraternities that did. What to do about the frats was a hot campus topic, and Dukakis knew what he would do: he committed himself to the campaign to get the local chapters of national fraternities that discriminated thrown off campus. Despite the best efforts of Dukakis and his political allies, fraternities that practiced racism nationwide were allowed to maintain integrated chapters at Swarthmore, although none of them ever got Mike Dukakis to pledge.

These were the days before Brown vs. Board of Education, and long before the civil rights movement got up a head of steam. Small, elite, suburban schools like Swarthmore were more than a decade from an aggressive program of recruiting non-whites. Blacks were admitted in small numbers, and foreign students from Nigeria, recruited by Quaker missionaries, helped pepper the student body at Swarthmore. But it was not a time of campus activism. Off campus, in the smug Republican suburb of Swarthmore, barbers did not cut kinky hair. The few American-born blacks on campus, accustomed to this form of racism, went into Philadelphia to get their hair cut. But the foreign students, less comfortable moving into and out of the big city, tended to stay on campus.

The dilemma for these students—how were they to get haircuts?—moved Mike Dukakis to take action. Here was a chance both to strike a blow for equality and to serve a social need—and, as a side benefit, to give the student with the father at home who was tight with the buck a little extra pocket money. Dukakis set up shop in his dormitory hallway. Before he knew it, he had a thriving business as he clipped away at the hair of the Nigerian students, some sympathetic white kids, and a smattering of Swarthmore town civil rights activists who were boycotting the local barber. Working two or three days a week, with sixty regular customers at sixty-five cents a cut, Dukakis was realizing a profit while compensating for injustice. The extra spending money was added to the earnings from his job busing tables at a campus cafeteria. His entrepreneurial dedication to social justice had its price; Dukakis offended his first special interest group. ''Not the favorite of local barbers,'' noted the Swarthmore yearbook beneath his photo.

During spring vacation of his freshman year, Dukakis and a college chum, Jerry Schiller, a philosophy major, hitch-hiked to Miami Beach. They left Philadelphia with fifteen dollars apiece and slept on the beach. ''We didn't talk philosophy because he wasn't into it, and we didn't talk politics because I wasn't into it,'' recalled Schiller, ''although Mike did tell me his ambition was to be governor of Massachusetts.'' By the time they began the trek up Route One from Orlando, with a bag of oranges to sustain them, they were nearly broke, save for the sixty-six cents Dukakis insisted they each save for a hunger-quenching breakfast at a Washington, D.C., diner he knew of.

''He always had a little compartment in his wallet where he kept his change,'' Schiller recalls. ''I was always impressed with that.''

After their freshman year, Dukakis brought Schiller back to the Boston area with him. The students worked as counsellors at a non-profit overnight camp on the South Shore, about forty-five minutes from Boston, in the wealthy town of Duxbury. The camp served underpriveleged boys from Boston, referred by social service agencies. Dukakis was a bunk counsellor, Schiller a swim coach. Dukakis started a two-day olympics at the camp which became an annual event, and he became active in discussions with the staff and directors organizing programs for the campers.

As a sophomore at Swarthmore, in the fall of 1952, Dukakis tasted presidential politics for the first time. Twelve years after he and Stelian had sat around the radio, charting and tabulating the Republican convention balloting, Dukakis threw himself into liberal Democrat Adlai Stevenson's underdog campaign against Republican war hero, General Dwight Eisenhower. Dukakis organized the campus for the intellectual governor of Illinois with youthful enthusiasm. On one occasion, he even climbed a water tower to rip down an ''I Like Ike'' banner. He replaced it with one that read simply, ''Adlai Stevenson.''

These were not easy times for liberals and all stripe of political activists to their left. The nation's post-war political disillusionment, in the manipulative hands of the anti-communist senator Joseph R. McCarthy, was easily shaped into paranoia. The United States had risen up in a supreme effort to crush the Axis powers, only to find that, somehow, in the process, it had negotiated away central Europe to the Soviet Communists, and now China had come under the control of Mao Tse-tung and his Communist party. As McCarthy waved his lists of alleged communists and communist sympathizers in the federal government, as Alger Hiss was convicted of perjury, as the Rosenbergs were tried, convicted, and executed for spying, fear drove liberals, leftists, socialists, communists and former communists underground—or out into the open to face public humiliation, black-listing, ostracism, or worse.

Simply to exercise one's First Amendment right to speak freely, "These were acts of political courage," Sieverts recalled. Dukakis, who had no illusions about communism, joined the local chapter of Students for Democratic Action, the campus affiliate of Americans for Democratic Action. ADA then was a relatively new group, formed as a liberal anti-communist response to former Vice President Henry Wallace's Progressive Party campaign for president in 1948, which was, as the ADA saw it, naive about the Soviet Union and communism.

"He wasn't doctrinaire, wasn't a part of the left-wing on campus—the Henry Wallace supporters, the anti-Adlai group that couldn't support Adlai because he had the support of Dick Daley," the boss of Chicago politics, recalled Carl Levin, a student at Swarthmore who was a year behind Dukakis (and who is now a U.S. senator from Michigan). "I viewed him as a political mentor of sorts. We were both Democrats interested in the same kind of politics." Dukakis was known around campus as a distinguished political advisor and campaign manager, was instrumental in bringing to Swarthmore artists and intellectuals, such as the leftist, iconoclastic author I. F. Stone and leftist folk singer Pete Seeger.

If it was the Joe Clark campaign that inspired Dukakis to consider what could be won in elective politics, it was McCarthy, the red-baiting demagogue, who taught Dukakis how fragile the democracy was, how easily it could be placed at risk, and how fearful were those prospects.

As he had at Brookline High, Dukakis also tried to keep the place clean; to do so, he called forth the students' responsibility to serve Swarthmore even as Swarthmore served the students. From his position of leadership on the student council, Dukakis organized what became an annual student activity, known as Work Day. One day each fall, students were recruited to rake the fallen leaves on campus.

Over the course of his college years, Dukakis never strayed from the academics that were his primary reason for being there, but he also yearned for a more practical education. During the first semester of his senior year, he signed on at American University's Washington Semester Program and spent the fall in Washington observing government agencies.

Set on his career path toward elective politics and the governor's office in Boston, Dukakis applied himself feverishly to the final rigors of undergraduate education. Swarthmore offered an honors program for its best students, and, naturally, Dukakis signed up. Under the two-year program, students who chose to participate took eight seminars, two each semester, including four in the major and two in each of two minors. Students were required to write a ten-page paper a week on average, but there were no exams. Final grades were based on a student's performance in eight oral exams, conducted by specialists brought in from outside the college, and eight papers. Of the few honors program graduates each year, no more than two or three did so with Highest Honors, the Swarthmore equivalent of *summa cum laude*. When the class of '55 picked up their diplomas in June, Michael Stanley Dukakis made his parents proud by graduating with Highest Honors. In addition, he had been selected to join the prestigious academic fraternity, Phi Beta Kappa, as his mother had before him.

The Swarthmore years had been peripatetic and formative. Now grounded in political science, Dukakis was ready to embark on a career in government. His political values had been formed and fixed in the reform wing—the Joe Clark wing —of the Democratic party. The times were soporific and lethargic. But Mike Dukakis left Swarthmore full of energy, anticipating the time when he could do what Joe Clark had done back in the fall of 1951: throw the scoundrels out on their ears.

The otherwise straight and narrow road to the governor's office that Dukakis set for himself at Swarthmore actually had one long detour. It took him halfway around the world to Korea. Selective service regulations at the time allowed for college graduates to continue their student deferments as long as they met class rank and grade requirements, which Dukakis obviously could do. But, as his plan dictated, he enlisted, along with classmate Jay Levine, because he wanted the political stripe and because, according to Levine, "He was tired of school, worn out, and in need of a change." After completing basic training at Fort Dix, New Jersey, Dukakis was sent for advanced training as a radio operator at Camp Gordon, Georgia. Then Dukakis and Levine were sent overseas to Korea as privates in 1955.

The fighting had ceased in Korea in 1953, two years before Dukakis was sent over to the United Nations base camp as part of a specialized army unit that provided support to the Military Armistice Commission in the U.N. effort to administer the cease-fire. Levine was stationed seven miles away. "He didn't like the army at all. He was too bright and smart for it. And he was subject to an immense degree of spit and polish. It was a chickenshit operation," said Levine who, along with Dukakis, whiled away his time until his tour of duty came to an end in early 1957. The two college buddies were sustained by the thought that, when their army days ended, they could both look forward to attending Harvard Law School, which had accepted them prior to their leaving for Korea.

Dukakis found the military routine tedious, and he was depressed by the harshness of the place and his isolation from the Western world. "It was desolate and cold," said Levine of the days when they were made to bunk in corrugated tin huts and tents. "We were always exposed to the cold." Dukakis's camp was barren and muddy, as well, with no vegetation to hold the soil. For the young man from Olmstead's Brookline and the plush green campus at Swarthmore, time passed slowly. Dukakis was ill-suited by temperament to perform the menial tasks to which he was assigned by the overabundance of officers, representing the various nations in the U.N. delegation. But he did his job, finishing with the rank of specialist, third class, bit his tongue, and thought about getting out of Korea and the Army as quickly as possible. He looked forward to the challenge of law school. The Army was a lost cause.

Chapter 4
The First Campaign

The Second World War ended the Great Depression and ushered in an era of vast changes in American society. The end of the war found Massachusetts, and its capital city, Boston, feeling pressured to change as well, but in the Bay State the pressure was building because the war had failed to lift up the economy as it had elsewhere in the nation. After the wartime industries shut down, Massachusetts was left with a lot of former workers and new residents, and a shrinking industrial base. The social fabric was beginning to attenuate.

The textile industry, which had helped drive the state's economy before the Depression, was abandoning the cities of Massachusetts as fast as it could build and open factories in the south; Dixie's aversion to unionism made for a more congenial climate. Lowell, Lawrence, Fall River—cities that seemed in their halcyon days like nothing so much as giant factories of brick—and many smaller mill towns that dotted the riverways and dam sites throughout Massachusetts, teeming with activity, were falling empty and silent, oversized brick crypts for the passing of the industrial age in Massachusetts. The fishing industry, in the beginning so central to the region's prosperity that a cod was chosen as the sacred symbol of the Commonwealth, was coming under increasing foreign competition after the war. Gloucester, to the north, and New Bedford, to the south, among the world's greatest fishing ports through World War II, saw their catches dwindle, and the onetime hectic pace on the waterfronts grow ever slower. The shoe factories and tanneries that brought jobs to immigrant Americans in Haverhill, Brockton and Beverly closed down; Massachusetts shoe and leather workers were among the first Americans after the war to feel the devastation of overwhelming foreign competition built on cheap labor.

In the economic stagnation, profound social changes brought on by the war were eroding old Boston. Soldiers and sailors who had seen the world and fought side by side with Texans and Brooklynites came home without the dedication to Southie or Fields Corner, or the parish church that had provided their parents and grandparents with a sense of security. In some instances, vast demographic shifts seemed to occur overnight. For years a large Jewish community had thrived in the city's Roxbury and Dorchester sections. During the war years, skilled and unskilled laborers streamed to Boston while the home fires were burning to supply the war effort. Boston's black population nearly doubled in size, from 23,000 to 40,000 between 1940 and 1950, and was concentrated in Roxbury and Dorchester. Suddenly, the Jews were gone, out to suburbs like Randolph and Sharon, to the west and south, and to Brookline and Newton closer in.

The political system, dominated as it was by the Yankee-Irish war that had been going on for almost a hundred years, all of a sudden seemed pathetically out of step with the times and dangerously incapable of dealing with the new realities. In sheer numbers, the Yankees were doomed. The Yankee-dominated Republican party could save itself only by appealing beyond its patrician base to independents and independent-minded Democratic voters. But the urban Irish domination of the Democratic party was also coming to an end.

It was to his credit that James Michael Curley, Boston's greatest boss, hung on as long as he did. First elected mayor in 1913, Curley dominated Boston politics for more than thirty years, logging three terms as mayor, five terms in Congress (with two interruptions) and one term as governor. He was elected mayor for the fourth time in 1945, in what would be his last hurrah. Curley was elected while under federal indictment for mail fraud; when his appeals were exhausted, the mayor of Boston, the greatest Irish politician in the city's history, was taken away to prison. A long and tumultuous chapter in the history of Massachusetts and Boston politics was coming to an end.

New personalities, already on the scene and ready to take center stage, would lift Massachusetts up and away from its obsession with the ethnic politics of an earlier age. In 1945 Archbishop Richard Cushing, a crusty political sort with an affable personality and earthy sense of humor, replaced the aloof and self-important William Cardinal O'Connell as the spiritual leader of Boston's Catholic population. In 1946 John Fitzgerald Kennedy began campaigning for Congress from the 11th district, where Curley had most recently served. And in 1947 Yankee Republican Governor William Bradford appointed John B. Hynes, a soft-spoken, dignified political unknown, as acting mayor until Curley got out of federal prison.

Though all of these men were Irish, each had an appeal that transcended his ethnicity. Cushing became a highly visible mover and shaker, as he reached out to embrace Protestants and Jews. So strong was Cushing's spirit of ecumenicism that he became, in truth, the cardinal of all Boston. Kennedy, with his clean-cut, well-tailored good looks and sophisticated wit, seemed to represent a break from the rough-hewn politics of the city. And Hynes, the epitome of professionalism, worked his way up the municipal ladder until he was appointed city clerk in 1945; his presence as acting mayor offered an alternative role model to that of the stereotypical Irish pol, one that appealed to the post-war generation of Irish and non-Irish voters.

President Harry Truman pardoned Curley in 1948, and he returned to take his rightful place at city hall down on School Street. But he would not be there for long. When Curley ran for reelection in 1949, Hynes ran against him, as a reformer. "Curley's day has ended. He has passed his peak," Hynes announced. "And I respectfully remind this tired and battle-scarred political warhorse that the majority of his votes are now in the cemeteries of an era long past.'' Hynes was supported by the reform-minded "New Boston Committee," which included progressive Yankee Republicans, middle-class Irish, Italians and Jews, and by groups of young voters like "Students with Hynes for Better Government." On election day, 1949, the reformers shocked the old boss and dispatched him from office for the last time. Hynes beat Curley by 11,000 votes out of 300,000 cast, and he beat him again in 1951, and for the last time in 1955. John B. Hynes had rung down the curtain on the nineteenth century in Boston. Finally, Massachusetts was ready for the future.

On a smaller scale, and, as befits a dignified high-class suburb, on a quieter one as well, the politics of Brookline were undergoing similar tensions to those in Boston. A new generation of political leaders was coming out of college. Inspired by the reformers' success in Boston, they were disconnected from the wealthy Yankee Republican establishment that, for the most part, owned the town, and from the working-class Irish who dominated the Brookline Democratic Town Committee. The Young Turks—who actually were similar in makeup to the "New Boston Committee" and included Jews, Greeks, Italians, as well as reform-minded Yankees and Irish—were nothing less than a body of political energy in search of an outlet.

In 1952 they found one, in the Democratic presidential campaign of Adlai Stevenson. His urbane rationality, his modest probity, his vast intelligence, and his sophisticated manner made him a hard sell in much of America, but he hit a responsive chord with young, educated progressives. While down in a suburb of Philadelphia, young Mike Dukakis was racing around campus organizing for Stevenson, back home in Brookline Sumner Kaplan and Bernard "Bunny" Solomon, the town's leading progressives, were doing the same. A rally for Stevenson produced a packed high school auditorium; it was the largest Democratic gathering to date in the town's history.

Kaplan and Solomon observed with growing frustration that the Democratic Town Committee had no real interest in the party's presidential campaign. What energy it had was devoted to helping the party's candidate for governor, the Irishman Paul Dever, in his fight against the Yankee Republican Christian Herter. Stevenson, who lost badly to Eisenhower in November, could not even carry Brookline, losing 19,000 to 13,000, though he ran ahead of Congressman John F. Kennedy, whose family homestead was on Beals Street, up in the northern section of town. Kennedy, while winning a seat in the Senate that year, nonetheless was beaten nearly 2-1 in Brookline by Yankee aristocrat Henry Cabot Lodge. Stevenson stirred enough interest in Brookline to illustrate that the Yankee majority and Irish minority political organizations did not speak for a third group that was straining to be heard.

Kaplan and Solomon maintained their political activism in Brookline after the presidential campaign ended. Kaplan, a young attorney interested in tenants' problems, proselytized for rent control, a new concept at the time. With the name he had made for himself through his direction of the Stevenson campaign in 1952 and his association with tenants, he set out four years later to win a seat in the state legislature. The traditional method of campaigning involved placing ads in newspapers and handing out leaflets on street corners; Kaplan eschewed that for a radical approach. Going door to door and ringing doorbells, the reformer succeeded where the complacent and somnolent Democratic regulars had always failed. When he was sworn in at the State House in January, 1957, Sumner Kaplan became Brookline's first Democratic state representative.

That next year, Mike Dukakis, twenty-four, starved for intellectual and political stimulation after his sedentary, cold, and lonely two-year tour of duty in Korea, came back to Brookline to prepare to enter Harvard Law School in the fall of 1957. His base of operations was home, at 210 Rangely Road in Brookline. He commuted on a motor scooter.

Dukakis proved a superb and consistently well-prepared law student. Though the pressure at the law school was legendary, and the faculty often ruthless in exposing errors of fact or logic with sarcasm and ridicule, "Mike was oblivious to the pressure, or else he didn't show it," said a classmate of Dukakis's, Francis X. Meaney. Meaney, who grew up in a town south of Boston and attended the University of Notre Dame on scholarship, first met Dukakis at a social hall for commuters. Dukakis, Meaney recalled, was usually seen carrying a copy of the *New York Times* along with his pile of law books. Dukakis never lost sight of his purpose for being in law school.

Dukakis soon met two other law school students interested in politics: Carl Sapers, another Brookline progressive and reformer, and Herb Gleason, from Boston's Back Bay-Beacon Hill section, a part of the city, like Brookline, that was controlled by wealthy Republicans. Gleason was chairman of the Harvard Law Graduate Democratic Club, which brought important Democrats, such as Eleanor Roosevelt and Adlai Stevenson, to campus to speak.

In the spring of 1958 the Law Graduate Democratic Club brought Senator John F. Kennedy to speak. A huge crowd, including many faculty, turned out to see and hear Kennedy. He walked in by himself, strode to the microphone and matter-of-factly announced: "My name is Jack Kennedy. I'm a candidate for president of the United States. Are there any questions?"

"He handled himself so superbly," Gleason recalled. "He was so articulate, so sophisticated. Mike said that's when he got tweaked about national politics."

If it was, it coincided with a time in which Dukakis was beginning to formulate his thoughts on the hottest social issue of the times: urban renewal. Urban renewal was the fifties' stock phrase for the razing of slums the post-war urban leaders of America—in politics, business and finance— found teeming with folks from overseas and far away. Often the net effect of urban renewal—if the poor were lucky—were new impersonal, antiseptic slums, usually run by a local, politically controlled agency. If the poor were not so lucky, a shiny new bank or office building revitalized their old urban areas.

In Boston the businesslike mayor, John B. Hynes, to the accolades of the business and financial communities, was pushing urban renewal as hard as he could. A new Government Center, to replace seedy old Scollay Square, was planned. Slum clearance in various neighborhoods was ordered. In 1957 a tenement district in the

"New York Streets" neighborhood of the South End was leveled to make way for industrial development in what was the first contribution of the newly created Boston Redevelopment Authority.

In 1958 the BRA turned its attention to the West End, a roiling melting pot that had absorbed waves of immigrants from Ireland, Italy, Greece and Poland. The inhabitants considered the West End a warm, familiar, Old World-like place, crowded but pleasant. Others looked at the West End and saw luxury apartment high-rises, shopping centers, parking garages, office buildings for the mushrooming state and federal bureaucracies, an expanded tax base, a renewal of business for downtown. The protests of West Enders to save their neighborhood and of protectionists could not stop the bulldozers, and one of Boston's most diverse neighborhoods became a part of history. The dark, destructive side of urban renewal that counted corporate profits ahead of human concerns had been exposed for all to see. Neighborhood groups united out of fear and a determination that the banks, bureaucrats and real estate developers would not do to them what they had done to the old West End.

In Brookline, an area known as "The Farm," just across a small pond from the Jamaica Plain section of Boston, and another parcel nearby in Brookline Village were up for development. Part of the heart of St. Mary's Parish, The Farm was a small area of wooden two- and three-decker apartment buildings whose residents were largely municipal workers. The Farm was not a slum, but it certainly was the poorest section of town, and a prime candidate for redevelopment. Taking its cue from Boston, the Town Meeting created the Brookline Redevelopment Authority to determine how the suburb would be developed. Mike Dukakis, whose thinking about development issues was being stimulated as a result of a law school course in property, a first-year requirement, decided to run for a seat on the redevelopment authority.

In 1958 Michael was not the only Dukakis dedicated to public service. Stelian, after much psychiatric treatment, had returned to Bates to get a B.A. in government, and a master's degree from Boston University, also in political science, in 1957. But Stelian and his younger brother shared many interests. Like Michael, Stelian appreciated classical music. Both boys were dedicated long distance runners. And while Michael was putting together his first political campaign, Stelian, who had been hired as the assistant to the acting city manager of Medford, a working-class city a little north of Boston, became a candidate for city manager.

At the core of Dukakis's campaign were his political buddies from the Law Graduate Democratic Club at Harvard, including Carl Sapers, Herb Gleason and Fran Meancy, as well as friends from Brookline, including Haskell "Hackie" Kassler, a first-year student at Boston University Law School.

Election day was cold and rainy, an especially harsh day even for early spring in eastern Massachusetts. Dukakis stood at the polls all day without a raincoat or gloves urging voters to put him, a young, independent, people-sensitive reformer, on the new board. But just as Stelian would not be selected city manager of Medford, Michael's effort fell short. Dukakis finished fifth, just out of the money, a

loser in his first off-campus political campaign by 127 votes. A well-established
"townie" from the Brookline Village section, not far from The Farm, and town
committee member Francis J. Hickey, who got 4,467 votes, won the last place on
the redevelopment board. But the campaign established Dukakis as "a bright, articulate guy who burst upon the scene," said Kassler. As a result of his campaign,
Dukakis came to the attention of Sumner Kaplan, the Democratic state representative and father of reform politics in Brookline. Kaplan's insurgency added a newly
returned and ardent member to its growing number.

Kaplan did not have to wait long before launching another assault on the complacency of Brookline Democratic politics. A redistricting required a special
townwide Town Meeting election in the spring of 1959; all incumbents, including
those serving multi-year terms, were required to run again. "This is the time. Run,"
he urged. Kaplan's crew, including Mike Dukakis whom he personally recruited,
won many seats. Winning a seat at Town Meeting was a modest enough achievement, but the significance of the election was found in the presence at Town Meeting
of a whole new crowd—a minority, to be sure, but more than a sprinkling. It was
a group of friends and associates who, unlike Town Meeting members in years gone
by, had not run in order to gain social acceptance and had no interest in joining
the old establishment. Many—like 26-year-old Mike Dukakis from Harvard Law
School, as well as a member of the Brookline Council on Planning and Renewal,
a director of the Brookline Community Council, and a neighborhood association—
were experiencing the pleasure of political success, and the taste of leadership for
which they had studied and prepared, for the first time. They did not want to
join the establishment; they wanted to shake it up and make it over.

Inspired by Jack Kennedy's presidential campaign, Michael Dukakis came up
with a bold idea in 1960: the reformers would put together a slate of their own
and try to take over the thirty-five-member Democratic Town Committee, which
had been closely held seemingly forever by the Irish crowd that controlled the town
agencies. To the ambitious and idealistic Dukakis, the comfortable Democratic old
guard had to be replaced if the party could ever think of nominating and electing
local figures the likes of Joe Clark, Stevenson and Kennedy to statewide office.
The Town Committee Dukakis targeted for ouster represented all that was wrong
with local politics. It discouraged broad representation and grassroots activism. It
demonstrated by its passive hostility to Adlai Stevenson that it had no interest in
progressive causes nationally. And it voted repeatedly to nominate hacks, still
fighting the Yankee-Irish Wars, for statewide office, thus allowing the Republicans
to attract enough independent support to remain in power despite a numerical
inferiority.

Kennedy's campaign for the White House, which began in earnest almost two
years earlier, seemed to inspire a new idealism in Massachusetts. Progressives and
reformers, such as Sumner Kaplan, Dukakis, Meaney, Sapers and Gleason, who
felt no affinity for the old Democratic establishment that had produced characters
like Curley, as well as gentlemen pols like U.S. House Speaker John W. McCormack, felt heartened that Massachusetts could thrust up onto the national scene,

a modern man, liberated from the past, free to define a new frontier. Young Irishmen, who did come out of the melting pot but who were alienated from politics because of the social stigma attached to it, saw John F. Kennedy as a cleansing agent. "Kennedy made politics a place of pride," recalled David Bartley of Holyoke in western Massachusetts, who studied education at the University of Massachusetts and was inspired to enter politics by the Kennedy presidential campaign. "We were sick and tired of the mediocrity of the Eisenhower era. We were the best and the brightest, and now we could go ahead and show people what we could do."

It did seem that there was a new political spirit abroad in the land, or at least in the Commonwealth of Massachusetts, during that very special year, 1960, when Kennedy ran for president and gave pride back to his state. Just as Dukakis was plotting his takeover in Brookline, Carl Sapers and Herb Gleason were putting together a progressive and reform slate to challenge for control of Boston's Ward 5 Democratic committee in historically Republican Back Bay and Beacon Hill. "We were interested in revising the way the party was organized," said Sapers. "There was no opportunity to bring qualified people in to run and be elected." Similar efforts were underway in the wealthy suburban town of Lexington, famous for its Revolutionary War history; north of Boston, in the blue-collar city of Waltham, where watches were made; and in communities scattered across the state.

Back in Brookline, Dukakis organized his slate and his campaign to take over Democratic politics in the town. Dukakis got the slate to agree to urge all supporters to vote for the entire slate by pulling the "Group Two" lever on the voting machines. Not only was it his idea and his organization, but it was his style—originally his mentor, Sumner Kaplan's style, door-to-door—and low-key so as not to arouse the slumbering opposition while the insurgency went forward. Dukakis's good friend and fellow progressive, Hackie Kassler, joined the slate, as did Bill Sapers, Carl's brother, longtime liberal activist Ben Alper, and Michael's brother Stelian. In all, Dukakis had lined up a slate of dedicated reformers and progressives who appealed to the young, politically independent crowd that had been moving into Brookline since the end of World War II. "It was generational and quasi-ethnic," said Kassler. "Many of the new people were Jewish and new to Brookline. But they came from places where they'd been active in politics."

Every member of the Dukakis slate won, in an election that shocked the town. "A maverick group of Democrats swept the incumbent Democratic Town Committee out of office in this week's election in the most amazing upset of recent political history," the *Brookline Chronicle Citizen* reported April 26 in its lead article. The paper's headline read: "Amateurs Score Big Upset in Democratic Town Fight."

The *Chronicle Citizen*, the only paper in town, was wrong. They may have been overlooked and underestimated, but Mike Dukakis and the new Democratic Town Committee were anything but amateurs. They were, in fact, the new professionals in politics: younger, smarter, more ambitious, and more idealistic than the tired crowd that they had retired from political leadership. "By 'amateur,' " said Kassler, "the paper meant 'non-establishment.' " Insurgents are always non-establishment, but this group meant to retire the old establishment and take over. Kassler recalled Dukakis's battle cry to the reform slate. "He said that it's about time the town committee serves as a base for candidates like Sumner. It should not be viewed as outside the mainstream. We have an opportunity to dictate what the mainstream will be."

No sooner had Dukakis digested his victory in Brookline than he and his cadre of political friends began planning feverishly to take their show on the road. Dukakis, Sapers and Fran Meaney, who was becoming Dukakis's political alter ego, decided that the insurgency in Brookline could be replicated across the state, that the Democratic party could be revitalized at the grassroots. Dukakis and his group believed that new blood, in the image of Dukakis's political role models, would assure that the party could come to govern honestly and fairly. The goal was nothing less than a new age of enlightenment.

The vehicle to bring this grandiose dream into reality was to be a statewide organization of reform-minded Democratic activists. This organization was not conceived of as an alternative or third party; instead it would exist within the Democratic party and, as Dukakis had done in Brookine, sieze control of the party systematically, community by community, office by office.

The organization was to go under the acronym COD. The founders—Dukakis, Sapers and Meaney—agreed that it was a good idea to have the organization remind the public of the historic symbol of the Commonwealth's prosperity, the Sacred Cod. It was Meaney who came up with the name, Commonwealth Organization of Democrats, which, if a bit of a stretch, did well enough to allow COD to be formally organized.

In preparation for the public announcement of the formation of COD, Meaney ran the idea past party officials, who had to approve of the use of the word "Democrats" in the name. The party leadership, having seen what Dukakis and his people had done in Brookline, had no intention of encouraging similar episodes across the state. "They're out to destroy the party," said the Democratic chairman at the time, while indicating why he was withholding the use of the name. Permission was refused.

But COD would not be deterred. The party regulars were, after all, dealing with a group that was about to graduate from Harvard Law School. Meaney had added to the organization's legal name the word "Incorporated" and told the party he would see them in court. The secretary of state issued the group its non-profit charter after a favorable court ruling.

After graduation from law school, Dukakis took off for the 1960 Democratic National Convention in Los Angeles, along with another law school friend, Paul Brountas, in Brountas's Volkswagen Karman Ghia. They had little hope of getting into the convention; they just wanted to be there, to be around for Kennedy's coronation, and to do some traveling, after the pressures of law school and the endless politics of the past three years.

With the conclusion of the convention, Dukakis and Brountas took a side trip to Acapulco. Dukakis had been there before. On one of the frequent spring vacation hitch-hiking trips he took while at Swarthmore, he and Jerry Schiller had hit Acapulco. While there in 1960, Dukakis, as coincidences would have it, met a woman from Springfield, a city in the western part of Massachusetts. Dukakis liked Pat Leahy very much, and he was thrilled to discover she was single and unattached. When Dukakis got back to the Boston area, he couldn't wait to call his friend, Fran Meaney. "I met the perfect woman for you," he told Meaney. "She lives in Somerville, and she's Irish, too." Dukakis urged Meaney, who lived in Somerville during his second and third years of law school, to call Pat. He did, and they began to date.

In December of 1960, in the aftermath of Kennedy's victory over Richard Nixon, Meaney, Dukakis and Sapers called the organizational meeting of COD in no less a site than Faneuil Hall, where Sam Adams helped foment the American Revolution. Many dozens of reformers and progressives showed up.

COD did not appeal to everyone who was dissatisfied with the choices the Republican and Democratic parties had been offering. Some felt it was elitist and referred to COD as "the clean neighborhood" group. Some felt it was indulging euphemistically in ethnic and class warfare. Others felt that the Democratic party was beyond redemption. But, for the most part, COD gave the Kennedy generation of political activists a way to express its energy that was compatible with its values and aspirations for American democracy. If the issues were vague, the goal—a better quality of democracy—was not. "We were not into causes," said Herb Gleason. "We were into reform and having better people elected."

Somehow, through all this, Mike Dukakis managed to graduate *cum laude* from Harvard Law School. Following his friends, Carl Sapers and Herb Gleason, who were a year or two older, Dukakis was recruited to join the prestigious Boston law firm of Hill, Barlow, Goodale and Adams. From a tiny cubicle of an office in downtown Boston, in 1961, Mike Dukakis mused about the world convinced more than ever about the genius of democracy. "We were all full of ourselves in those days," Sapers said. "We came out of Harvard Law School and thought the world wanted to hear what we had to say."

Chapter 5
The Insurgency

In Massachusetts, JFK's "New Frontier" meant the suburbs. And the suburbs, in the early sixties around Boston, meant those communities caught in the loop of state highway Route 128. Completed in 1951, Route 128 formed a sixty-three-mile "C" around Boston, from the fishing port of Gloucester on the North Shore to the sprawling town of Braintree in the south. There was a certain irony in the fact that Old Irish Governor John Dever and the all-powerful Public Works Commissioner William F. Callahan, "the shadow governor," were responsible for the post-war highway boom, and its centerpiece of the circumferential highway, Route 128. These proud defenders of the old order didn't know it, but they were building the roads to political extinction for their urban-based Democratic party.

After World War II, an exodus to suburbia was underway throughout the nation. But the suburbanization of Boston had certain unique elements which yielded an economic revival as well as a profound political realignment. Route 128 was the lifeline for both.

Ever since President Franklin Roosevelt had called on Vannevar Bush, the vice president and dean of engineering at Massachusetts Institute of Technology, to preside over World War II related research, the Boston area had been a mecca for defense contractors. Located in Cambridge on the banks of the Charles River, MIT has stood as one of the nation's foremost centers of technology. Its faculty was encouraged to apply creative thinking to profitable purposes, and its relationship with the Pentagon has long been cozy.

After the war the steel mills and factories reconverted to peacetime products, and the dizzying pace they had kept during the early forties slowed down. But the government, ever fearful of the Soviet Union in the new Atomic Age, maintained its commitment to the research and development of weapons and defense systems. Washington found a willing ally in Cambridge. Some of the best scientific minds in America were setting up small companies in and around Kendall Square, where MIT is located, or in the basements of their suburban homes.

As Route 128 was being completed, MIT and the U.S. Air Force embarked on a joint venture in research and development. Lincoln Laboratory was situated near Route 128 in historic Lexington. As scientists and engineers pressed the technological horizon rapidly outward, firms seeking to develop and market new ideas spun off from Lincoln Lab and other first-generation high-tech companies. A research assistant at Lincoln Lab became convinced that digital computers would be the wave of the future; in 1957 Kenneth H. Olsen left to concentrate on the development of his idea, which was to become Digital Equipment Corporation.

In the former farm country around Route 128, for the most part less than twenty miles from Boston proper, the fields were so rich with entrepreneurial thinking that mind-boggling high-tech successes seemed to pop up like mushrooms. Just as DEC spun out of Lincoln Lab, Data General spun out of DEC—and so it went. Impressed by the government's interest in research and development, the billion-dollar Bank of Boston and local venture capitalists, who had amassed their fortunes during the days of the China trade and the development of the western railroads, decided the high-tech field was no longer risky and began making loans to the start-ups and spin-offs. This pioneering soon attracted venture capital from out of town.

Sputnik and the space race kicked the region's first high-tech boom into high gear. Back in Cambridge, in 1961, MIT got its first Apollo contract from NASA. Its task was to develop a guidance system for a rocket that would land a man on the moon by the end of the decade, as President Kennedy had challenged the nation to do.

When high technology's founding fathers were ready to exchange Cambridge for more expansive quarters, Bill Callahan's Route 128 provided the access route. And with the opening in 1957 of another Callahan project, the Massachusetts Turnpike, which ran east and west across the state for 123 miles, intersecting Route 128 in Newton, a short ride to downtown Boston, a vast swath of eastern Massachusetts was suddenly accessible to the city.

The fusion of the highway boom with the high-tech boom created a demographic explosion. Boston's population in 1950 was 801,444. Twenty years later, it was down to 628,215; in a generation, 173,229 people had moved out of Boston. Political power shifted with the population. In the sixties alone, a lesser Boston was forced to give up thirteen seats in the state legislature to Greater Boston.

The suburbanization of the region was bad news for the old Republican and Democratic parties. In the GOP, which had finally surrendered control of both houses of the legislature to the Democrats in 1958, its number was down to ninety in the 240-member House of Representatives and declining sharply. And while the Democrats were enjoying an unprecedented blessing of numerical riches on Beacon Hill, the Democratic leadership was nonetheless losing control. Too many of these new, suburban Democrats behaved with a decided independence. They were sent to the city to represent the interests of the town, and they often found themselves pitted against those of the prevailing power structure, often in alliance with the Republicans.

As the inner suburbs began to fill out, a managerial elite, without ties to either Yankee or Irish clans, took up residence in newly constructed ranch and split-level houses on subdivided lots a short drive from the office or lab. Many of the new suburbanites were drawn to the Boston area—frequently from around the world—to study at its great universities and, afterwards, to begin professional careers.

Mike Dukakis, Fran Meaney, Carl Sapers and Herb Gleason were fortunate. The mountain was coming to Mohammed.

Dukakis's gospel of rational, logical and clean government appealed to the cultural values of the new suburbanites. It was a pitch that did not speak directly to *what* government should be doing so much as it focused on *how* government should be be doing it. The suburbanites were less dependent on direct government services and on local government agencies for employment; the "good government" pitch of Dukakis and his COD co-founders struck a sympathetic chord outside the city.

The COD philosophy was predicated upon a politically aware and active electorate, which would participate in a vigorous democracy and produce responsible, issue-oriented candidates. COD's vision, not surprisingly, was of a society very much like Brookline's. The organization placed great faith in party nominating conventions—the forum for the expression of enlightened citizen activism—and favored the "Connecticut challenge primary," in which a candidate must receive at least 20 percent of the vote at the convention to be allowed to run for nomination in a party primary. At this time in Massachusetts the ballot often was absurdly long. Besides local races, six State House offices were filled by statewide elections: governor, lieutenant governor, attorney general, state treasurer, secretary of state and state auditor. Without some control over nuisance candidates and "straws," the ballot would continue to resemble a local phone book. More than once, voters found John Kennedys, and people with names that were close to those of other prominent Boston politicians, running for one thing or another. (In fact, a John F. Kennedy, fortuitously named by parents who had no blood relationship whatsoever to *the* Kennedys, did get himself elected state treasurer, in 1954, and he remained in office until 1961.)

COD also stood for a strong local party that cared about national issues and fought for them with the national party. And COD, very much in the Hamiltonian tradition, was convinced that the key to a successful democracy was a strong chief executive. The bequest of the Irish-Yankee war was precisely the opposite. The cultural and political fragmentation of Massachusetts had produced an equally fragmented government filled with semi-autonomous agencies and commissions—fiefdoms insulated from executive or legislative oversight. Remarkably, the books of Bill Callahan's turnpike authority were closed to the eyes of the state auditor, *by law*, for more than a decade after it was created.

Dozens of agencies and departments had fixed terms of service for their administration, and some positions actually had statutory life tenure, leaving governors emasculated and frustrated. In such a decentralized and balkanized governmental organization, corruption was encouraged; the hand was always open. An informal secular tithing of citizens doing business with the government became an accepted custom. Callahan, the road builder and boss of the DPW and, later, of the turnpike authority, though unelected, was unquestionably the most powerful man in government during the years following World War II, and he brought more than one elected governor to heel.

Among the reforms COD proposed to strengthen the executive were a four-year term for the governor, who had been required to run every two years, and another that required candidates for governor and lieutenant governor to run as a ticket. COD also believed that minor statewide elective offices, which were primarily ministerial, should be eliminated and their duties transferred to the governor to shorten the ballot and bring about real accountability.

In 1961, after the buoyant start in 1960, the heady successes of 1960, the young men from COD aimed to take their gospel on the road. They wanted a beachhead in the legislature, and they wanted a statewide membership of local Democratic leaders who would in turn proselytize for good government and political activism. The COD crusade gave Dukakis, then twenty-seven, a reason to move constantly around the state as early as 1961. He and Meaney spent most of their available free time, especially weekends, on the road, making converts as they went.

At this time, Sandy Cohen was living in Brookline as Sandy Kohn, as the result of her marriage five years earlier. The Kohns' apartment was right across the hall from the apartment of Harry Ellis Dickson, a soft-spoken, easy-going violinist with the Boston Symphony Orchestra, and his wife, Jane. Kohn had known the Dicksons' elder daughter, Kitty, even though Kitty was only a freshman when Sandy and Mike were leaders of the senior class. Kohn, who was still considered part of the family by the Dukakises, always kept her eye out for young women her friend Mike might enjoy meeting. It had been ten years since their high school romance, and Mike had not had a serious girlfriend since.

After high school, Kitty Dickson, who loved to dance and had been teaching dance since the age of fifteen, went off to Penn State in the fall of 1955 to study dance, following her mentor, Betty Jean Ditmar, a dance instructor whom she had met in summer camp in Maine when she was eleven. Ditmar was on the staff of Camp Newfound, and Kitty went back each summer for nine years to study with BJ, as she was known. Now, Kitty could resume her studies with Ditmar at Penn State.

While there, Kitty got to know John Chaffetz, whom she had met earlier, while both were counseling at different camps on the same Maine lake. They decided to get married. She left Penn State and followed her husband to California where he was stationed during his military tour of duty. The newlyweds had a son, John, in 1958. But Kitty and John Chaffetz had not chosen well, and that was quickly apparent. Only months after young John was born, the couple separated. Until she could make plans to return home with her infant son, Kitty moved in temporarily with actor and conductor Danny Kaye, who was a friend of her father.

Dukakis, still in law school, called Sandy Kohn about this time to complain that "there wasn't anyone out there to date, and did I know anyone nice," Kohn said. From the Dicksons, she had learned that Kitty would soon be back in town, and Kohn thought she might have a match. "Do you remember that adorable Kitty Dickson?" she asked Dukakis.

Kitty and Mike had first met when she was thirteen and he was seventeen. Although he did not recall the encounter, it had been an exciting event for Kitty, a high school freshman; she spent much of that night calling friends and telling them she had met Big Man On Campus Mike Dukakis.

Dukakis told Kohn he did recollect meeting Kitty while home on break from Swarthmore, several years later, when he was a senior and she was a freshman at Penn State. They met at Symphony Hall, where he was in line to buy "rush" tickets, the heavily discounted 175 tickets that go on sale just prior to each Friday matinee and Saturday evening concert, a bequest for the benefit of area students.

Dukakis called Kitty Chaffetz, and they had their first date in October of 1961. He was almost twenty-eight, and she was almost twenty-five. She was living with John, who was now three, in an apartment on Everett Street in Cambridge, opposite Harvard Law School and down the street from Lesley College, which specializes in early childhood education. Kitty was working part-time and attending Lesley while John was in nursery school at Lesley-Ellis, the college's laboratory training school.

The couple hired a babysitter to stay with John, who cried as they went out, hoping to keep his mother from leaving. Kitty assured Mike that her son would stop crying soon, and off they went. John, meanwhile, ran from window to window, trying to keep Kitty in sight as long as he could. They had dinner at Maison Robert, a moderately priced French restaurant then located among the handsome, turn-of-the-century brownstone townhouses in Boston's classy Back Bay section. After dinner, they walked across Copley Square and bought tickets at an art theater to see the Italian movie *Rocco and His Brothers*. They hated the movie, left before it was over, and went back to Kitty's apartment for tea.

She was crazy about the handsome, idealistic Dukakis, who had spent most of their first evening together talking about his plans to run for the legislature. To Mike Dukakis, who had not spent his adolesence in the throes of puppy love, the young woman with a passion for dancing and classical music and an interest in politics was everything he had ever imagined in a mate. He fell completely and immediately in love with Kitty. She was especially taken with her new date's interest in her son—soon after their first date, he would babysit for John while Kitty studied for her exams—and by the way young John seemed to embrace his mom's new friend. This, Kitty told friends at the time, was what sealed her relationship with Dukakis.

The families were more cautious. The Dicksons were not pleased that Kitty was getting involved with another man so soon after the breakup of her marriage, and with someone who wasn't Jewish. As for the Dukakises, "it was a problem," said Euterpe Dukakis, "because, in those days, divorce was not a common thing. Certainly not among us, not in our families or background." The issue of Kitty's being Jewish "never came up," she said. "Divorce, yes. But not that she was Jewish.

"And it was difficult to take, with a little child and all. You wonder always, if there is a divorce, whether a second marriage will be successful. But as we, my husband and I, discussed it and talked about it, I said, 'Look dear, this is a fact.

He's not a young boy. He's grown up. He's twenty-eight years old. Almost twenty-nine. Do we want to alienate our child? This seems to be serious.'

"I had met Kitty. I liked her very much. So he said, 'Alright. I think I ought to meet Kitty.' I said, 'Alright. I'll arrange for it.' "

With John in tow, Kitty had gone to visit Euterpe a number of times—always while Panos was at the office—as her relationship with Michael deepened. The introductory meeting between Kitty and Dr. Dukakis was full of tension. "He was most severe when I first met him," Kitty Dukakis said. "He was a very straight-laced person. Everything was done by the book."

In their racing around the state, Dukakis and his political pals had put together a formidable reform phalanx for the campaign of 1962. They had more than a thousand members, including a handful with legislative experience, plus advisory committees composed of academics and professionals. COD boasted more than one hundred ward and town committee members, eight school committee members and four city councilors, plus the mayor of a growing western Massachusetts city and a half dozen state reps.

In the fall of 1962, COD targeted seventeen candidates—including co-founder Mike Dukakis from Brookline—for election to the House of Representatives. The effort was focused in middle and upper middle class suburbs within Route 128. Many of the towns, like Brookline, had traditionally voted Republican, but the rapid suburbanization of the new managerial middle class was overwhelming tradition.

In the Republican party, John Anthony Volpe, a first-generation Italian-American, reigned supreme. Volpe, who first won the governorship in 1960 was running for reelection. A pious Catholic with a warm, winning smile, a former hod-carrier who had become a heavy-construction magnate, Volpe was hardly the stereotypical stiff-lipped Brahmin that the GOP had been spewing forth with regularity since anyone could remember.

It was the Democratic party that offered the voters of Camelot a chance to elect a Yankee governor. Young and handsome, Endicott "Chub" Peabody from Cambridge, an All-American football star at Harvard who was the very embodiment of Kennedyesque "vigor," wrestled the nomination away from Edward McLaughlin, who, in the absurdity of Massachusetts politics, had been elected, as a Democrat, to be the Republican Volpe's lieutenant governor two years earlier. Peabody expressed the energy of the reform movement. His campaign emphasized that he had worked in Kennedy's historic West Virginia primary two years before and that he was a "real Democrat." It also emphasized that he was the only hope for the party to recapture the governor's office from a generally well-liked Republican incumbent.

The Volpe-Peabody fight was unlike any recent gubernatorial election in Massachusetts, and it generated unusual public interest. There wasn't an Irishman to vote for—or against.

Nor was ethnicity a deciding factor in the U.S. Senate contest that year. How could it have been when the choice, effectively, was between scions of the state's two most esteemed Irish families, the Kennedys and the McCormacks? When Jack Kennedy resigned his Senate seat for the White House, a close family friend was appointed to keep the seat warm for Teddy Kennedy, who would be thirty by the time of the 1962 election and, therefore, just old enough to serve, according to the U.S. Constitution.

Running against young Kennedy was Edward J. McCormack, nephew of the U.S. House speaker, and the attorney general of the Commonwealth. The contest posed a real dilemma for all Democrats. McCormack, from the Old Irish South Boston neighborhood, had achieved an admirable record on civil rights and economic opportunity. Kennedy, while having accomplished next to nothing, represented a family success story, and an assimilation for Irish voters that was a dream come true. The liberal group, Americans for Democratic Action, endorsed McCormack overwhelmingly; among the reformers a debate raged. The case for Kennedy was that only he could lead a united party to victory up and down the ticket in the fall. The case against Kennedy was that his presence in the race represented a sophisticated version of the kind of familial and personal politics that was anathema to the reformers. (The presence in the November general election of a peace and disarmament candidate, Harvard Professor H. Stuart Hughes, gave some reformers a convenient and principled escape from the Teddy-Eddy dilemma.)

McCormack did quite well against Kennedy in the suburbs where COD was strong, especially in Brookline, the home of Sumner Kaplan, his statewide campaign manager; Dukakis helped his mentor and backed McCormack. But elsewhere in the state, Kennedy charisma carried the day over substance from South Boston. In the November general election, Peabody beat Volpe by the narrowest of margins—five thousand votes—but he needed help from President Kennedy and a close association (on bumper stickers) with Teddy, as well as campaign management from Congressman Tip O'Neill, to recapture the governorship for the Democrats. Along with Teddy and Chub, ten COD candidates, including Mike Dukakis, were elected to the House. In a race with five others for three seats, Dukakis ran third, two votes behind another young politician, Beryl Cohen, but safely ahead of the fourth-place finisher. At twenty-nine, Mike Dukakis was going to the State House.

Through Governor-elect Peabody, the call for reform became a battle cry. The House of Representatives which Mike Dukakis was about to enter in January of 1963 was in a tumult as a historic power struggle was reaching its climax. Since 1958, John F. Thompson, a legendary pol from the western Massachusetts town of Ludlow, had been running the House—and, in the view of genteel observers, running roughshod over it. Thompson, a World War II veteran, was a swaggering, charismatic drunkard whose brand of personal politics and style left reformers appalled but inspired. Here was the enemy incarnate; he was known as "The Iron Duke."

There was more than a bit of Jack Armstrong in Chub Peabody; even before he was sworn into office, he threw himself into a campaign to unseat Speaker Thompson. Of course, Peabody's unprecedented decision to commit the prestige of the governor's office to an internal legislative election, while couched in righteous language, was at least an equal part self-serving power politics.

Peabody's candidate for speaker was Michael Paul Feeney, from Boston's Hyde Park section. The chairman of the Boston Democratic City Committee, Feeney was a pleasant enough sort, but he was hardly a reformer. What he was was a key part of the Peabody campaign, and he had delivered a key block of delegates to Peabody at the state Democratic convention. Peabody's commitment to Feeney in his fight against Thompson smacked of a deal.

On the first ballot, when the House convened on January 3, 1963, Thompson had ninety votes among the 236 cast, leaving him twenty-nine short of the simple majority needed to retain the gavel. The Republican floor leader had eighty-eight votes. Feeney was third with forty-four votes. Cornelius Kiernan, another regular Democrat, had eight votes. Former FBI agent Paul Menton, a second term representative and young reformer, received two votes. Half of his support came from extreme idealist Mike Dukakis, the other half from attorney and civil libertarian William Homans, Jr., a Democratic Boston Brahmin and reformer. Dukakis and Homans had concluded together that Menton would make the best speaker. Somewhat less naive and more realistic was Menton himself. He did not consider himself a candidate nor did he even vote for himself. He was supporting Kiernan.

Dukakis had eschewed the power struggle on principle. By bucking Thompson—and Peabody and his pragmatic colleagues who backed Feeney—"Dukakis demonstrated his remarkable self-confidence, plus an ability to articulate it intelligently and forcefully. People were attracted to that," said James Segel, a liberal Brookline activist.

There would be two more, equally inconclusive, ballots on January 3 as the struggle wore on. On the second ballot, Thompson lost a vote, Feeney stayed at forty-four, but Menton attracted a third vote. Thompson was stuck at eighty-nine on the third ballot, Feeney showed some movement up to forty-nine votes, and the non-candidate, Menton, lost all but Dukakis's vote. After the third ballot, the House adjourned for the day.

The next day a ceasefire was declared for the combattants to watch Peabody take the oath of office. Overnight, Dukakis decided that he had made his point and switched to Kiernan. Finally, around 9:00 p.m., Thompson was reelected speaker on the sixth ballot. The House fight had afforded Dukakis the immediate opportunity to express his reform philosophy: no compromising, government by principle. It was there for all to see in his lonely votes for the progressive Menton.

Dukakis, who wrote a roughly five hundred-word column, "Rep. Dukakis Reports...," at the end of each month for the *Brookline Chronicle Citizen*, devoted his entire space on March 28, 1963 to the battle for the speakership. Dukakis wrote that his participation in the largely quixotic challenge to Thompson was, in his opinion and in the opinion of many freshmen, "the first step on the road to the reform of the Massachusetts legislature....

"All of us knew that we were risking legislative suicide in challenging Thompson. Most of us realized that only a minor miracle would defeat him. Nonetheless, the challenge had to be made, if only to demonstrate to the people of Massachusetts that there were at least some legislators in the Commonwealth who would not stand for the kind of government we had been getting on Beacon Hill.''

While Thompson survived, his victory was a Pyrrhic one, as Dukakis accurately noted. ''Already signs of a reform bloc are appearing in the House of Representatives as key bills come out of committee and on to the House floor,'' he wrote. ''Speaker Thompson himself has won a victory but appears to have lost the war. He has little or no control over the Democratic members of the House. He has made almost no attempt to enforce party discipline on major issues and, if he did, he would not succeed.''

Chapter 6
First Tests of the Reformer

Even though he was a freshman state representative, Dukakis was determined to take full advantage of the vacuum of leadership at the top of the Massachusetts House. While Speaker John Thompson hung on for pride's sake, Dukakis maintained a fevered pace trying to change the rules for a more enlightened future.

He continued to press the COD agenda for four-year terms for the governor and lieutenant governor elected as a team, so as to create a strong executive. He pressed for legislation to give the governor broad powers to reorganize government agencies and to expand home rule for Massachusetts municipalities; for more funds for mass transit and for a halt to highway spending; and for the abolition of the Governor's Council, an anachronism from colonial times when representatives of the Crown passed on matters of the purse and other details of government—in the sixties it was a low-visibility body filled with political hacks who routinely sought to extract favors from the governor in exchange for their ratifying judicial nominations and for approving various expenditures. He opposed the expansion of horse-racing dates and an amendment giving the state personnel director life tenure. And he pursued an investigation of shadow governor Bill Callahan's vast public works fiefdom.

At the end of the 1963 legislative session, Dukakis sent a newsletter to his Brookline constituents. In it he expressed pride that he had lived up to his campaign promise to fight for better government. "It has been a year in which my conviction that there is a place for integrity and high ideals in the General Court was put to the test....I can report to you that I haven't changed my mind....The fight to pull Massachusetts government out of the morass into which it has sunk goes on....I haven't fixed a ticket. I have refused to become enmeshed in the [public works] patronage net....The important thing is that public officials and citizens of good will have begun to fight, and fight effectively." If Dukakis had not slain the dragon in his first year in office, neither was he mauled by it. He had proved to himself—and to his constituents and colleagues—that he could enter the house of the beast and come out whole.

Many reform initiatives slipped past the weakened old guard. The four-year term, the teaming of the governor and lieutenant governor and home rule all passed.

So did metropolitan planning. In the final days of the session, the legislature voted to reorganize the Department of Public Works and bring it under the control of the governor. And half a million dollars was appropriated for a crime commission to conduct a crash investigation of Callahan's long unreformed DPW.

A personal note appeared at the end of the newsletter. "One other event made this the most important year of my life—and that, of course, was my marriage to Kitty on June 20. What with a grueling legislative session and the demands of a law practice, we had a quick four-day honeymoon on [the island of] Nantucket and hurried back to town to take up the battle once again."

The newlyweds and young John Chaffetz set up housekeeping in an old but spacious apartment at 93 Perry Street in Brookline which they had purchased around the time of the wedding. "My bride is already up to her ears in the hectic pace of public life. She seems to be thriving on it," Dukakis continued. "The welcome mat is out for all of you here at 93 Perry, and if by chance you are in the neighborhood, we would be delighted to have you drop in and say hello."

The end-of-year newsletter closed with a postscript: "All of us have been touched this holiday season by the tragic passing of two men who were rare in public life." Dukakis was referring to his inspiration, and that of a generation, President John F. Kennedy, who was assasinated on November 22, a little more than a month before, and to Mike Galvin, Dukakis's state senator who had died unexpectedly in December, eleven months after being elected to his first term. "I hope that we do not forget these two men," Dukakis wrote. "Together, they served as living examples of what competence, integrity and dedication really mean in public life."

If Dukakis's attention in the first year of the term seemed scattered—as if the kid in the candy store wanted to try everything—it began to focus in 1964, his second year in the House. The focus was on housing, but with one notable distraction for Dukakis and the entire House.

On May 8, 1964, Speaker Thompson was indicted by a special Suffolk County grand jury on bribery and conspiracy charges. A crime commission named Thompson and a former Democratic speaker, along with twenty-four persons and nine small loans companies in 137 indictments.

On May 11, three days after the indictments were handed down, Boston Republican Gordon D. Boynton presented an order to declare the chair vacant. Thompson, who barely had survived the insurgency of January 1963, would face another, even tougher vote. The motion to vacate posed a special problem for the Democratic reformers, who despised the scornful Thompson. But something always seemed partisan about the crime commission; it gave off the scent of Yankee Republican class condescension. Its targets were always the Irish, as if the ghosts of Brahmins past would yet haunt them to their graves. Moreover, Thompson was owed the presumption of innocence, wasn't he? On the motion to vacate, no easy answers came to the reformers. The reform impulse was on a collision course with cherished legal rights.

Thompson was willing to do almost anything to keep the title of speaker. He put out the word—and told the reformers personally—that if he were allowed to keep the gavel, he would never use it again. He promised that he would never return to the rostrum if the House voted not to vacate the chair. Thompson, the bully, was begging. When the roll was called on Boynton's motion to vacate, the reformers were split. Bill Homans, Paul Menton and Al Kramer, a passionate liberal from the poor, melting-pot city of Chelsea, just north of Boston, led the reform group that voted for civil liberties and said "no." Dukakis voted "yes"; on the basis of an indictment, Thompson should be removed. To Dukakis, the zealous reformer, the respectability of the institution took precedence over the rights of an individual.

Boynton's order was defeated, 115-101, and a second Republican effort to remove Thompson failed by an even greater margin, 117-97, with Dukakis once again voting with the Republicans.

Meanwhile, Dukakis was doing everything he could to see that affordable housing was available, and would remain available, for the middle and working classes. It was the same concern that moved him to run for the Brookline Redevelopment Authority six years earlier. Housing had for years been a sensitive issue in Brookline. Because of the town's high-class reputation and its location, so close to Boston, a residence in Brookline was constantly in highest demand. Houses were mainly in the more rural south side; in the north, close to Boston, apartment buildings predominated. The tenants, for the most part, were long-time residents—including a good portion of elderly—who were rooted in Brookline. "Transients," as Brooklinites called them, had always been a nuisance. Students from nearby Boston University and other Boston-area colleges wanting to live off-campus and willing to cluster in cramped quarters in a pleasant neighborhood were driving up rents and pushing out town residents.

Dukakis's dedication to preserving Brookline for Brooklinites was tireless. As he jogged about town, which he did often, he would memorize the addresses of buildings where mail slots listed the names of more people in residence than the zoning by-laws allowed. After running, State Representative Dukakis reported the violations to the zoning board.

At the same time, to help hold down rents, Dukakis sponsored rent control legislation, pushing the legislature to allow Brookline to impose it. In addition, to help low- and moderate-income renters afford a homestead, Dukakis came up with the then-novel idea of condominiums. He filed the first bill to allow apartments in the same building to be sold individually as a way of allowing renters to purchase their dwelling units at a reasonable price.

For a first-term legislator to even propose so bold an innovation as the condo law was extraordinary. Remarkably, Dukakis, the lone vote for Paul Menton for speaker a year earlier, managed to push the condominium bill through the House and Senate and, with the signature of Governor Peabody, into law before he began to campaign for reelection in the fall. Dukakis was particularly pleased with the accomplishment. "It is, I believe," he wrote in his session-ending newsletter, "the first real breakthrough in many years in the effort to speed construction or rehabilitation of middle-income housing."

In 1964, during his campaign for a second term, Dukakis was shocked by a bizarre incident which dramatized the gulf that had been growing between his brother, Stelian, then thirty-four, and himself. Stelian had always had a mind and a body that was the envy of his younger brother, yet he had never been able to conquer his emotional problems. Despite years of therapy following his suicide attempt at Bates nine years earlier, he continued to exibit mood swings. At times, in the view of family friends, he seemed deeply resentful of his stolid, stable brother and his great successes. On one such occasion, Stelian distributed leaflets in a section of Brookline—urging voters *not* to reelect Mike Dukakis to the State House.

Michael Dukakis was out of town when Kitty received a call informing her of Stelian's leaflet drop. She immediately called Fran Meaney, who organized a group of campaign workers to go door to door and retrieve the embarrassing scandal sheets. Meaney's group was effective; they even were able to fast-talk their way into the mailbox of the Longwood Towers apartment complex to pick up the fliers before most of the residents got home from work that day. So successful was the retrieval effort that few Brookline voters were ever aware of the sad and disturbing episode.

Friends of Michael Dukakis back then say he never discussed his brother's differences with him, or his brother's illness. They say they felt that Michael Dukakis had a difficult time expressing his deep feelings. Some friends back then say Michael seemed shaken and frightened by Stelian's emotional problems, fearful that they might befall him as well. He responded, they say, by imposing an even tighter emotional grip on himself than he had before—and moving on. Later that election year, Stelian Dukakis announced to the press that he would challenge Congressman Thomas P. "Tip" O'Neill in the Democratic primary, although he never filed nomination papers for the race.

By the fall of 1964, the first-term legislator who was responsible for a major innovation in housing and who had emerged as a leader of the reform movement in the Massachusetts House had become the unquestioned political leader of Brookline. Dukakis did not have difficulty getting reelected. He was the leading vote-getter from Brookline in both the 1964 Democratic primary for state representative and again later in the November general election, when he far outdistanced the second-place finisher.

It was in 1964 that Dukakis and Meaney decided to close down the COD office. Meaney, then an attorney with a Boston firm, was serving as the unpaid director of the organization. The job not only took up too much of his time, what with the constant calling and chairing of meetings, but after three years of weekends on the road, the routine was beginning to wear him out. "We'd achieved as much mileage as we could," Meaney recalled. By the time the office closed down for good, after spending hundreds of hours driving thousands of miles on Bill Callahan's highway system, Meaney had a list of two thousand activists whom he and Dukakis had, for the most part, personally recruited in their crusade to make over the state Democratic party. And it was coming up on the time that Dukakis himself would run for statewide office.

Dukakis and the reformers had succeeded in pushing much of their reform agenda into law. The 1966 election would mark the first time the governor and lieutenant governor were required to run as a team, and the winners of the '66 statewide elections would enjoy the luxury of four-year terms, instead of the two-year terms that had demanded almost constant campaigning and made actual governing next to impossible. After the reforms come the reformers, so Dukakis believed and hoped.

Along with two-term secretary of state Kevin White, Dukakis was the acknowledged rising star of the reform wing of the Democratic party. In 1965 he prepared to run for state attorney general. The incumbent, Edward W. Brooke, a young, handsome black man who had made his reputation in the Republican party as an enemy of Democratic corruption, had let it be known that he was going to try to integrate the U.S. Senate, so the attorney general's office would be empty at the end of the term. In early January 1966, 32-two-year-old Mike Dukakis announced to the assembled media that he would be a candidate for the vacated position. At the press conference, Dukakis said that it was his belief that his party wanted to rid itself of "tired Democratic voices."

There was a better, sharper, more riveting way to express the raison d'etre for Dukakis's campaign for attorney general, but he had yet to sieze upon it. Dukakis was still searching for the issue that could galvanize his campaign, and he found it through his long-time colleague at Hill and Barlow and a co-founder of COD, Carl Sapers: sweetheart deals and political corruption, the meat and potatoes of Massachusetts politics. Curiously, though the reforms he had pushed were aimed at raising the quality of government, until the run for attorney general Dukakis had never emphasized the venal and corrupt nature of state government in Massachusetts in his appeals for reform. But it was right in front of him in the headlines, and it had been for years.

It was also near at hand. Carl Sapers was representing a family named Worcester when Thomas Worcester, an engineer, came to Hill and Barlow for advice on how to avoid paying taxes on $275,000 of earnings he was about to pay to an influence peddler in order to get work from the state's Department of Public Works during Bill Callahan's final term. Sapers advised Worcester not to pay the bribe and admonished that if he did pay the bribe, he should find another law firm. Worcester paid the bribe and found another law firm. In 1961, when he was indicted for income tax evasion, Worcester returned to Hill and Barlow for representation in federal district court.

After Worcester was convicted, a federal judge offered to release him in exchange for sworn political testimony on political corruption in Massachusetts. Worcester agreed and provided powerful evidence that the state was for sale. The Worcester case moved Governor Volpe to propose a crime commission, and the public outrage left the legislature with no real choice but to accede. Sapers took a partial leave from Hill and Barlow to serve as assistant counsel to the Gardner Commission, as it was named, after chairman Alfred Gardner. Sapers for years had kept his friend and young associate at the firm, Mike Dukakis, informed about developments in the corruption cases.

In 1961 the Boston Common Underground Garage scandal exploded before the public. The head of an independent authority created to build a public garage under the Boston Common and his co-conspirators, through an intricate web of phony companies and middlemen, had figured out how to fleece the public of millions while building the garage. From then on, as the reformers pushed to strengthen their position in the legislature, political corruption was always in the air, thanks to the crime commission and Attorney General Edward W. Brooke. In 1964 it was small loans cases and dozens of indictments. And as recently as April 1965, a grand jury, acting on evidence developed as a result of the probe of the Department of Public Works that Dukakis had helped instigate back in 1963, returned fourteen more indictments relating to Bill Callahan's administration of the turnpike authority. Though Callahan was dead by this time, he was named posthumously as an unindicted co-conspirator. In all, a veritable herd of politicians, including two former speakers of the House, a judge, two members of the Governor's Council, the former head of the state police and a former governor, Foster Furcolo, had either been indicted or convicted on corruption charges as Dukakis began his campaign for attorney general.

Although Furcolo was acquitted and few of the indictments resulted in convictions, the stench was so strong it attracted the attention of the *Saturday Evening Post*. The June 5, 1965, issue contained a major article by Boston native and author Edward R. F. Sheehan. The cover tease told America about "Corruption in Massachusetts, a state on trial." Inside, on a two-page spread, were four photos. One was of Callahan. "The late William Callahan ('the shadow governor') had the legislature under his thumb," read the cutline. The second was of Executive Councillor Sonny McDonough, above a cutline that read, "I've broken a few rules and will again—to help a friend." The third photo was of Brooke. "Edward Brooke, the nation's highest elected Negro, is leading the campaign against corruption," the cutline read. The fourth photo was of Mike Dukakis, with the cutline "Men like young Rep. Michael Dukakis may save the scandal-ridden legislature."

As Dukakis campaigned for attorney general, a new scandal was dominating the local news. This one involved allegations of bribes, illegal campaign contributions and architectural and engineering contracts for the state medical school. At the center of it was the governor, John Volpe. After a two-year hiatus, he had been returned to office in the 1964 election. Volpe had wanted a rematch after his close loss to Peabody in 1962, but Peabody's fellow Democrat, the ambitious and independent lieutenant governor, Francis X. Bellotti, denied him the opportunity for revenge. In a move that was considered outrageous even by Massachusetts' standards, Bellotti challenged his own governor in 1964 and beat Peabody in a brutal primary battle. Again, neither party had nominated an Irish candidate for governor, nor was there a Yankee to vote for, or against, this time. The upstart Italian-American, the candidate of a party bleeding from fratricidal warfare, fell to Volpe, the better-known Italian-American, in November.

Back in office, the co-founder of the Volpe Construction Company embarked on a huge project to build a state medical school. The trustees of the University of Massachusetts selected The Architects Collaborative (TAC) of Cambridge to do the design work, but, in the spring of 1965, Volpe's commissioner of administration and finance substituted his choice for that of the trustees. A political fire storm erupted. The Democrats in the legislature immediately impaneled a special investigating committee. Attorney Beryl Cohen, Dukakis's friend from Brookline who had been elected to the state senate, was the committee's most aggressive and resourceful interrogator. Within weeks, witnesses were testifying that the governor's brother, Peter, who had no govermental authority, had been choosing architects and contractors for the medical school project—and had been accepting campaign contributions from them at the same time.

Carl Sapers, at Hill and Barlow, was part of the team that was representing TAC at this time. As a result, Sapers was privy to aspects of the matter that had not, and possibly would not, hit the papers. From Sapers, Dukakis began to learn in meticulous detail how payoffs were made in Massachusetts for public works contracts, how bad things really were. Even reformer Peabody had been actively fundraising from architects and contractors who designed and built for the state, Dukakis learned. The corruption was virtually open, and almost everywhere.

Dukakis saw the revelations as compelling evidence of the need for reform; he had found the theme for his campaign. He ran for attorney general dedicated to prosecuting and purging political corruption from the system. A new element had been added to the reformer's agenda. Soon, newspaper headlines were reporting revelations from the Dukakis campaign. He charged that more than a dozen contractors and architects had gotten state work after making contributions to Volpe, and he did not make idle claims. He named names, just as Joe Clark had done in Philadelphia fifteen years earlier when he had swept the corrupt old Republican machine from power at City Hall with the help of Swarthmore freshman Mike Dukakis.

Meanwhile, throughout the spring of 1966, the medical school scandal dominated the local news. Newspapers ran lengthy transcripts of testimony, and the storyline was damaging to Volpe. An architect, who had been told formally in a letter from the state that he would not get a medical school contract, testified that he was subsequently selected to do the work after Peter Volpe personally intervened. Another architect, David Shields, testified that he went to the Malden office of the Volpe Construction Company to give the governor's brother a thousand dollars in cash and to discuss state contracts. Shields told the committee, "I found that the system called for anyone who wanted anything like a contract to contribute to the campaign. This is the system."

Dukakis's campaign literature reiterated the now-standard Dukakis pitch: his election would bring courage, dedication, knowledge and experience to the attorney general's office. But the boldest type was saved for quotes from the *Saturday Evening Post*.

"Dukakis is a 'forerunner of what must become the predominent mood of Massachusetts politics'."

"He is 'animated by a vision of the good society'."

"Men of his caliber will...take over."

But not in 1966. Frank Bellotti, the former lieutenant governor and loser in the 1964 governor's race, was a tireless campaigner and overwhelmed the field to win the convention endorsement in June.

In losing, Dukakis did nothing to hurt his reputation or his future. He received the first-ever endorsement of the state's principle disarmament and peace organization, MassPax, which urged its members to support Dukakis as "the peace candidate." Coming from nowhere and charging forward with the good-government standard held high, he finished a distant second to Bellotti. Consistent with the COD reform philosophy that conventions of party activists—and not primary voters—should choose the party's candidates, Dukakis paid his respects to the winner and bowed out of the race for attorney general, declining to run in a primary election, as was his prerogative. Besides, as Fran Meaney noted, Bellotti enjoyed far greater name recognition, and the less well-funded Dukakis was not prepared to run statewide as an underdog.

Instead, Dukakis took out reelection papers and was returned to the House of Representatives. Because he had refused to brand Bellotti as a party-wrecker for having run as a lieutenant governor against Peabody two years earlier, Bellotti was gracious in victory. "He handled himself with real class," Bellotti commented on the Dukakis campaign. It had been a long time since such had been said about a leader in the Massachusetts House.

Chapter 7
Early Successes

Professor Robert Keeton of Harvard Law School remembered Michael Dukakis as an excellent student. Dukakis had taken torts from Keeton in his first year, back in 1957-58. In 1966 Keeton, who had spent six years investigating why Massachusetts had the highest auto insurance rates in the nation, was on the phone with his former student, trying to interest him in sponsoring a reform that Keeton was certain would bring relief to the beleaguered Massachusetts motorist.

Keeton had received a grant from a research institute to study auto insurance, and then had convinced a former student, Jeff O'Connell, to come back to Massachusetts from the University of Iowa to work on the problem. The two had finally reduced the incredibly arcane legal and actuarial gibberish to a couple of relatively simple points that explained the cost of insurance. First, Massachusetts had a law that required all drivers to buy what was known as "compulsory" personal injury insurance. Massachusetts was the first state to make such a requirement, and one of only three states in the early sixties to do so. Under compulsory insurance, an insurance company insures a policyholder against personal injury judgments by the courts. Second, Massachusetts also required a legal judgment that an auto accident was the fault of another party before an injured motorist could collect for personal injuries.

In combination, the two laws insured that Commonwealth courts would be constantly jammed with tort cases as the motorists of Massachusetts, who had earned a reputation for bad driving, spent an inordinate amount of money and time trying to prove that someone else was responsible for the accidents that had caused their injuries. Routinely, cases were delayed for three to four years, and often, after all that time, many motorists who had been victimized could not prove it in court, so they received nothing for their suffering. For consumers, the system was a nightmare, but from the point of view of the Massachusetts attorney with a tort practice, the system was functioning quite well. And insurance companies, which were only paying out about forty-four cents on the premium dollar in claims, were not complaining, either.

After Professor Keeton's presentation, Dukakis began thinking of the reform possibilities. "Because he is so bright, it was not difficult for him to understand what we were talking about," Keeton (now a U.S. district court judge in Boston) recalled. "He quickly agreed to sponsor our bill."

What Keeton and O'Connell proposed to Dukakis was unique to the nation, though the Canadian province of Saskatchewan had a somewhat similar system. First, a motorist's own company would provide some compensation without regard for fault; and second, a partial tort exemption would be created, eliminating the least significant claims for the least significant losses. Under such a "no-fault" system, in the vast majority of accidents—the routine fender-benders—involved motorists would simply file claims with their own insurance companies.

The accident attorneys would lose a good deal of work, but the companies theoretically would not suffer. Their rates were set by the state on the basis of a complicated formula involving their recent experiences in losses. The general public would benefit greatly; under no-fault, drivers would have their minor accident claims settled quickly and efficiently without resort to nightmarish civil litigation.

Dukakis was ecstatic. The problem and the solution were classic, and tailor-made for him, his reform program, and his political agenda. A system based on the solid legal philosophy of negligence that was originally created to protect the individual from financial catastrophy had, over time, been corrupted by a special interest, the tort bar, which was well represented in the legislature. Time, effort and money from the tight family budget was being wasted and the consumer was being plundered.

Dukakis filed the no-fault bill of Keeton and O'Connell for the 1967 session and began organizing a reform coalition inside and outside the House of Representatives behind it. Meaney and Gleason organized a lawyers' group in support of the reform. At a time when the civil rights movement was setting off sparks (and fires, all over the Los Angeles ghetto of Watts in the summer of 1966) and the anti-Vietnam War movement was beginning to push hard against the Pentagon, a crusade to reform auto insurance laws seemed a rather parochial exercise and, given the entrenched interests it threatened, one not likely to yield much in return for the effort. As the youth of America were taking over the times, the 33-year-old Dukakis took on an adult issue, a bottom-line numbers issue. But in the effort to reorganize a complex, politically sensitive system to eliminate abuse and waste, he was commiting himself to precisely the kind of challenge he had always coveted.

Dukakis was fortunate not to have made it onto the Democrat ticket in the 1966 election; he was much better off back in the old state representative's seat where he could continue his reform crusade. Nineteen sixty-six had not been a kind year for Democrats. Rebounding from the Goldwater debacle of 1964 in Congress, the GOP won an additional forty-seven seats in the U.S. House and three in the Senate in the mid-term elections. In California, the Republican tide brought Ronald Reagan, who had been running against Mario Savio's Free Speech movement in Berkeley, to the governor's mansion in Sacramento. Back in Massachusetts, the internecine Democratic warfare of recent years and the patina of corruption that covered the party's general reputation had done nothing to help mitigate the national trend back toward the GOP, and Republicans captured every important statewide office that they contested. For the first time in fourteen years, they even made progress, albeit minuscule, in the legislature; they gained two seats—up to fourteen—in the forty-member Senate, and two seats—up to seventy-one—in the 240-member House of Representatives.

The Republicans put up candidates who fit the time-tested model; they nominated political moderates who would appeal to independents, and the Democrats concentrated on the middle-class suburbs. Ed Brooke, the corruption fighter, attracted voters imbued with the spirit of the civil rights movement, and Massachusetts, with palpable pride, elected the first black since Reconstruction to the U.S. Senate. Brooke's opponent, Chub Peabody, was overwhelmed. Eddie McCormack, U.S. House Speaker John W. McCormack's nephew, was less appealing in his final fling at elective politics than he was as the darling of the reformers in the 1962 U.S. Senate primary against Ted Kennedy. Volpe, despite his tarnished reputation, overwhelmed McCormack to retain control of the governor's office. And why not? If Volpe was not squeaky clean, at least he was not a thieving Democrat. The 128-based economy, working overtime with space- and Vietnam-related work, was humming. In rolling up a record 524,683-vote margin over McCormack, Volpe even carried Boston, the first time a Republican had done so in more than forty years.

Elliot L. Richardson, a veritable block of Brahmin rectitude who resembled Clark Kent, was elected attorney general to watch over the Democrats and keep the graft to a minimum. Richardson had no trouble beating Frank Bellotti, and he probably would have had an even easier time with the lesser known Dukakis had his convention effort paid off. It was going to be the Republicans who would be the first beneficiaries of the COD-inspired reform of four-year terms. Volpe, Frank Sargent, the lanky Yankee outdoorsman and conservationist who had won the nomination to run for lieutenant governor, and Richardson would be around for four long Republican years. Or so it seemed.

While the GOP was making a comeback with ethnic and racial diversity, the old days in the legislature were passing, finally, from the scene. Speaker John F. Thompson finished out the 1964 term but did not run for re-election as speaker in 1965. John F. X. Davoren, Thompson's floor leader, was elected to succeed him, and he appointed Thompson chairman of the Ways and Means Committee. Thompson died a few months later of acute alcoholism. At the age of forty-five, Davoren was not a strong leader, and the reformers continued to thrive in the vacuum. Before the term ended, Dukakis had pushed the Keeton-O'Connell no-fault bill through the House, a notable achievement, although it was stopped in the Senate.

Meanwhile, in Boston, COD co-founder Herb Gleason was in the midst of working in a campaign for mayor that promised to have transcendent importance for the city's future. Kevin White, re-elected secretary of state for the fourth time in 1966 and bored by his low-visibility job, was running for mayor. The office was being vacated by John Collins, a conservative who had vastly extended the redevelopment efforts of John Hynes and now after two four-year terms was stepping aside. Vying with the sparkling White in the 1967 fall finals was a frumpy School Committee member, Louise Day Hicks. The contest was steeped in racial overtones. Hicks was an Old Irish politician, but now, with power and prosperity out in the suburbs, virulence was taking the place of Irish conviviality. Her enemies were liberals, the suburban middle class that had abandoned Boston, leaving the city to be fought over by blacks and the poor whites whom it fell to Hicks to lead. White, by contrast, represented liberal enlightenment.

It was the time of the city, black urban activists were making sure of that. Young, energetic, liberal white mayors, like John Lindsay in New York, were for a while at the forefront of social change. White, the cosmopolitan son of an Irish politician, seemed perfectly cast for the role. Against a backdrop of urban riots during the summer of 1967 in Detroit and Newark, and a smaller riot in Boston's black Grove Hall section, the nation watched closely the direction Boston would choose for itself. It chose enlightenment, but just barely. White won by 12,429 votes out of almost 200,000 cast. Boston would have a reform mayor. When White resigned his state post, House Speaker Davoren retired into the secretary of state's position; House Majority Leader Robert Quinn then became speaker.

There was a populistic streak in the ambitious Kevin White, who attracted young, idealistic political activists such as Barney Frank, then the executive secretary of Mike Dukakis's Young Turks, known more formally as the Democratic Study Group, and Fred Salvucci, then working with the Boston Redevelopment Authority. Frank was a brilliant, fast-talking political junkie and whiz kid from Bayonne, New Jersey, who had a special affinity for outcasts and underdogs. Salvucci, a vegetarian and former Rhodes scholar who lived in a triple-decker in working-class Brighton with his large family, was well connected to neighborhood activists; the city's most knowledgeable critic of urban road-building and an acknowledged expert on transportation.

For years before White's election, citizens all over Greater Boston had railed against what was known as the Inner Belt. It had been decided, without community input, that an eight-lane highway was going to cut through the neighborhoods of Roxbury, the Fenway, the town of Brookline, and the cities of Cambridge, Somerville and Charlestown. According to Bill Callahan's Master Highway Plan of 1948, the Inner Belt would feed a number of radial roads and generally cut Greater Boston to shreds. Citizens directed their frustration and anger at the seemingly inevitable highway, unaware that the culprit was a political system that had given the late public works czar vast authority while freeing him of accountability to the people. The Inner Belt was to have been the centerpiece of the Master Highway Plan.

Its purpose was to allow motorists to go *through* the Boston area without having to go *into* it. To fulfill Callahan's vision, more than five thousand units of housing would have to be taken. Close to half of the people who would be displaced were poor enough to qualify for public housing, although the masterplan contained no provision for replacement housing. Much land, including a long swath through the southern end of Boston, was taken by eminent domain, and some houses had already been demolished.

In each community threatened by the highways, grassroots opposition emerged; these urban populists expanded their base by making alliances with like-minded activists from communities that were also scheduled to be cut by the Inner Belt. The insurgency organized itself, grew in power, and prepared to fight. The neighborhood opponents to the highways found themselves in alliance with political activists who were developing a new understanding of the term "the environment." Salvucci, a card-carrying union bricklayer, was deeply dedicated to an environment in which people could live with a minimum of fumes from auto exhausts, noise from jets, and traffic in the streets.

With White in office, the community-based, anti-highway insurgency found that, for the first time, it could communicate with the powers that be. So long as Volpe, a man who made his fortune in heavy construction, was governor, the protestors believed they were fighting a rear-guard action aimed at delaying and minimizing the desecration of their neighborhoods—but at least they could get a hearing at City Hall.

In the town of Brookline, which would be dissected, opposition to the Inner Belt was intense. Dukakis, who had identified Callahan and all he represented as the ultimate symptom of what ailed democracy in Massachusetts, had been fighting the state Department of Public Works and the turnpike authority from the time he took office in 1963. To Dukakis, dedicated as he was to citizen involvement in government, affordable housing, mass transit and local home rule, the Inner Belt and all it represented was evil incarnate.

In March 1963, in his column in the *Chronicle Citizen*, Dukakis extolled a report to Governor Peabody by William Griswold, Peabody's special assistant for mass transportation. Griswold proposed a halt to highway construction and an expansion of trolley and subway service, including construction of an Inner Belt subway. "Griswold's proposals would not displace a single family or business," Dukakis wrote. "What's more, they can be achieved for a fraction of the cost of the Master Highway Plan."

Two months later, Dukakis became furious at plans to give the turnpike authority the power to lease air rights over the highway as it cut through Newton, Brookline and Boston. Dukakis charged in a press conference that the turnpike authority planned and built the extension of the toll road through the three municipalities "in such complete disregard of the public interest that it would be utter folly to permit the authority to retain control over the leasing of air space over the highway extension.

"The authority has in case after case ruthlessly kicked homeowners, tenants and businesses out into the street without the slightest shred of relocation assistance. . . . Not content with the irresponsibility it has displayed on the construction phase of the project," Dukakis told the press, "the authority now proposes under its latest air rights bill to lease air space above the extension free from local controls which apply to all other types of construction in Boston and free from any determination by the three communities involved that the buildings to be constructed are in accordance with their comprehensive plans."

During this time, Dukakis had a weekly radio show on a local station. One day he called Salvucci, whom he had never met, and invited him to go on the air with him to discuss the Inner Belt. "People said we should meet," Dukakis told Salvucci. "People tell me there's a civil engineer who's a transportation professional who's opposed to the highways. People tell me I'm crazy to fight the highways. People say we should like each other."

People were right. Intellectually and philosophically, and in their choice of simple, family-oriented, work-obsessed lives, Salvucci and Dukakis matched beautifully. They began working together to stop the highways. Now the community insurgents—through Salvucci—were connected with the legislature's leading reformer as well as with Boston's mayor.

Though he had not been able to stop the air rights bill from becoming law on the signature of Governor Volpe, by the end of the 1967 legislative year Dukakis was becoming recognized as the Commonwealth's most outstanding legislator. This conclusion was formalized by the New Bedford *Standard-Times*, which polled the House and Senate membership. More respondents named Dukakis as "most outstanding in terms of ability" than any other member.

Along with his concern for affordable housing and mass transportation, and his opposition to the highways as threats to both, Dukakis was working hard on Keeton-O'Connell as a means of lowering auto insurance rates and on a method of lowering electric rates. Dukakis and three other House colleagues were developing a program to encourage the municipal electric companies created by some towns to unite and expand in order to compete more effectively with the private utilities, thus forcing down prices throughout the market.

Concentration on such technocratic matters, important as they were, was becoming more difficult as the 1968 presidential election year began. The candidacy of Senator Eugene McCarthy of Minnesota was stirring a lot of local excitement in Brookline; a furor arose after the Brookline Democratic Town Committee voted in January to endorse McCarthy and his anti-war insurgency against President Lyndon Johnson. A number of Johnson supporters on the town committee, led by State Representative Jack Backman, protested vigorously that the Dukakis-led committee had taken the vote on an unpublicized motion on a night when half the town committee was absent due to a snow storm. The schism was so deep that Backman organized an entire slate and ran against the incumbent slate of "opportunists" and "puppets," as he called them. The pro-McCarthy slate—including Dukakis, Kassler, Alper, Meaney and Sumner Kaplan—was reelected by a two-to-one margin, but inflamed feelings persisted on both sides.

In January of 1968, the Tet Offensive, an audacious thrust by Vietnamese Communists into the cities of South Vietnam that demonstrated the vulnerability of all parts of the country and shattered all American pronouncements that victory was in sight, turned a majority of the American people irrevocably against the war. With McCarthy's surprisingly strong showing in the New Hampshire primary two and a half months later, Robert F. Kennedy's entrance into the race four days after that, Johnson's shocking announcement three weeks after Kennedy's move that he would not run for reelection, the assasination of Martin Luther King in April, and the assasination of Kennedy in June, the nation was becoming unglued. With much of the nation's inspiring leadership gone, many Americans were rejecting the system—and trying to tear it down. But Dukakis never wavered in his attempts at recruiting participants *into* the political process in order to change it.

Massachusetts Democrats and many independents as well had worked up a serious dislike for Nixon during his campaign against their favorite son, John F. Kennedy, eight years before; therefore, news of Nixon's victory in November was not greeted with widespread jubilation in the state, which supported the Democratic ticket more strongly than any other state. As the despised Nixon entered the high office taken from Jack Kennedy with a bullet, the hand of fate was preparing one of its more spectacular contortions. In the disappointment of Nixon's victory, none of the reformers—not Mike Dukakis, not Professors Keeton and O'Connell or their allies, none of the urban populists, not Fred Salvucci or the anti-highway crowd—could see ahead of them, just weeks away, the creation of nothing less than a new order in Massachusetts, one that would draw together all the political forces of the state in a unique and short-lived commitment to common ends. As Massachusetts had been plagued by a hate-filled hundred years' political war that left the state wasted, the government corrupted and the people alienated, so now, in an almost miraculous reversal, Massachusetts would be blessed for a while as its reformed government responded energetically to the expressed aspirations of an indiginous populist insurgency. The results would be a spectacular flowering of democracy, just as the reformer, Mike Dukakis, had always dreamed they would be.

Nixon's role in all this was simple and straightforward. He wanted some Republican talent from Massachusetts to help run his administration. Two days after Nixon took the oath of office, John Volpe accepted an offer to join Nixon's cabinet as secretary of transportation and resigned as governor. With Volpe's departure, Lieutenant Governor Francis W. Sargent became acting governor. The next day, January 23, Elliot Richardson resigned as attorney general in order to become the number-two man at the state department in Washington. On Beacon Hill, the House of Representatives had the pleasure of filling vacant statewide offices by a vote of the members. Speaker Robert H. Quinn was elected attorney general, and immediately afterwards the House elected David M. Bartley, the floor leader, to be speaker.

By the time the music stopped and the players plopped down into their chairs, a new generation of leadership suddenly found itself in charge on Beacon Hill. The new leaders were different in important ways from their predecessors. In 1966 the voters of Massachusetts elected a roadbuilder governor; thanks to Nixon, they ended up with an environmentalist. An MIT graduate with a degree in architecture, Frank Sargent had joined the ski troopers and fought in Italy during the war, then came home and opened the Goose Hummock sporting goods shop on Cape Cod; the new governor also ran a charter fishing boat and dabbled in commercial fishing. Before winning the nomination to run with Volpe, Sargent served as state director of marine fisheries and director of the Federal Outdoor Recreation Resources Review Commission.

In a reformed, post-Callahan DPW, Sargent was in charge of waterways; later, on a Volpe appointment, he headed the agency. He did not question the assumption that the Master Highway Plan would be followed, that the roads would be built, but he also had a deep affection for the environment and a determination to do it as little harm as was humanly possible. Otherwise, Sargent came to power with a lustful taste for politics, a broad smile and an open mind that was expressed in a Boy Scout-like determination to do good deeds. In his young Al Kramer, a one-time state rep who, like Salvucci and Barney Frank down at City Hall, was a dedicated populist, Sargent had an open line to the people—even if he was not completely aware of that fact.

Over in the House, David Bartley, the young speaker from Holyoke who was not quite thirty-four, was a bantamweight of cocky self-confidence, suggesting the kind of leadership that had been lacking in the two Speakers who had followed Thompson. Bartley, who entered the House with Dukakis in the class of '63, had voted down the line for Thompson. Bartley and Thompson were both westerners, and Thompson's tenure, if nothing else, had been good for the western part of the state. He was an unreconstructed party regular. He fought bitterly with reformers, the *Globe* and the League of Women Voters, who were trying to cut the size of the House. He believed in an old-fashioned liberalism coming from an active and caring government, and he wanted an appropriate measure of respect for the institution he had just taken over. There was a rough edge to Bartley, who laughed heartily and cussed repeatedly, but his commitment to public service was sincere. He had studied political science at the University of Massachusetts and had gotten a master's degree in education before entering politics.

Over in the Senate, Maurice Donahue ("Mossie," as he was affectionately known) was wrapping up a six-year term as president and presiding officer. A child of the Depression, Donahue was a New Dealer and a quite serious student of government. He was a gentleman, and was widely respected, even revered for his rectitude and idealism. Donahue, who earned a master's degree in education and studied public administration at Harvard, was more the scholar than the rough-and-tumbler. Donahue and Bartley lived in Holyoke; to Bartley, Donahue was a mentor, a political godfather. As a result, the House and Senate acted in lock step during this time.

Donahue's ambition was the element that seeded the cloud of liberal, progressive and populist programs, laws and actions that were about to shower down from Beacon Hill. Donahue, the laconic bastion of stability who wanted to be governor and had tried once before, this time was going all the way—up or out. One way or another, he would be leaving the Senate at the end of the 1969-70 session. In the meantime, if he were to go up, he would need a strong liberal record, and he would be well served by reminding voters that Sargent was a Republican, like Nixon. If Sargent was to have a term of his own, he would have to beat Donahue or some other Democrat, maybe Kevin White. In Boston, municipal elections are held the year after state elections, so White could run for governor without giving up City Hall.

As for Dukakis, he too was planning on a statewide campaign in 1970, and with Quinn settled in the attorney general's office, certain to run for a term of his own, Dukakis's aim was clear. Rather than challenge an incumbent from his own party (as Lieutenant Governor Bellotti had done in wresting the 1964 gubernatorial nomination away from Peabody) and run a second time for attorney general, Dukakis decided he would run for lieutenant governor.

On September 26, Dukakis, along with twenty members of the Democratic Study Group, called a news conference to condemn the Master Highway Plan and call for Sargent to declare a moratorium on all highway construction within Route 128. The event marked the first time elected officials publicly acknowledged membership in the anti-highway coalition. "What Dukakis did with that news conference was to invigorate the grassroots," said Salvucci. "It gave people courage. It showed them that they'd been heard by the political system."

Dukakis's characteristic passion for causes was expressed over the highway fight, for the entrenched interests, the arrogance of Callahan and the roadbuilders were threatening the foundation of the idealized society to which he was dedicated. Dukakis and his Young Turks released to the press a letter that they would send to Sargent. "Unless current transportation priorities are reversed," the reformers said, "a series of highway projects in eastern Massachusetts costing a billion dollars will, by 1975, destroy almost five thousand units of housing, displace thousands of jobs, pave over dozens of green spaces and parks, further befowl the air and only exacerbate the tragic traffic problem in our core cities."

Much of the coordination with Salvucci now had been delegated to an aide, Steve Kinzer. Until then, Dukakis, like most of the state reps, worked without the luxury of a staff. The presence of Kinzer, a brilliant young man cast in Dukakis's mold, radically increased his capabilities.

Like Dukakis, Kinzer attended Brookline High, where he was editor of the school paper. Kinzer (who is now on the staff of the *New York Times*, where he reports from Managua, Nicaragua) had antagonized the school authorities with his strong anti-war slant, and they tried to rein him in. But Kinzer would not be censored. He set out to start an independent newspaper. Approving of his spunky independence, Dukakis gave Kinzer his fundraising list. To the fourth estate was added another voice, and a long friendship began. On December 17, Mayor White, having reached the conclusion that he had problems with practically every component of the Master Highway Plan, joined Dukakis in calling on Sargent to declare a moratorium on highway construction.

What time Dukakis and Kinzer did not dedicate to the anti-highway fight was spent in the lush Republican towns and villages, like Beverly Farms and Prides Crossing, and the grittier old cities—Peabody, Lynn, Salem—that made up the Sixth Congressional District on what is known as the North Shore of Massachusetts Bay. Republican Congressman William Bates had died suddenly in early summer, and the special election contest to succeed him quickly became a *de facto* referendum on the Vietnam War, as well as an opportunity for the Young Turks to promote one of their own from the State House to Congress. The Republican hawk was, in fact, one of the district's leading gentlemen, State Senator William Saltonstall, son of former U.S. Senator Leverett Saltonstall, the ultimate Brahmin Yankee. The dove was State Representative Michael Harrington, an active member of Dukakis's Democratic Study Group (and one of "the two Mikes," as they were known at the State House) who happened to be the son of one of the North Shore's legendary politicians, Joe Harrington.

As anti-war pressures built and active members of the area's huge counterculture prepared their vans and VWs for the westerly trek on the Mass Turnpike toward Woodstock, New York, at the end of the summer for a marathon concert and convention, Dukakis was going door to door for Mike Harrington. In the heat of the campaign in August and September, Dukakis subordinated all else to the anti-war and reform crusade. He gave Harrington his volunteer and fundraising lists and sent out literature of his own to North Shore residents appealing for their help. "It was an anti-war statement *a la* Duke," Kinzer said. On September 30 the anti-war and the reform movements had reason to celebrate. Harrington narrowly beat Saltonstall 72,029 to 65,052.

Two weeks later the anti-war movement turned out across America for Vietnam moratorium demonstrations in vast numbers. The war was the transcendent issue around Boston as 1969 drew to a close. More than a hundred thousand people came together on Boston Common to participate in the moratorium in what was the largest massing of people in the city's history. Anti-war activity seemed boundless.

Hidden by all this grassroots activity were the makings of a more local political upheaval. The governor and the leaders of the legislature were about to begin a contest of liberal, progressive, populistic one-upmanship as they raced toward the state elections of 1970, pushed and prodded by Mike Dukakis and the Young Turks. A year-long outpouring of liberalism was about to begin, the likes of which had never been seen before and has never been seen since.

(left) The 57th-place finisher in the 1951 Boston Marathon. (courtesy Sandy Bakalar)

(below) In the early fifties: Bunk counsellor speaking to Camp Wing assembly. (courtesy Camp Wing)

(above) Swarthmore student council: Victor Navasky (top), Frank Sieverts (second from right); Dukakis (left). (courtesy Frank Sieverts)

(left) State Representative Mike Dukakis and family in the late sixties. (courtesy *Brookline Chronicle Citizen*)

1968: As state representative, with Francis X. Bellotti (to Dukakis's left) and close friends Allan Sidd (second from right) and Joan Hertzmark. (courtesy Joan Hertzmark)

1971: The Brookline Democratic Town Committee "mafia" with Father Robert Drinan. From left to right: Fran Meaney, Bill Sapers, Joan Hertzmark, Father Drinan, Dukakis, Dan White, Joan Lamphier. (courtesy Joan Hertzmark)

Brookline Democratic Town Committee unveils 1974 gubernatorial campaign slogan. (courtesy Joan Hertzmark)

With tennis partner Billie Jean King, at a charity event in March 1976. (photo © Ellen Shub)

1977: Posing for a newspaper feature on famous refrigerators. (photo © Clif Garboden)

Taking the "T" to work during his first term, 1977. (photo © Jerry Berndt)

1977: With parents, Euterpe (third from right) and Dr. Panos Dukakis. (courtesy Joan Hertzmark)

September 19, 1978: Defeated by Ed King in the Democratic primary, with wife Kitty. (photo © Jon Chase)

January 1979: Leaving the legislature in the final minutes of his first term. (photo © Michael Grecco)

Chapter 8
The Organizer

Governor Frank Sargent was no fool. He understood that the Democrats were trying to force him to act like a Republican at a time when Massachusetts had become an incubator of the anti-war movement. Under the growing influence of chief policy adviser Al Kramer, a disheveled liberal populist and a former Young Turk from the early sixties, he had no intention of ceding the left or the moral high ground to the Democrats. Sargent opened the election year, 1970, in dramatic fashion by proposing an Environmental Bill of Rights to the state constitution. He argued that "a healthy environment is as fundamental a constitutional right as free speech." He went on to talk about the preservation of housing: "Small neighborhoods are the environment for all of us, and we disturb that social, even spiritual, environment mindlessly when we demolish housing without replacement in that same area."

On January 9 Mike Dukakis found that his long crusade on behalf of rent control was beginning to pay off. Sargent adopted Dukakis's point of view and filed a rent control bill of his own. Not to be outdone by the governor, Bartley and Donahue became notably more sympathetic to Dukakis's long crusade, even as the real estate lobby, a powerful force on Beacon Hill, became apoplectic with fear and rage.

The first major test Donahue and Bartley were considering for Sargent was nothing less than a bill to prohibit the President from sending citizens of Massachusetts to fight in an undeclared war. To require citizens to fight in undeclared wars—i.e., wars not declared by Congress, which has the Constitutional responsibility to make war—was to deny citizens their constitutional rights. This was the legal theory on which the legislation was based. It was an interesting approach, developed by a Unitarian minister and filed by a freshman reformer. Massachusetts is a "free-petition" state: the state constitution guarantees citizens the right to put any proposition before the legislature. In adapting to this guarantee, such off-beat bills were the kind that legislators had long ago learned routinely to process through to the trash bin without a second glance.

But these were not normal times, not with "46,000 American troops in Thailand, more than double the number that were in Vietnam in 1964. Do we commit *these* troops and our nation to war?'' asked the Reverend John Wells, the bill's author, at a press conference on January 26. "Do we do so by the action of a President alone? Such a course is both unconstitutional and immoral. As a religious person, I protest. As a lawyer, I seek a legal remedy." Bartley and Donahue were becoming interested. Both supported the anti-war effort, and they saw the potential for this bill to create unique difficulties for the Republican governor. But they were concerned that the bill was frivolous and might further bring the battered legislature new embarrassment.

As the legislative leaders pondered constitutional questions of war and peace, Dukakis was busy fighting highways, along with Fred Salvucci and the neighborhood insurgents. Around Salvucci and Dukakis were drawn political activists with connections in both the mayor's and the governor's inner circles. Communication and coordination were efficiently accomplished, since all three political leaders—Governor Sargent, Mayor White and reform leader Dukakis—were, in effect, relying on the same pool of political talent: Salvucci and his neighborhood leaders. Now that White had made a highway moratorium the city's official position, it was time for the showdown.

The Young Turks' bill to freeze highway construction inside Route 128 was scheduled for its hearing before the legislature's Transportation Committee on February 3. The leaders of the insurgency wanted to create a massive demonstration that day behind the Dukakis bill and against the failure of the governor to commit himself on the issue. But Al Kramer talked them out of it. He argued that Sargent would, in the end, come to adopt their point of view, and would do so more easily if it did not seem that he had been bullied by a mob. The organizers agreed not to mobilize a demonstration. Instead, they packed the hearing room in what the *Boston Globe* in its lead story the next day called "the strongest and longest protest against new expressways" in more than fifteen years.

In kicking off the hearing, Dukakis did not equivocate. He told the committee that what he wanted was a "complete cancellation" of the highways of Callahan's masterplan, including those on which the state, through the DPW, had already invested millions in land-takings and construction contracts. He called the masterplan "folly, expensive [and] destructive." What Dukakis proposed instead of highways was a vastly expanded system of mass transit, to be financed by diverting gasoline tax revenues to amortize a mass transit bond issue. However appealing, the idea, as Dukakis acknowledged, was of questionable constitutionality.

The *Globe*, which was becoming the region's dominant newspaper by riding and pushing the spirit of citizen empowerment and reform, editorialized strongly in support of the highway moratorium. Sargent was getting the same arguments from a special task force he had created to restudy the masterplan. A week after the hearing on Dukakis's bill, Sargent went on statewide television to announce that he had ordered a moratorium on highway construction within Route 128. "Nearly everyone was sure highways were the only answer to transportation problems for years to come," he told the people of Massachusetts. "But we were wrong."

Along with the halt in the destruction of housing for the construction of highways came a bipartisan commitment to build new housing. The state, in partnership with cities and towns, was encouraging construction from the often half-abandoned and derelict housing projects, monuments to the mindless urban renewal of the fifties, that would avoid concentrating the poorest citizens in one area and immediately forming new slums.

A leading thinker on public housing was Democrat Jack Nason, thirty-six, the director of the housing authority of the city of Melrose, a middle-class city north of Boston, and, it was widely assumed, its next mayor. Nason had ties to Senate President Donahue and was working part-time as a driver and communications aide for Mike Dukakis in his campaign for lieutenant governor. Reformers working on housing issues had successfully pushed for legislation requiring private developers who took advantage of favorable state financing programs to reserve a quarter of the units for fully subsidized renters and additional units for partially subsidized renters. Nason helped push through legislation for rental subsidies and had worked for legislation requiring that housing authorities like his own treat applicants without discrimination on grounds of race. Early in 1970 Nason convinced Sargent to require local housing authorities to set aside 5 percent of their units for the physically handicapped.

In 1968, in Chicago, police hordes made sure that the protesters in the street were kept far away from the media spotlight as the Democrats nominated Hubert Humphrey for president. But in Massachusetts, on February 11, 1970, the street protesters were jammed into a legislative hearing room—eight hundred activists in a room with six hundred seats—trying to convince the members of the General Court to join them in a legal, responsible, even elegant initiative toward the ending of the war. When a succession of legal scholars testified before the Judiciary Committee that the anti-Vietnam war bill raised profoundly important constitutional questions, and septuagenarian former senator Ernest Gruening of Alaska, one of the two dissenting votes on the Tonkin Gulf resolution in 1965, added his personal prestige to the effort, the Democratic leaders were emboldened. What better way to remind voters that Sargent was a Republican than to challenge him to sign a bill declaring, in effect, that his president—the leader of his party—was conducting an illegal war?

When the Shea-Wells bill (named for its author, the Reverend John Wells, and its sponsor, representative H. James Shea of the liberal town of Newton, just west of Brookline) passed Bartley's House, 136-69, on March 16, Chairman J. William Fulbright of the Senate Foreign Relations Committee offered his "compliments to the great Commonwealth of Massachusetts...for showing great leadership." With Donahue working the chamber and the anti-war activists working the phones, the bill passed the Senate easily and went to the desk of the governor. On April 2, 1970, with the network cameras rolling, Sargent made it the law of the Commonwealth that a citizen of Massachusetts could not be made to fight in a war undeclared by Congress. So much for the Democrats' effort to outflank Sargent on the left and to make him into a Nixonian Republican.

At the end of the month, on April 29, Nixon's invasion of Cambodia began, and a week later, college students protesting the invasion were shot and killed by National Guardsmen on the campus of Kent State University in Ohio. In Massachusetts, to protest the killings, thousands marched on the State House. Sargent came out to speak to the protesters. When a violent confrontation with police threatened, Sargent ordered the American flag lowered and removed. Massachusetts had become an alternative capital of the nation, a mecca for liberal and progressive causes—a place where Nixon had never been, and would never be welcomed.

In such tumultuous times, it was more than a little ironic that the climactic political battle of the legislative session would be fought over auto insurance. But Dukakis and his professorial allies had worked the legislature tirelessly on behalf of the Keeton-O'Connell bill. Now Sargent was sifting through the House and Senate calendars for liberal and progressive initiatives to support, and he threw his weight behind Dukakis's no-fault insurance bill. The *Globe* chimed in, and yet another reform movement took wing.

For years Dukakis had had a difficult time lobbying his peers in the corridors of the House, for the subject was complex and tedious, and the influence of the bar was immense. After he became speaker in 1969, Bartley named attorney Ned Dever, the nephew of former Governor Paul Dever, to chair the Insurance Committee. Although Dukakis had gotten no-fault passed by the House in the previous term, Dever did not know enough about the issue or the proposed reform to have a firm position yet. So, in 1969, Dukakis did not get committee support for no-fault. In 1970, again, "there was very strong opposition to this from the attorneys," Dever said. "For them, it meant less clients and less claims. Also, it works against the philosophy of negligence. But we were the highest-rated state in the nation. I was convinced by Keeton and Michael that something had to be done." The Insurance Committee gave no-fault its blessing.

On July 29 the House passed no-fault, but the Senate refused. Lending urgency to the building crisis was the upcoming expiration of a freeze in auto insurance rates. If something was not done, rates for 1971 would go up by as much as 30 percent. With the Senate still balking, Sargent, who was determined to build his favorability ratings for the gubernatorial campaign had yet another good reason to take to statewide television a week later, on August 5. He attacked the tort lawyers and insurance industry lobbyists, whom he said had been jamming the State House corridors for the past two weeks as the public interest had been "ignored and trampled." Declaring that "my patience is at an end," Sargent promised that he would not approve an adjournment for the legislature until auto insurance was reformed. "I don't care if the session runs until hell freezes over," he added with a flourish.

At last, the Senate passed an amended no-fault bill, and it went to a conference committee. Bartley named Dukakis as one of the three members of the House conference committee, but removed him in favor of Dever when Dukakis's refusal to compromise jeopardized the committee's chances of reaching agreement on a version that could be approved by both branches.

The amendments, to which the House finally agreed, made the reform even more odious to the industry. One amendment mandated a 15-percent cut in *all* auto insurance rates, not just on the compulsory bodily injury coverage, as Dukakis had wanted. Another amendment gave drivers the right to automatic renewal of their policies no matter how many accidents they had had in the previous year; this too had not been part of the Keeton-O'Connell bill. In response to the compromise that emerged, Lumberman's Mutual joined Aetna Casualty Insurance Company and Employers Commercial Union in threatening to stop writing insurance policies in Massachusetts if the amended no-fault bill became law. As the *Globe* noted in the lead of its top story on the legislature's sending the governor the no-fault compromise, Sargent's response would determine "whether the state's 2.5 million motorists will have lower insurance rates next year or no auto insurance at all." Dukakis was constantly on the telephone to his friend Al Kramer in the governor's office, "telling me what the administration should be doing. This was Dukakis's baby," said Kramer (now a state district court judge).

Would Sargent sign the flawed bill, calling the industry's bluff, and risk chaos? Or would he send the bill back with corrective amendments, a more moderate and, many felt, more responsible step? Sargent again asked for and received statewide TV time on August 13, the night after he finally got the bill; he wanted to speak to the people about the auto insurance crisis. What Sargent would do with the bill was a closely held secret. Even Dukakis was kept in the dark.

Sargent began his address by outlining all the benefits of no-fault. Then he explained the amendments to which the industry objected. If the companies did leave, he said, he was prepared to create a state insurance fund. And with that, the governor said, "I will sign the auto insurance reform bill." On the spot, on television, he signed the bill, slamming down his pen in dramatic fashion. "And now the crisis is upon us," he said ominously.

Sargent could have said, "And now the election has been decided," and he would have been equally accurate, for in standing up to the insurance industry and the tort lawyers, Sargent was standing up for the little guy in a big way. The Democrats were not going to get to Sargent's left.

On September 15 Kevin White sent State Senator Maurice Donahue into political retirement by beating him for the Democratic gubernatorial nomination, 231,605 to 218,665. Meanwhile, Mike Dukakis, the reformer who had presented Sargent with two huge opportunities—with highways and auto insurance—to show the voters that he too was a liberal, a reformer, a progressive, and a populist with a flair for the dramatic gesture and courageous action was catapulted onto the statewide ticket as the Democratic nominee for lieutenant governor. Dukakis got the appreciative support of the anti-highway populists within the urban areas of Eastern Massachusetts. And motorists everywhere on the Democratic side who understood the importance of auto insurance reform were ready to give a vote of thanks to the reformer, too.

Dukakis's opposition in the Democratic primary was weak. None of the candidates had anything more than a countywide base, and none could boast of anything like the landmark achievements that had put Dukakis on the political map. Dukakis's crack statewide organization, which had practiced at identifying and recruiting reform-minded political activists since the COD days, ensured for Dukakis a place on the statewide ticket.

The leading candidates at the convention, held on a summery June weekend on the campus of the University of Massachusetts, were Dukakis and Beryl Cohen, good friends and neighbors and longtime allies on the Brookline Democratic town commitee. The loser of the two at the convention would not take the contest further. Cohen, the sponsor of the Racial Imbalance Law, was less a reformer and more a traditional liberal than Dukakis. He was also more comfortable with the Beacon Hill crowd.

From Frank Bellotti's mastery over Dukakis in 1966, when both sought the endorsement of a state convention, and Bellotti, after falling short on the first ballot, surged to victory with new delegate support that appeared as if by magic, Dukakis had learned the first commandment of conventions: Know Thy Delegates. It was a lesson Beryl Cohen had been spared. He was relying on his twenty-six Senate colleagues, including President Donahue, to deliver their delegations for the senator from Brookline.

Dukakis, on the other hand, revealed himself as the great organizer he had become as he prepared for the convention. Before delegates were even elected, he was campaigning before ward and town committees, urging them to send delegates pledged to him. "He visited every ward and town committee and every delegate to the last convention, some more than once," said Kinzer. In one small town southwest of Boston, the town committee conducted a non-binding straw poll of Democrats to get a sense of the preferences of the local party rank-and-file before the town committee picked delegates. Dukakis organized a full-fledged campaign to ensure that the results of the straw poll were favorable to him. It was a success. "Michael didn't call the senators and reps to say, 'Get me your ten delegates.' He called the senators and reps and said, 'Give me the names and addresses of your delegates,' " said Bartley. "Then he called them and met with them all personally." Said Dick Giesser, a friend and fundraiser for Dukakis, "He had memorized their names as if it were an examination in school."

Unlike 1966, when Bellotti's greater experience at conventions caught them unaware, Dukakis, Meaney and company were prepared down to the most minute detail. The wives of the campaign's brain trust—Pat Meaney, Connie Giesser, Kitty Dukakis, among others—all wore similar, contemporary tight dresses and hats, as if in uniform. Dukakis distributed Chinese fortune cookies to the delegates lest they even consider the notion that the cerebral reformer did not understand the kitschy spirit of conventions. "Dukakis, that's the ticket—well one half anyway" was one fortune. Another read, "Mike D. Thanks for your support. Have another cookie."

On the morning of the balloting for lieutenant governor, Beryl Cohen called his Senate colleagues together under a tree outside the Curry Hicks Cage, the convention center, after being told by a Donahue aide that neither he nor Dukakis would be the nominee. He was shocked to learn that the senators would offer no help. Donahue, who had secured the convention endorsement for governor the previous day, had decided he did not want to run with Beryl Cohen, another senator. That much was clear. Less clear was what influence, if any, Donahue wanted to have in the voting for lieutenant governor. Bartley, who presided at the convention but was not hiding his support for his mentor, said Donahue maintained a strict neutrality. "Delegates would come up to us and say, 'This guy, Dukakis, came to my house and talked to me for thirty minutes. And I'd kind of like to vote for him.' And we'd say, 'You're on your own.' " But Cohen, Meaney and Kinzer insisted that Donahue had put out the word that he wanted his supporters to swing the convention toward a late entrant, state representative Anthony DiFruscia.

No machinations, however, had the potential for stopping Dukakis's reform juggernaut. In 1970 it had not yet dawned on the old-style politicians like Bartley and Donahue that the activists who had gone door to door for Eugene McCarthy in 1968, and afterward continued to pursue the kind of local political goals that had made the present legislative session a high-water mark for liberalism in Massachusetts, were the new party regulars. And, for 1970 at least, their candidate was Mike Dukakis for lieutenant governor. As the voting began, Geraldine Pleshaw of Boston, a delegate and a state committee member from Boston, moved to dispense with the polling and endorse Dukakis by acclamation. Bartley ruled the motion out of order, but not before it set off a two-minute "We want Mike!" demonstration. When the voting was over, Bartley announced that Dukakis had beaten Cohen 697-428, with DiFruscia and the other candidates far, far behind.

Conventions had always played a central role in Dukakis's vision of a reformed Democratic party, a party infused with the energy and ideas of high-minded political activists drawn together to focus their intentions and choose their leaders. Ten years after setting out, through COD, to make that happen, Dukakis stood before the convention, the realization of his own vision. Beaming from ear to ear, Dukakis accepted the convention's endorsement "with great gratitude and deep appreciation." His graciousness to "a great guy and a great candidate" did nothing to ease the pain of Beryl Cohen, who had assumed the loyalty of his Senate colleagues.

After such a convention, the primary was anticlimactic. The leading challenger to Dukakis in a field of four was a little-known candidate from Arlington, a Boston suburb. Dukakis beat him by a 4-3 margin in his hometown, and statewide ran ahead of him almost 2-1. In Brookline Dukakis received 92 percent of the vote.

At the top of the ticket was Mayor Kevin White. White and Dukakis went back more than ten years together, and through Herb Gleason and Fred Salvucci, among others, they remained connected. But they had never been close friends; instead, a rivalry of sorts had developed between them, the two most successful local products of the JFK inspiration. When the Democratic nominees sat down together to organize themselves into a team, it became clear that White saw himself as "the ticket," with Dukakis a constitutionally required add-on. Dukakis successfully negotiated from White an agreement that Dukakis would be responsible for transportation issues, which would be developed by Salvucci and Kinzer under his aegis. But as for the politics of how to beat Governor Sargent, White, who after three years in office—and in klieg lights—was already attracting national attention, would take care of that.

At one early meeting of White's and Dukakis's top staff members, called to work on the two staffs' integration, Kinzer and Jack Lawton, Dukakis's official campaign manager, walked into White's headquarters to find themselves in a room with forty people, including campaign consultant Joe Napolitan, who was splitting his time between two big-time politicians, Kevin White and Ferdinand Marcos of Manila.

Given the events of that extraordinary year, all the talent in the world was not going to help White beat Sargent. The mayor could not appeal to urban populists by citing his opposition to the Inner Belt because Sargent had stopped it. He could not try to beat Sargent by campaigning against Nixon's war because Sargent had signed a bill declaring American participation in it to be illegal. And he could not complain that Sargent was Republicanly soft on big business because he had stood up to the lawyers and the insurance companies on no-fault.

In fact, even if he had had a theme and a message, White could not have campaigned against Sargent for a critical ten days in the middle of the campaign season. In mid-October he was hospitalized with a bleeding ulcer and did not return to the trail until a week before the election. All in all, the mayor could have stayed in bed for all the good winning the Democratic nomination did for his political career.

Sargent's victory margin in November was 259,354 votes, a 57-43 percent trouncing. In a remarkable year of populism, idealism, liberalism and reform, Sargent had become the embodiment of them all; he was the unquestioned political master of the moment. ''The administration reached out to the times,'' said Kramer. ''It gave power to the voices of the previously disenfranchised.''

Chapter 9
The Fading of the Old Guard

Election day, November 3, 1970, happened to be Mike Dukakis's thirty-seventh birthday, but no one in the Dukakis campaign for lieutenant governor expected to be celebrating. They had no illusions about what Kevin White faced at the polls, and in this election, his fate was their own. But like their leader, Dukakis campaigners took their medicine stoically and made the best of it. The chairman of the Melrose Housing Authority, Jack Nason, a Dukakis speechwriter and communications advisor, had set up TV interviews for Dukakis with several news stations. At least the defeat would afford Dukakis a chance to raise his visibility. At the end of a long and depressing day, Dukakis balked at going through with the final TV interview, with the UHF station WKBG-TV, Channel 56, located on Morrissey Boulevard in Dorchester, a fifteen-minute drive from downtown. But the 36-year-old Nason had made a commitment. So the losing candidate for lieutenant governor, with his wife and Fran Meaney in one car, and Nason, Kinzer and two other aides in a second car, dragged himself down to Channel 56 for the final interview of the day around midnight.

At 1:30 a.m., after the interview, Dukakis and his companions left for Brookline. To do so, they had to make a reverse turn at a light on Morrissey, just south of the *Boston Globe* building. The Dukakis car was far enough ahead of Nason's that no one in the lead car heard the sickening crash as a rented truck, driven by Thomas J. Houton of Peabody, smashed into Nason's car as it negotiated the reverse turn on a green light.

Houton had grown up in Ward 13, a heavily Irish, heavily political working-class section of Dorchester; Ward 13 had many triple-deckers, wooden three-story apartment buildings in which three families typically lived, one on each floor. There was a lot of celebrating going on in Ward 13 on election night. Favorite son Robert H. Quinn, who had been elected by his colleagues in the House to succeed Elliot L. Richardson as attorney general when he resigned to join Nixon's state department in January 1969, on this day had won a four-year term of his own, swamping a minor Republican. The Houtons were quite close to Bob Quinn, who had also grown up in Ward 13. Quinn had attended Boston College, where many of the brightest sons of old Boston went to get a Jesuit education, and had advanced to

Harvard Law School. One of Tom Houton's brothers, Jack, had worked for Quinn for years, back when he was the Speaker of the House, handing out summer jobs and other patronage appointments, and he continued that work for Quinn as an assistant attorney general.

Tom Houton, the youngest of three brothers, also dabbled in politics. He had spent at least part of the election night in downtown Boston at the headquarters of his other brother, Dan. Running as an independent, Dan Houton was a loser that night in a three-way contest for a congressional seat. From downtown, the preferred route home to Ward 13 ran south, down Morrissey Boulevard and just past the *Globe* building, and turned right and west into Dorchester's Savin Hill section, which was Ward 13.

Two Metropolitan District policemen raced to the scene. They sent the injured aides to the hospital in an ambulance and a cruiser, and smelled the strong odor of alcohol on the breath of the 26-year-old Houton, who staggered around the accident scene glassy-eyed, speech slurred. One officer told Houton he was being placed under arrest for being drunk and read him his Miranda rights. Then the officer searched Houton and found a can opener in a pocket. At the scene, the officers gave Houton written citations charging him with operating under the influence of intoxicating liquor and operating to endanger.

It was not until they were back at home in Brookline that the Dukakis's received word from the emergency room at Boston City Hospital. Michael and Kitty Dukakis and Fran Meaney got down to the hospital fast, racing into the ER. Kinzer, drifting in and out of consciousness, was lying on a cot with blood pouring from his head. He heard Fran Meaney telling him Dukakis was there. "Hello, Michael," Kinzer said, before fading away one more time. Dukakis fainted on the spot, collapsing to the floor. Kitty tended to her husband.

Meaney could not stay. He was needed in the morgue to identify Nason's body. He had been declared dead at 3:15 a.m.

It took seventy-five stitches to close the wound in Kinzer's head, and he also suffered multiple broken ribs. Later, Nason's widow, Rita, who had left her three children alone in Melrose for the thirty-minute ride to Boston City Hospital, arrived.

Houton was arraigned the next day before Judge Jerome Troy, the presiding justice of the Dorchester District Court. Troy ruled, rather than presided, over the working-class neighborhoods in Dorchester. His capricious and autocratic manner was legendary, and Troy had a reputation for setting exorbitant bail for defendants who were not friends, or friends of friends, and taking a cut of the profits from the grateful bail bondsmen. The people of Dorchester lived in fear of Judge Troy. Jerome Troy had made himself the law, and a citizenry raised to respect authority bit its tongue and muddled on with a monster in its midst. So outrageous was Troy's behavior that a group of anti-war activists turned community organizers, led by Michael Ansara from Harvard and Students for a Democratic Society, had begun organizing a grassroots opposition to Troy called The People First months before Houton came before Troy for arraignment.

The police sought manslaughter and dangerous driving charges against Houton, but Judge Troy refused to issue the complaints. Instead, he decided to charge Houton with driving under the influence of alcohol and released him on one thousand dollars' personal recognizance.

Dukakis was deeply shaken by the tragedy that had befallen his aide Jack Nason, whom he had known for five years. Nason was a reformer like Dukakis. His great accomplishment, as director of the Melrose Housing Authority, was leading the way toward construction of the city's first public housing project, a 155-unit apartment building for the elderly that was set to open in January of 1971. "The kind of dedication and tireless effort which Jack gave my campaign was of a quality and intensity not often seen in political life," Dukakis said in a statement that was released to the press.

"This was a tragic accident that took the life of a good man who worked so hard to make the political system work because he strongly believed it could work responsibly only if people became involved. He was a man to be admired. I mourn for him, his wife and three children and all of his family."

Three days later, on Saturday, November 7, the religious, political and business leadership of Massachusetts gathered in Boston for the funeral mass for Richard Cardinal Cushing, who had died two days before election day. Michael and Kitty Dukakis could not attend because of a scheduling conflict. They were in Melrose at the Incarnation Church for the funeral mass for Jack Nason.

On December 11, Thomas Houton went on trial in Dorchester District Court, not on the manslaughter and dangerous-driving charges the police had sought, but on the reduced charge of driving under the influence.

Despite the obvious potential conflicts of interest the system created, Massachusetts at the time allowed practicing attorneys to sit as judges and hear cases. The judge who was to hear the Houton case and to render a verdict in the absence of a jury at the district court level, as was then the law, was one of these "special justices." The favored few, as a result of their special justice status, earned more money and had considerably more influence in the court system when they were wearing their other hats as trial attorneys. It was a system that encouraged abuse, and although the reformers had identified the special justices for elimination, the law still allowed governors in 1970 to select "specials," and they could be called to the other side of the bar at the discretion of a court's presiding judge.

To hear the Houton case, Judge Troy selected a special justice, James J. Mellen. Attorney Mellen practiced criminal law mostly in the Charlestown District Court; he came across town to Dorchester to try the Houton case. The two police officers at the scene and the booking officer testified as to the shape Houton was in at the accident scene. One officer testified, "I detected a very strong odor of alcohol. His speech was slurred and his eyes were glassy." The second officer at the scene testified that "... his speech was thick. His eyes were glassy, and I noticed a strong smell of alcoholic beverage, one which I am familiar, beer, from his breath." The booking officer testified to having made the same observations about Houton, and he added, "In my opinion, he was drunk."

J. J. Sullivan, a shrewd and experienced Boston attorney, represented young Houton at his trial. Sullivan recalled that he was asked to take the case by Bob Quinn or his aide, Jack Houton; Sullivan and Quinn, who had shared office space together, had been friends for years. Sullivan called only one witness in Houton's defense: Michael Donovan, a long-time friend of Houton's dating back to grammar school. Donovan had done political work for Quinn; now, in his mid-twenties, he was an assistant clerk for the superior court in Boston. Donovan testified that he had been with Houton at his brother's campaign headquarters until about 1:00 a.m. on election night, and that Houton was despondent over his brother's election loss. Long after the polls closed, Houton worked the phones, compiling returns, Donovan testified. He said Houton had been sober as of 1:00 a.m., when Donovan closed the office, and that "he couldn't" have been drinking because "there wasn't" anything alcoholic to drink at Houton headquarters.

After more than an hour's testimony, Special Justice Mellen rendered his verdict. He explained, "There is no criticism of the intent of a police officer in the course of his duties in the courtroom and the elements that go into the drunkenness and the observation by the second and third witness that succeeded him, the lieutenant as I recall it, and they were emphatic in their allegation; their opinion, that the defendant was drunk, but there is no drunkenness charge in front of me, and they either did not seek the complaint for drunkenness or had it denied, I do not know which is the case, but that might weigh to a great degree the effect of such testimony because the charge is not drunkenness. So I have to as a matter of law minimize that testimony and take it to the lower degree of it, if he had any alcohol on him; and whether or not it was sufficient to perceptively affect his operation of the motor vehicle."

On the other hand, Special Justice Mellen found witness Donovan convincing: "I was impressed with his truthfulness and his accuracy and his frankness, and that culminates my opinion that the defendant is not guilty."

With that, Tom Houton, the driver of the truck that had smashed into the Jack Nason's Ford Maverick, killing him, was a free man.

Five days later, in the evening of December 16, Mike Dukakis was the master of ceremonies for a Jack Nason memorial evening at a resturant on U.S. Route 1, fifteen minutes from the Nason home. Mayor Kevin White, the losing candidate for governor, also attended, along with scores of reform-minded political activists and friends.

With the tragedy compounded by travesty, the sad times for Rita Nason and her family became even harder. Her oldest son, John, who was eleven, took things especially hard. Laurie, who was nine, dealt with the tragedy by absorbing and trying to remember everything. Robert, who was two, was too young to comprehend. The Dukakis family drove out to Melrose from Brookline almost every Sunday during the holiday season. By then Kitty's son John was thirteen and had since the second grade been using his stepfather's surname. And to play with the Nason kids, in addition, was Andrea, who was five, and Kara, who, like Robert Nason, was just two.

On January 7, 1971, the *Boston Globe* published the entire transcript of the Houton trial across one full page of the broadsheet and onto a second. The next day, the registrar of motor vehicles suspended Tom Houton's license "indefinitely." Ansara and The People First capitalized on the *Globe*'s courageous exposure of the case by organizing opposition to Troy in the neighborhoods of Dorchester, using the published transcript of the trial as evidence that things were seriously amiss in Troy's court.

For Bob Quinn, the next step up the political ladder was the governor's office. No higher-ranking Democrat stood in his way. He gave little or no thought to the possibility that he would have trouble in 1974 with his old adversary from the House, Mike Dukakis, or from any other Democrat, for that matter, so Quinn made little effort to put together a statewide organization. He had never forgotten the essence of ward politics—you help your own. It had stood him in good stead as he made his way up the legislative leadership ladder, and it had helped him get to the attorney general's office. In the run for governor, he was confident he would get all the help he needed from "his own."

Though badly shaken by the Nason tragedy, Mike Dukakis wasted little time after the election before embarking on an effort that was designed to yield an election victory four years later. Over the previous four years, Dukakis had lost a convention fight and later won one, and he had run a statewide race on a losing ticket. Now he was ready to take charge of his fate in a second statewide run.

His eye was on the attorney general's race in 1974. The local political world believed that Bob Quinn would vacate the position to run for governor. Dukakis and Fran Meaney were confident that they would have no Democratic opposition. "Nobody would challenge him," Meaney recalled, "since he was such a star." To Steve Kinzer, to run for attorney general made all the sense in the world. "He was a lawyer, he had run for it once before, and next to governor, it's the job with the most clout."

So convinced was the Dukakis inner circle that the race for attorney general would be a "gimme" that Meaney told Dukakis that he wanted to stay out of his race for attorney general in order to concentrate on helping an old Meaney-Dukakis ally, Congressman Michael Harrington, who was planning to challenge Quinn for the Democratic gubernatorial nomination. "I told Dukakis that the experience would come in handy when he ran for governor later," Meaney said. The Dukakis brain trust believed Sargent, riding high as a liberal reformer, would crush either Quinn or Harrington three years later in 1974.

With Dukakis's approval, Meaney attended a couple of planning sessions of the Harrington brain trust and heard a strategy unfolding that he found disturbing. In order to run unopposed, or at least without major Irish opposition, Harrington was planning to announce early, with the endorsement of such political luminaries as Harrington's House colleague Tip O'Neill, and others. If Quinn could be sufficiently intimidated, he might opt to stay on as attorney general.

If Harrington carried through with his plan, it could have left Dukakis with the option of running against Quinn, an incumbent Democrat, for attorney general, or against his friend Mike Harrington for the party's nomination for governor, and Meaney and Dukakis thought running for governor was premature. Meaney withdrew from the Harrington group and came up with the strategy to clear the way for Dukakis to run for attorney general. In the Machiavellian way of politics, the idea was that Dukakis would immediately begin spreading the word that he was going to run for governor. Hopefully, Quinn would then decide to announce for the top spot on the ticket for fear of being left behind by Dukakis and Harrington. "You can always drop down," Meaney counselled Dukakis, "but you can't go up" once a lesser office is announced for.

The only trouble with the strategy was that Quinn did not take the bait. He would not advance his timetable, which had him announcing for governor early in 1974. To further prod Quinn into publicly declaring, Meaney passed the word to Quinn that Dukakis had established a deadline for him to declare his intentions; if he did not, Dukakis would. Again, Quinn demurred. With the passage of time, as Dukakis and Meaney began talking up a race for governor, newspapers duly reported that Dukakis was a candidate, possibly a strong one. The idea, initially a strategic ruse, began to take root. And the more Dukakis and his allies traveled the state speaking with supporters from the 1970 campaign, the more encouraged they became.

The Dukakis inner circle at this time was led by Meaney, Steve Kinzer, Kitty Dukakis, who was an active partner in planning Michael's moves, and Allan Sidd, another close friend from Brookline. In the great demographic shift that turned one of Boston's most Jewish communities into a black community in the forties and fifties, Allan and Shirley Sidd had moved from the Roxbury section of Boston to Brookline in 1958, shortly after Mike Dukakis returned to town from Korea, and they became friends almost immediately. During the Depression, the Sidds were young radicals, idealists dreaming of an egalitarian world. In 1948, just married, they were barely old enough to vote for Henry Wallace, the candidate of the Progressive Party for President. And their poor and working-class oriented politics were still notably to the left of Dukakis's middle-class reform focus.

The burly, gruff-talking Sidd, a veteran of the garment industry who eschewed physical exercise for chain smoking, seemed the antithesis of the proper, cool and cerebral Dukakis. But mutual friends said the ascetic Dukakis seemed to take some vicarious pleasure in Sidd's mild self-indulgences: cigarettes, food, gambling and politics. His style of politics was simple and human. One friend described Sidd as "the caricature of the old Jewish ward boss." In his post as town treasurer, Sidd became a powerful figure in Brookline by accumulating information, the currency of politics, and using it judiciously. It was Sidd, back in 1969, who introduced the Dukakises to underground student publisher Steven Kinzer. Sidd characteristically was amused and pleased that Kinzer was bucking the high school establishment and encouraged the effort.

The run for lieutenant governor gave Dukakis an opportunity to meet still more potential supporters, but with the loss, he was out of office for the first time since January of 1963, so he would have to find new ways to remain in the public's eye.

Ralph Nader, the uncompromising consumer advocate who was shaking up Washington with his investigations of the Interstate Commerce Commission and the Federal Communications Commission, gave the ever-resourceful Dukakis an idea.

On November 24, less than three weeks after the 1970 election, Dukakis announced in a *Boston Globe* interview that he was forming an agency to monitor the performance of Governor Frank Sargent's administration of the state, and to make recommendations for reforms. The idea, developed with Kinzer, who had been released from the hospital but now was required to wear glasses as a result of injuries suffered in the accident, was to create a volunteer organization modeled on Nader's national model. Researchers, investigators and writers would be drawn primarily from the ranks of area law schools and law firms; young, good-government activists from the same environment from which Dukakis himself had come would emerge to form a shadow government.

And just to make sure nobody missed the point of what Dukakis was trying to accomplish, he labeled his group "the Raiders," after Nader's Raiders, as they were popularly known. Dukakis told the *Globe* that *his* Raiders would probe state agencies in much the same way that Nader's Raiders probed federal agencies. "Nader has developed a mechanism nationally for keeping people on their toes," he said. "The same kind of thing is necessary on the state level." In the *Globe* article, which also mentioned Dukakis as a "possible" Democratic party gubernatorial candidate in 1974, the newest Raider indicated that his group would focus on state regulatory agencies "to find out why they've been so sleepy for so long. In most cases, regulatory agencies tend to get very close and chummy with the industries they're regulating."

The Dukakis Raiders went officially into action after a well-publicized press conference in February 1971 at the Parker House Hotel. Over the next year and a half critical reports were issued on the Outdoor Advertising Board (the billboard regulators), the personnel and insurance broker licensing policies of the state Division of Insurance, the employment of a highly paid lobbyist at the Massachusetts Port Authority (a quasi-public agency that runs the seaport, the airport and a toll bridge) and the Port's refusal to promote mass transportation, the city of Boston's meat inspection efforts, and the housing policies of the state Department of Community Affairs. In July the *Boston Globe* called the former state representative a "poor man's Ralph Nader" and judged the reports to be "credible." The effort, with Kinzer coordinating the research and writing efforts, actually took up very little of Dukakis's time, but it served to keep him up to date on what was happening in much of the Sargent administration. The project never grew, however, to have the same cachet and impact Ralph Nader enjoyed at the national level, in part because Dukakis was too busy earning a living.

Dukakis had maintained his part-time position at Hill and Barlow since graduating from Harvard Law School more than ten years before, but while Kinzer ran the Raiders, for the first time he began practicing law full-time. He did so with characteristic zeal and responsibility, although he never got much satisfaction from representing the real estate developers who made up his basic clientele. Dukakis and his friend and fellow COD co-founder Carl Sapers had been made partners in 1965.

With three growing children, the apartment the Dukakises occcupied in the building they had bought at 93 Perry Street in 1963 was getting a bit cramped. When the two-family dwelling at 85 Perry Street, immediately adjacent to their six-unit apartment building, went on the market in 1972, they decided to buy it with some friends who were active in Brookline politics and who were also looking for another home. Michael, the father of the Commonwealth's condominiumization law, now had an opportunity to be one of the first to use the law that he had written. Characteristically, he practiced what he preached.

He decided that, rather than sell the building as a whole and risk its falling into the hands of an absentee landlord some day, he would convert the building into condominium units, which he did, selling four to residents and two to additional buyers. In characteristic Dukakis fashion, he priced the units modestly, at $13,500 each—below the market—and sold his building for $81,000. When the Dukakises bought 93 Perry, they took out two mortgages, totaling $51,000. Dukakis had enough of a profit from the sale to buy 85 Perry, and a few more residents began paying property taxes in Brookline. "He wanted to give people who lived there a chance to be secure," said Dan White, one of the buyers. "It was typical of him to find a way to do it creatively."

Meanwhile, Alan "Lanny" Johnson, a student at Northeastern University's School of Law, was traveling the state for Dukakis, augmenting the file of supporters for the 1974 campaign. Johnson had begun working for Dukakis in the 1970 campaign as a driver and, after election day, he began to develop a field organization that would be second to none. Often accompanying Johnson on the road on weekends was John Dukakis, by now a young teenager.

Working for a candidate with a near-photographic memory could be frustrating, Johnson found. From time to time, he would return from the road to report on his efforts, only to have Dukakis throw a name back at him that he had recalled from previous campaigns. After a three-day trip to the city of Haverhill, which Dukakis knew especially well because his mother's family lived there, he gave Johnson a mild rebuke. "Don't tell me you've organized Haverhill if you haven't met Bill Wrenn. He runs the Amoco Station on White Street, and he's worked for me before." Johnson returned to Haverhill, an hour's drive to the north, to make sure Bill Wrenn had been signed up for the next campaign.

Dukakis was widely assumed by the press to be the reform candidate for governor in 1974, but in 1972 he was fortunate to be organizing his campaign in relative anonymity; with all eyes trained on the presidential election, Dukakis could once again, as he had done in 1970, quietly go about the business of organizing state convention delegates. During a raging presidential campaign, who could think of a state election more than two years off?

An army of anti-war college students produced a groundswell for Senator George McGovern, the peace candidate from South Dakota. His Midwestern moral outrage at the war in Vietnam touched a responsive chord throughout New England, especially on the region's many college campuses. In Massachusetts, the state that responded to Eugene McCarthy in 1968 with near-religious fervor and the state that had challenged the constitutionality of the war in 1970 (a challenge the Supreme Court later rejected), McGovern was a folk hero. In February McGovern shocked the nation by far exceeding expectations in the New Hampshire primary. Though he lost to Senator Ed Muskie, 46-36 percent, McGovern's campaign ignited interest within his party.

As the acknowledged leader of the Democratic establishment, Attorney General Bob Quinn led the Muskie slate of delegates in the March primary. Dukakis, the reformer who would remake the establishment, bringing the outside in, also ran as a Muskie delegate, the Democratic establishment's anti-war candidate. In 1971 Dukakis, already known in Washington circles for his organizational abilities, had been asked by Muskie's campaign manager to serve as New England coordinator for the campaign, an offer Dukakis declined. But he did maintain a close link to Muskie; Paul Brountas, his Harvard Law School classmate and friend, was an active fundraiser, strategist and delegate coordinator for the Maine senator.

Back on the campaign trail, Lanny Johnson was constantly on the move. What pleased him was that he was not coming across Quinn organizers out on the hustings, nor was there evidence that Congressman Michael Harrington was putting together an organization. "As far as I could tell," said Johnson, "they weren't prepared to do the work. They probably thought the pols could deliver for them, but they could not deliver the ward and town committees any longer. Our position all along was that those days were over. This was the grassroots era." As Johnson secured the commitments of the Bill Wrenns of the Commonwealth, the early believers gathered for monthly organizational meetings, which were held in the Dukakis living room in the apartment at 93 Perry Street. With each passing month during 1971 and 1972, the meetings were becoming larger and larger. The Dukakis organization was growing, though its members could still jam themselves into one room in 1972.

For the most part, they were political activists who had no stake in traditional party politics. Predominantly young people, who chose grassroots political activism to express their protest at old government, they shared a belief in Mike Dukakis. He was the channel for their alienation from the cynical, corrupt politics of the back room, and he was the embodiment for their optimism in the idea of progress; they worked tirelessly to give him a chance. And they were beginning to attract people from the city neighborhoods where, just a few years before, the word "reform" referred to the kind of school to which the neighborhood punks ought to be sent. Some of the urban volunteers for Dukakis had come to know of him through the long fight against the highways; others had met him on the campaign trail and were impressed.

The latter was the case with Bill Geary, who in 1971 was fresh out of graduate school and yearning for a career in public service, not simply politics. Like the Houtons, Bill Geary grew up a working-class kid in the city's Dorchester section, not far from Ward 13. And like the Houton brothers and so many others in Boston, he was bitten by the political bug. Geary worked days and attended Boston State College at night, where he earned his bachelor's degree in political science. He was driving a cab and studying for a master's degree in public administration at Northeastern University in 1970 when he was introduced to the campaigning Dukakis.

After Geary finished with his courses, he looked up Lanny Johnson and volunteered to join the effort. Geary told Johnson that he would do anything that was needed. ''I thought Michael had no chance of winning in '74,'' said Geary. This was Dorchester. Everyone was working for Quinn. He could be seen driving down Dorchester Avenue in his big rented Cadillac, confident, and with every reason to be.

''My sense of Dukakis, what I found attractive, was his incredible integrity and that he stood for principles. Even though I didn't think he had a chance of winning, working in the campaign was appealing because I could do an apprenticeship. It was a very small group. They were thrilled—I was from Boston and I was Irish. Besides, I knew the cast of characters around Bob Quinn and I wasn't impressed with them.'' Bill Geary began to organize like-minded Bostonians for Dukakis in 1971. Mike Dukakis was bringing his crusade against the old politics into the city and right to the doorstep of the three-deckers.

There, the Dukakis campaign crossed paths with Mike Ansara and The People First, who were campaigning to get Judge Troy removed from the bench. When The People First found the political establishment standing firm to protect Troy, Ansara and his colleagues and allies at the *Boston Globe* began to pressure the Massachusetts Bar Association for disbarment. Only when it became obvious that The People First were not going to go away did the Bar Association cave in. With Troy disbarred, the Supreme Judicial Court had no choice but to deal somehow with Troy, and it moved to open hearings on the Troy matter. On July 26, 1973, when the hearings were over, the state's highest court found Troy guilty of perjury and ''consistently and palpably'' neglecting his duties as a judge along with a shopping list of ''extremely serious charges.''

Still clinging to the notion that the legislative leadership would take care of him in his hour of need, just as he had taken care of their interests when they were in trouble, Troy refused Governor Sargent's request that he resign. It was not until November 7, 1973, that the House, by a 204-17 vote, and the Senate, 34 to 1, voted to remove Jerome Troy from the bench by a petition for address. Jerome Troy, a product of the old politics and an expression of its values, exaggerated and magnified by his arrogance and ego, was undone by a citizens' reform movement. Change was in the wind, the old order was crumbling, even in Jerome Troy's and Bob Quinn's Dorchester.

Ten months before the 1974 primaries, the toppling of Jerome Troy by The People First augured ill for Bob Quinn's hopes of capping his career in politics by a term in the Corner Office up on Beacon Hill. But he remained oblivious to the signs around him.

Chapter 10
Ushering in the New Era

Joe Grandmaison, the 27-year-old son of a local politician and union organizer in Nashua, New Hampshire, was regional director of George McGovern's masterful slalom across New England in the late winter of 1972; this is when Grandmaison first took note of Mike Dukakis. "Most of the pols were with Muskie," said Grandmaison. "During the Massachusetts primary, I was struck by the fact that Dukakis had committed himself to Muskie and he was the only pol who kept plugging away even when the Muskie campaign was falling apart. Although I'd never met him, I had a lot of respect for that."

Grandmaison was in Washington in mid-April 1973, still recovering from the McGovern campaign, when Pat Caddell, a pollster and an advisor to Dukakis who had worked closely with Grandmaison in the McGovern campaign, brought them together.

Dukakis needed a campaign manager for his next statewide campaign, and Grandmaison needed another campaign. Lanny Johnson met Grandmaison at Logan International Airport. Grandmaison was not impressed that it took Johnson forty-five minutes to find his car in the parking lot, but the two finally got to Dukakis headquarters, a three-room basement office at 18 Tremont Street in downtown Boston. Grandmaison interviewed with Kinzer and Johnson, and the next day with Dukakis. Already the campaign had "Dukakis for Governor" letterhead and was financing the shoestring operation by circulating a pledge book among the volunteers. In the book, supporters indicated their willingness to send in a small amount monthly, generally five or ten dollars, with their signature.

Grandmaison had been told the campaign had budgeted twenty thousand dollars for a campaign manager, but in negotiations, Dukakis asked Grandmaison if he would do the campaign for less. When he refused, Dukakis agreed to the twenty thousand, and for the first time Dukakis had a professional campaign manager—one of the architects of the grassroots campaign that had steamrolled Mike Dukakis's candidate for president, Ed Muskie. Along with Caddell, who worked out of Cambridge and was already recognized as a brilliant and audacious strategist, Grandmaison had learned and practiced the mechanics of grassroots insurgent politics from McGovern's campaign manager, Gary Hart.

None of this registered over at the Quinn campaign. "They laughed when Dukakis hired Grandmaison," said Marty Burke, a product of Ward 13; when he was a teenager he used to get summer jobs with the state in return for doing campaign work for Quinn. Burke had grown up, gone off to the service, returned and attended college, and was serving as assistant press secretary for Quinn. "They thought Grandmaison was a joke, a nobody."

Nor did it register with the Quinn campaign that in Mike Dukakis they had an opponent who, without spending a cent, had developed vast and extremely positive name recognition, thanks to non-commercial, educational television. Quinn's opponent was nothing less than the moderator of "The Advocates," something he had been doing weekly since October 1972. "The Advocates" was a Public Broadcasting System's public affairs show, a joint production of WGBH-TV in Boston and KCET-TV in Los Angeles.

The format of "The Advocates" combined elements of a trial and a debate. Liberal and conservative positions on controversial national public policy issues were presented by two advocates, aided by research staffs; most often they were conservative William Rusher, publisher of *National Review* magazine, and liberal law professor Howard Miller of the University of Southern California. During each show, the advocates would call upon witnesses of their choosing to buttress their ideological positions; the witnesses would then be cross-examined by the opposing advocate. At the end of each show, viewers were invited to write in with their "yes" or "no" vote on the question being discussed that night. The results were tabulated and forwarded to the White House and to members of Congress, among others.

The role of the moderator was to keep the show moving smoothly, on time, and according to previously agreed-upon lines of argument. The moderator was the only on-air personality who was aware of the testimony of the witnesses and of how they would be cross-examined by opposing advocates. If a witness or an advocate strayed, it was up to the moderator to get the show back on track. And if a witness or an advocate engaged in personal attacks, the moderator was supposed to jump in to keep the show from degenerating into a shouting match. The work of the moderator required an ability to think and react quickly, and to serve as the anchor for the show.

Not surprisingly, the intellectually gifted and quick-thinking Dukakis was a superb moderator. It was a wonderful opportunity for tens of thousands of Massachusetts residents to become acquainted with Dukakis in an impressive setting. Among the approximately two hundred stations nationwide that carried "The Advocates" into the homes of more than one million people was a public TV station in Springfield, in western Massachusetts, as well as WGBH-TV in Boston. Because of the state's deep involvement in the issues and politics of the times, "The Advocates" had a large and loyal following in Massachusetts.

When he was first offered the job of moderator, Dukakis demurred. He was afraid that the required time commitment—nightly reading of background materials prepared by the show's research staff, meetings with producers and the two advocates, plus the two days a month that he would spend at KCET in Los Angeles and two more days in the studio in Boston taping the four monthly segments—would detract from his ability to prepare for the 1974 election. In addition to the practice of law and his monthly meetings with his political organization, Dukakis had committed himself to at least three trips around the state each week to meet with potential recruits and with local newspapers and radio stations. For all the work the show entailed, the producers could only pay him four hundred dollars per segment, an amount just slightly higher than the union minimum wage.

Always the pragmatist, it was Fran Meaney who, among others, convinced Dukakis that he should do the show; the visibility would be the envy even of politicians still in office, and Dukakis could take advantage of working with the show's technical crew to fine-tune his broadcast and speaking skills. They were entering the era of broadcast politics, and Meaney felt that Dukakis could only gain by the experience. Dukakis agreed.

Greg Harney, executive producer of "The Advocates," said that Dukakis learned the job quickly. He was speaking in increasingly concise and punchy sentences, and he made good eye contact with the camera, rarely looking away—one of the prime faults with inexperienced on-camera television personalities. "He already knew how to work a crowd," said Harney of Dukakis's prior experience as a political candidate. It was an important skill, since the show was taped before a live audience of up to three hundred studio guests and shown without edits. "Very seldom would we get calls about the moderator," Harney said, "and that's a sign that he was handling it with considerable class."

Dukakis and the show were impressive. Letters flowed in from United States senators and justices of the Supreme Court, as well as from the less famous. Wrote viewer James Stell of Danville, California: "Last night I had the opportunity of seeing your show covering the lettuce boycott issue. It was my first experience but certainly not my last. Your moderator handled a difficult task in an outstanding manner. You are to be complimented for making available the opportunity for everyone to get the facts separated from the emotion. You have won my support for the future."

Dukakis opened as the regular moderator of "The Advocates's" fourth season on October 5, 1972. It was one month to the week before the presidential election between Richard Nixon and George McGovern. The question to be debated on the first show of the season was: "Should you support McGovern's defense proposal?" For the next four weeks, "The Advocates" honed in on major campaign issues: McGovern's tax reform plan, Nixon's Indochina policy and management of the economy, and finally, whom to vote for. In anti-Nixon, anti-war Massachusetts, these episodes of "The Advocates," featuring Michael Dukakis, racked up impressive viewer numbers.

By the time the gubernatorial campaign was gearing up in mid-1973, Dukakis had made himself prominent in Massachusetts both as a TV star and as a man of wisdom and balance. He had sat behind his desk, center stage, as he was beamed into the homes of voters; he had held his own with the nation's best and brightest; and he had accomplished all this without having had to take a single position on a single controversial issue. His job simply was to see that the shows went sharply and crisply. And most of the time they did.

Dukakis demanded that his own campaign be run the same way: crisply and sharply, and in ways that were consistent with the reform values that had fueled his entire career. Dukakis insisted, for example, that he personally review all incoming checks from contributors lest a lobbyist or representative of a special interest slip one through. "I explained to him that if I didn't have our morning checks at the bank by 2 p.m. every day," said Grandmaison, "we'd be bouncing all over eastern Massachusetts." Demonstrating fiscal irresponsibility and mismanagement was as bad as getting a contribution from a lobbyist, so Dukakis agreed to a compromise. After checks were deposited, he would review a prepared list of the sources of the checks and order refunds sent to undesirables. Several refunds were ordered and mailed despite the fact that the campaign, relying almost exclusively on small donations from individual supporters, was living on a tight margin.

Dukakis was also determined to return to Perry Street for dinner with his family and an hour with the children each day unless he was west of Springfield—a ninety-minute drive on the turnpike. Grandmaison at first thought this requirement was absurdly rigid and wasted valuable time. But, said Grandmaison, "when he got back on the trail in the evenings, he was completely refreshed and a much better candidate and I came to see that he was right."

The principles of the candidate as translated by the campaign came off as self-righteous and arrogant to some non-believers. The campaign's slogan was simple: "Mike Dukakis Should Be Governor." It could be inferred by the line that Dukakis assumed he was living in a utopian meritocracy in which he had already demonstrated his superiority. Actually, the line was meant to be part of an advertising campaign that was to have set up a series of parallels ("This Is The Way It Is In Massachusetts" and "This Is The Way It Should Be In Massachusetts") that was going to have as its punch line: "Mike Dukakis Should Be Governor." But, due to lack of funds, the campaign just bought the last line and had it printed on tens of thousands of bumper stickers. Even though the inference of hubris left by the line was an unconsidered result of the campaign's financial poverty, the impression of presumptiveness that it conveyed was accurate; in Dukakis voters really did have a candidate who believed he "should" be governor, because he *knew* he was better.

Boston in 1974 was preparing for court-ordered busing, which seemed an unavoidable consequence of a federal court finding that public schools were segregated. Busing loomed as a potentially explosive campaign issue. In this environment, Mike Dukakis, who as a student at Swarthmore cut the hair of black students when the local barbers refused to serve them, ended his support for old friend Beryl Cohen's Racial Imbalance Law in May 1974. Instead, he proposed community control of the schools and fully integrated cultural and educational resource programs *outside* the classrooms.

This shift might have helped Dukakis with conservatives, but it infuriated many civil rights activists, who felt betrayed by a friend. "It was like saying we're not going to integrate the schools, so let's integrate the museums," one critic told the

Globe. Dukakis's was not a campaign steeped in hypocrisy or cynicism so much as it was a campaign that fell beneath the expectations of ardent leaders of the New Politics, who were applying to Dukakis the standards of political idealism Dukakis himself applied, to great effect, to his opponents. These were the standards embodied in Gene McCarthy and George McGovern which had produced political epiphanies in their adoring followers. Of course, McCarthy and McGovern, though they overflowed with idealism, had lost their races.

The only commodity the campaign lacked was money. Dukakis began the election year with only eleven thousand dollars in the bank, and the money was spent as fast as it came in. As a result, the campaign aired only one television ad, but around that ad Grandmaison built an elaborate mechanism that generated vast publicity, raised significant sums and, most importantly, exercised the large but untested field organization. On a single spring night, Grandmaison challenged the campaign to hold two thousand house parties around the state, for a couple of dozen people each. At 7:30 the hosts would turn on their TVs so the guests could watch a simulated thirty-minute house party, on tape but unrehearsed just like "The Advocates"—at which Dukakis would speak.

The campaign wanted a celebrity to host the mock house party and ensure the maximum audience. A campaign aide was assigned the task of writing a letter of invitation that would convince Leonard Nimoy, "Star Trek's" Dr. Spock, to agree to do the show. Nimoy was selected because he was a native of Massachusetts and had been deeply involved in the McGovern campaign two years before. At Kitty's insistence, Pat Collins, a former Boston TV news reporter then working in New York, was invited to co-host. Both celebrities agreed, and the event went off like clockwork. Grandmaison was able to garner massive publicity for the effort by showing reporters and camera crews an impressive-looking map of the Commonwealth with two thousand vari-colored stickpins in it; the field organization got an early workout, and the war chest got an infusion in funds from the guests who were asked to kick in a nominal sum.

Up in the state attorney general's office, Bob Quinn was building his campaign the old-fashioned way, around the Beacon Hill political network, "the patronage net" that freshman representative Dukakis proudly told his Brookline constituents in 1963 he had avoided in his first year in the House, and that he had pledged in the campaign for governor to abolish. The clout marshalled behind Quinn was significant. House Speaker David Bartley of Holyoke, who had followed Quinn up the totem pole, was dedicated to the cause and was a power in the western part of the state. Maurice Donahue's successor as Senate president, Kevin Harrington of Salem, was equally ardent and had vast influence on the North Shore. Together they mobilized the majority of the 280 reps and senators, who in turn mobilized local and county officials and so on down the line. The leaders of organized labor, home to blue-collar, urban, ethnic Democrats since before the Depression, were central cogs in the old political machine.

The only notables not on board were U.S. House Majority Leader Tip O'Neill and Boston mayor Kevin White. O'Neill stayed out of the governor's fight because his eldest son Tom was running for lieutenant governor and he did not want to risk creating trouble for him later by backing the wrong horse. As for White, he also declined to endorse, although, as he said, "Not endorsing either was an endorsement of Dukakis."

The clashing of these two coalitions, the old politics and the new, was a culmination of a culture's political struggle that had been years in the making. It is traceable back at least to 1959, when 26-year-old Mike Dukakis, a student at Harvard Law School, organized a reform slate to sweep the old order from the Brookline Democratic town committee. Now, fifteen years after that skirmish, the battle was being drawn for control of the entire state Democratic Party. There was no confusing the stakes.

The conventional wisdom into the summer was that Quinn was in front. As an adherent of the conventional wisdom, Quinn ignored Dukakis and aimed his brickbats at the Republican governor, Frank Sargent. If Quinn could win the nomination without alienating the reformers, he would be that much better off in November. His strategy was elementary: he would put together a coalition of Democratic regulars by attracting an overwhelming majority of the Irish voters plus an overwhelming majority of the state's Italian voters by campaigning in Italian sections of the state with his wife, Claudia, who was part Italian on her mother's side.

But in sections of Massachusetts, especially in the cities and towns just north of Boston with masses of voters of Italian descent, Dukakis was strong. Many of these communities had been threatened by the highways and continued to be threatened and aggravated by the insensitive and expansionist policies of the Port Authority. Many anti-highway activists, through Dukakis's friend and transportation advisor Fred Salvucci, recalled that Dukakis had been an ally against the highways and that he was an ally again in the fight to curb the Port Authority's expansion of Logan Airport into the same communities.

Quinn's issues advisors argued with him that it was both good policy to rein in the Port Authority and good politics to do so if he expected to make his Irish-Italian strategy pay off. But Quinn refused to act on what he acknowledged was sound advice. Quinn's college buddy from Boston College, Ed King, was the executive director of the Port Authority, and Quinn would say nothing critical of his friend. Besides, King was too valuable a fundraiser to antagonize, Quinn decided.

Some local Italian political leaders felt patronized and condescended to by Quinn's exploitation of his wife's ethnicity. In Revere, a heavily Italian and Jewish city on the coast only a few miles north of Boston, it was suggested that Quinn might do well if he would campaign in person. The Revere pols, who were secretly backing Dukakis—it was the only city whose mayor backed the Brookline reformer—suggested a campaign route through Revere that Quinn could follow if he wanted to maximize his local support. The campaign agreed with the plan, and while Quinn campaigned up and down Revere Street, shaking hands with patrons of the city's most notorious bookie joints, the local pols had a good laugh for themselves.

By Labor Day, the race was considered a tossup, with 30 percent undecided. Dukakis asked for a debate. Quinn refused; it would divide the party and help

Sargent, the Quinn campaign said. Dukakis then began criticizing Quinn's administration of federal crime-fighting grants from the U.S. Law Enforcement Assistance Administration. Quinn had done a credible job with the LEAA grants and was proud of his work; the attack bothered him. What also bothered him was a *Sunday Globe* poll published nine days before the the September 10 primary. It showed that Dukakis had pulled ahead, 39 percent to 32 percent, with 29 percent still undecided.

Having blithely ignored Dukakis for the entire campaign, and having turned down an invitation to debate him only a week before, Quinn, in the last week of the campaign, ordered a 180-degree turn in strategy. He reached for "the elephant gun," as a Quinn aide described the shift. He bought time on television the Wednesday before the primary for ads claiming that Dukakis was an "advocate" of abortions. The ad was timed to connect with Catholic viewers who had received at mass the previous Sunday reaffirmation of the Church's vehement opposition to abortion. Only a year after the Supreme Court had given legalized abortions constitutional protection in the *Roe* vs. *Wade* decision, abortion was a burning issue in heavily Catholic Massachusetts. The charge against Dukakis was based solely on his having filed a bill to legalize abortion in Massachusetts "by request" of a private citizen, birth control and pro-choice advocate Bill Baird, when Dukakis was a representative. John Wells's bill challenging the constitutionality of the Vietnam War was filed the same way, by a legislator who chose not to endorse the bill, but who served as the conduit for a citizen to exercise his state constitutional right to have his petition heard by the legislature. Meanwhile, Quinn had authorized a leaflet drop across Boston, reminding voters that "Bob Quinn has always opposed busing" and pointing out that Dukakis had voted for the Racial Imbalance Law—without mentioning that he had recently shifted from that position.

Grandmaison called the ad a "last minute desperate attempt to smear Mike Dukakis." The candidate himself said, "This is the kind of hack politics that has been hurting the state for forty years." Dukakis said that when he filed the bill for Baird he did not support it; by the same token, he did not in 1974 favor a constitutional amendment to reverse the 1973 *Roe* vs. *Wade* decision.

Quinn decided to withdraw the ad, but the Dukakis campaign would not let the issue die. On the Friday night before the primary, while using his portion of free TV time—a local tradition at a Boston television station—Dukakis deviated from his prepared text to say that "voters are sick and tired of mudslinging and character assassination." Since he was being severely battered for ads that were no longer being broadcast, Quinn reversed himself again and ordered that the ads run, in printed form, in daily newspapers in seven cities on the weekend before the primary. Dukakis said he considered the ads defamatory, and Fran Meaney, Dukakis's campaign chairman for the third time since 1966, sent a telegram to the seven publishers. Meaney wrote, "We are confident that you as a responsible publisher will not publish or assist in the dissemination of any false or misleading information concerning Michael Dukakis."

In the heat of battle, Dukakis used his righteousness as an offensive weapon. In criticizing Quinn's management of federal crime-fighting funds, he was reaching. Had Quinn done a perfect job there? No, but he had done a credible job. However, it was convenient for Dukakis to find fault, and he did so with a full complement of moral outrage.

Dukakis tolerated the political game as an unavoidable obstacle to his missions. But, as he approached everything else in life, he was a tough and tireless competitor. He entered the campaign for governor with a Boy Scout's reputation and a killer's instinct. He found himself the target of attacks from Quinn that suggested a desperate, tawdry and unfair effort to portray an upstanding, responsible and moderate candidate to be an abortion-loving, busing-loving left-winger. In responding with a fusillade of hackneyed ad hominems of his own, he had secured the moral high ground and was able to kick some dirt in the face of his enemy at the same time. If Mike Dukakis had been a boxer, he would surely have been a counter-puncher. All in all, Dukakis's campaign against Quinn was quite a performance for the scholar and good-government reformer.

As the residents of Massachusetts arose on the morning of Monday, September 9, the day before the primary, and opened their morning newspaper, it did not matter whether they got the liberal, crusading *Globe* or the conservative *Herald American*. The headlines were precisely the same: "Ford Pardons Nixon." Around Boston, the news was greeted with shock and a lot of anger, especially among the anti-war crowd of McGovernites. A lot of anger was also expressed later that morning when Ted Kennedy stepped to the podium to address a crowd of eight thousand on Boston's City Hall Plaza who were protesting the court-mandated busing that had been ordered to desegregate the schools, and that was scheduled to begin on Thursday. In an ugly scene, Kennedy was shouted down, objects were thrown at him, and he withdrew before speaking.

That Monday, the *Globe*, deviating from its policy of not endorsing candidates, urged voters to support a small number of reformers, including Dukakis. While praising him generally, the *Globe* noted that "Mr. Dukakis has developed a plan for community schools in Boston which would have the effect of preserving segregation." After observing that Mr. Quinn was "timid on corruption," the paper moved on to comment on other contests.

On election day, the Dukakis machine, which had been tested in June with the house-party exercise, performed as it never had before. At Dukakis headquarters, Grandmaison and Jack Walsh, a top-flight political organizer on leave from Mayor White's operation, were supremely confident. But the Quinn campaign also felt optimistic. During the day, Walsh called Grandmaison from City Hall. Someone whom he knew who was with Quinn had put up ten thousand dollars for a bet on the outcome of the race. Did the Dukakis campaign want to cover it? Grandmaison raced down to the bank and withdrew a thousand dollars. Around the office, staffers and volunteers dug into their pockets. Kitty Dukakis got two hundred dollars together. When the ten thousand dollars was gathered, it was delivered to Walsh to hold pending an official verdict from the voters. Kitty Dukakis was

furious that Grandmaison had not given her more notice so that she could have
raised a much larger sum to wager on her husband. Her puritanical husband was
furious that wagering of any kind had infected his campaign. Walsh was amused
that the Quinn supporter could so easily be parted with his money. Kitty and the
Dukakis campaign workers had made a bet, but there was no gamble to it.

When the results began to come in after 8:00 p.m., after the polls closed, it
was clear almost immediately that Dukakis had won. This did not come as a shock,
since he had been leading in the final polls, but what *was* shocking was the enor-
mity of his victory. Citizens who felt independent of the old-boy network, but united
in a reform spirit, were expressing themselves by pulling the Dukakis lever all across
the Commonwealth.

In blue-collar cities like Brockton, once the shoe capital of the nation, Dukakis
was a winner. In the fading fishing port of Gloucester, Dukakis was a winner. In
the heavily Italian blue-collar suburb of Saugus, where many heavy construction
entrepreneurs moved from the city to enjoy the first flush of success, Dukakis was
a winner. In the mill city of Haverhill, where Lanny Johnson had finally found
Bill Wrenn, Dukakis was a winner. And in working-class Revere, with its bookie
joints on Revere Street, Dukakis was a winner. Even in Boston, Bill Geary and his
mates had found plenty of people ready for a new politics. Favorite son Bob Quinn
won in the big city by a razor-thin edge, 49,478 to 45,328. And of his 4,150 margin
in Boston, 1,875 votes came from Ward 13 alone. Along with his home ward, Quinn
carried two other wards of Dorchester and won in anti-busing South Boston and
Charlestown, and one other ward in a conservative section. In all, Quinn was the
choice in only seven of Boston's twenty-two wards. For the most part, Boston, too,
wanted a new politics.

Statewide, the Dukakis tide flooded the Commonwealth. He beat Bob Quinn
and the boys from Beacon Hill, 444,590 to 326,385, a 58- to 42-percent landslide.
The margin of victory was 118,205 votes.

At the 57 Hotel, where the campaign had set up for the election night festivities,
Michael and Kitty Dukakis, Dr. and Mrs. Dukakis, the Dicksons, friends and top
campaign aides took in the great news by TV and telephone. Before the man of
the hour led the victory party downstairs, the Democratic nominee for governor
promised his intimates, "I'll never let you down." Dukakis graciously accepted
Bob Quinn's concession and pledge of support, and thanked the people for placing "your trust in my ability." He promised a "dawn of a new era" and an end
to "the buddy system of politics on Beacon Hill." The next day the *Globe* observed in an editorial that "the mantle of the Democratic Party has shifted" from
"working class three-decker neighborhoods" to "the more affluent and more liberal
single family homes of suburban Massachusetts. . . . Since 1960 Michael Dukakis
has been one of the flagships of this change. It is fitting that he is the standard-
bearer on the day on which it is obvious to all that the transition of power in the
Democratic party is complete."

Chapter 11
"Mike Dukakis Should Be Governor"

The Democratic nominee for governor slept for only three hours after the excitement of his primary-day conquest of Bob Quinn. Mike Dukakis could hardly wait to get to headquarters to begin planning the final ascent to the summit of Massachusetts politics.

Four years before, he had been surprised and disappointed when the head of the party's ticket that year, Kevin White, had brushed him aside, without so much as a token nod to the "team" concept. Dukakis would not make that mistake. His second would be fully integrated into the campaign for governor.

Beginning the integration process was the first order of business on September 11, the day after the primary. Down at headquarters, Dukakis, campaign manager Joe Grandmaison and Steve Kinzer, Dukakis's chief policy advisor and his protégé, began merging their campaign with that of the nominee for lieutenant governor. The previous day Democratic voters, conveniently for Dukakis, had chosen none other than Thomas P. O'Neill III, a thirty-year-old first-term state representative, to be Dukakis's running mate. Tommy O'Neill's primary appeal to Democratic voters was in his name and his bloodline. Though he was quite inexperienced, he had the genes of a thoroughbred pol, and he campaigned with a passion that made his father proud.

The Dukakis campaign had maintained an official neutrality during the primary, but privately it had been praying for O'Neill to top the large field of Democratic hopefuls and win the nomination. In the primary race with Quinn, Dukakis had studiously avoided attacking the old machine that stood united behind him, even at the expense of some frustration among purists in the reform camp, because he knew he could win the governor's office only at the head of a united Democratic party. In the minutes after Quinn was vanquished, Dukakis issued the order of the day to the campaign brain trust: "Now we have to marry the regulars."

Tommy O'Neill had had too many advantages to really be a "regular." Regulars do not usually run for lieutenant governor after only one term in the House. If they do make a run around the track, it is to get their names out and to test the footing; the efforts do not usually pay off as Tommy's had. He was something even better, the son of the ultimate regular, Tip.

The elder O'Neill was a local political legend. From his working-class neighborhood in North Cambridge, he moved through the Massachusetts House until he was elected speaker in 1949. When Jack Kennedy moved up to the U.S. Senate in 1952, O'Neill was elected to take his place in the U.S. Congress. By 1974 he was majority leader and almost certain to cap his career as Speaker of the U.S. House.

Tip O'Neill was proud of Tommy's political success and resolved to do everything he could to see that his son was elected lieutenant governor, which, of course, meant doing everything he could to see that Mike Dukakis was elected governor. With Tip pulling the regulars together—organized labor and the legislative network—a united Democratic party was possible. Grandmaison was so excited about the possibilities that he ordered Dukakis and O'Neill banners unfurled in the ballroom of the 57 Hotel before O'Neill's victory had been made official on primary night. Dukakis's campaign manager wanted viewers of the news at 11:00 to see signs of the big ticket.

With effort, the old politics/new politics coalition might be held together for the eight weeks of a general election campaign. After all, the Democrats, thanks in part to fratricidal feuding, had only held the governor's office for two of the previous fourteen years. As for Dukakis's oft-repeated insistence that he would end the patronage games and the back scratching, that was just Mike's rhetoric, the old guard told themselves; he would come around to face reality once he had to. How Dukakis dealt with the regulars would determine the long-term viability of the campaign coalition, but that was down the road. First there was an election to be won.

At Dukakis's direction, the O'Neill campaign organization was completely incorporated into his. They were housed together, down at Dukakis headquarters, and all paid and voluntary workers now toiled for the Dukakis-O'Neill ticket. Dukakis chose Mary Fifield, a young veteran of the McGovern campaign who had been O'Neill's press secretary, to be the official spokesperson of the campaign. Tommy O'Neill and his charming, savvy wife, Jackie, hit the road for the ticket, working the Irish, Catholic and blue-collar voters who had backed Quinn in the primary.

The Democrats had the perfect ticket: reform on top, regular on the bottom. And Dukakis's popularity coming out of the primary was remarkable. A *Boston Globe* poll taken at the start of the general election campaign gave Dukakis an 18 percent lead over Frank Sargent, who had been in office for almost six years. Even more impressive was the attitude of voters toward Dukakis; seventy-six percent of those polled said they had a favorable impression of him, while only 11 percent held an unfavorable opinion of him. Seventy percent thought of him as a "fresh new face," even though he was in his second statewide general election campaign, and 76 percent thought of Mike Dukakis as very capable and bright.

Under such buoyant conditions, 1,400 Democrats paid five hundred dollars a plate on October 15 to have dinner with Dukakis, O'Neill, Ted Kennedy and other party luminaries at Anthony's Pier 4, a landmark restaurant on the Boston waterfront. It was Tommy O'Neill who drew the loudest applause of the night when he told the crowd, "In touring around the state this year, I find there is one magic word—Democrat—and then I find there is a more important magic word—and that is Michael Dukakis."

Dukakis's final obstacle in the quest for the governor's office—the job that he had discussed with his college roommate Frank Sieverts during their undergraduate days at Swarthmore more than twenty years before—was the relaxed, lanky, Yankee governor and Great Society Republican, Frank Sargent. The reform and liberal outpouring of programs that had begun to flow from his office in 1970 when he whipped Kevin White to win a four-year term continued in 1971 and '72.

Not only had Sargent stopped the highways and signed the no-fault insurance reform, the constitutional challenge to the Vietnam war and the environmental Bill of Rights add-on to the state constitution, but he had put students on the boards of trustees of the state's colleges, decriminalized alcoholism, and created a Commission on the Status of Women. He had granted prison inmates many rights and privileges, such as a liberal furlough program and, in one county prison, conjugal visits, and moved thousands of mental-health patients from state institutions, where they had languished like animals, back into society. He had jacked up welfare benefits and eased the process of qualifying. He had instituted a program for bilingual education of public school students, and another one requiring cities and towns to adapt their public schools to educate their students with "special needs"— kids with learning disabilities and mental, physical and emotional problems—instead of shipping them off to special schools or institutions. He had created a statewide school lunch program and a program to get lead paint removed from dwellings where children lived. He closed the state reform schools and signed privacy laws. He refused to allow state agencies to exchange information electronically with the FBI, and he vetoed bills to reinstitute capital punishment. To no avail, he vetoed bills to repeal the Racial Imbalance Act, and he insisted that a Senate redistricting be done in such a way as to insure that a black was finally elected to the forty-member upper chamber. He vetoed bills to restrict the legal availability of abortions, and he tried unsuccessfully to have snub-nosed handguns, known as "Saturday-night specials," banned, without success.

Most of those battles were fought in the first half of Sargent's term; for the most part, he and his top advisors had spent the last two years of his term fighting a rear-guard action to keep the liberal reforms in place. And they had been fighting in an increasingly illiberal environment as a result of circumstances that were well beyond their control.

The national economy, which overheated during the Vietnam War, was cooling into a recession in 1973. As a result of the state's reliance on military and aerospace manufacturing and high-technology research and development, Massachusetts was inordinately hard hit. In 1970-71 the National Aeronautics and Space Administration's budget shrunk, and many contracts with MIT-related firms were not renewed. Locally, as many as twenty thousand scientists and engineers found themselves unemployed. In the wind-down of the Vietnam War, work slowed around Route 128, dubbed by this time "America's Technology Highway." President Nixon, out of vindictiveness, many local observers thought, toward Massachusetts, "the one and only" state to vote for George McGovern and against him in 1972, had closed five major military bases in the state during the early seventies, including two in Boston. These closings put thousands of blue-collar workers in the unemployment lines. The national recession years, beginning in 1973, found Massachusetts in worse shape economically than at any other time since the Great Depression. Unemployment was rising steadily, from 4.6 to 8.1 percent thoroughout Sargent's four-year term, and by the end of 1974, around election time, it was exploding toward double figures. Massachusetts lost 38,000 military- and defense-related jobs during this period.

In the fall of 1973 the Arab oil embargo only made matters worse for the state. New England was at the very end of the domestic oil supply line; as a result, the region had become overly dependent on imports. Before the embargo began, in September 1973, fuel oil was selling for 22.9 cents a gallon. In January 1974 heating oil was up to 34.2 cents a gallon—an increase of 49 percent in four months. An energy conservation crusade, scared up by Governor Sargent, began immediately. The lights were going out all over Massachusetts. Next to the Charles River, a huge Coca-Cola sign, a local landmark, fell dark. On February 2, 1974, Sargent ordered gas rationing. Cars with license plates ending in odd numbers were allowed to buy gas only on odd numbered days, and vice versa. People panicked and began filling up their tanks more often; long lines formed at the gas pumps every day.

The election year began with Massachusetts cold, dark and full of angry, frustrated people. But if the people could have seen inside Sargent's administration at the start of 1974, they would have been even more upset. The government was in a shambles, especially in the human services agencies that accounted for more than 40 percent of the state's budget in agencies such as welfare, mental health and corrections. Even the best administrators would have had trouble handling all the new reforms and programs Sargent and the liberal times had been dealing out to the bureaucracy to manage. For some agencies, Sargent had hired zealots, not managers. Sargent's commissioner in charge of youthful offenders was called before a legislative committee early in the term and asked to explain his ideas for reforming the prisons. The commissioner explained that he did not want to reform the prisons; he wanted to "bulldoze" them. A conservative legislator heard that and literally had a heart attack on the spot.

As a result of the process of emptying the mental-health hospitals, people who had not been on their own for decades, in some cases, were wandering the streets of Massachusetts. The idea had been to put the mentally ill in professionally staffed community settings, reintegrating them slowly into society, but the state went forward without the resources in the communities to make the reform work. Worse still, mental hospital employees had union protection and could not be laid off. As the state spent millions on community-based services, largely to non-profit social service corporations, it continued to pay to staff emptying hospitals.

Reforms such as these were enormously expensive. As the deinstitutionalization of the mental patients was taking place, Dukakis fumed about mismanagement and waste. To capture the absurdity of the situation, he focused his ire on the goatherds, civil servants who had been employed for years to supervise the goats who kept the vast grounds of the hospitals trimmed and continued to do so after the institutions were emptied. "Are we still paying the goatherds?" was a favorite Dukakis wisecrack, one he always delivered with a snarl of derision.

The government and the spending of the Sargent administration was careening out of control. A sad symbol for all this was the corrections commissioner, John O. Boone, a soft-spoken black reformer from Georgia who came to Boston on December 21, 1971, to take charge of the system and implement Sargent's prisoners' rights program. His appointment brought an acute case of apoplexy to the state's prison system. To the prison guards, who were an element of the old Democratic politics, reporting to a black boss from the South—who had been brought in to help the inmates, no less—was beyond their ken. For the inmates, Boone's arrival set off a revolution of rising expectations and escalated damands for better conditions. By March 13, 1972, inmates were threatening to riot and guards were threatening to strike. According to a poll commissioned by Sargent in 1973, John Boone had the fourth highest name recognition in the state, just behind Ted Kennedy, Sargent himself, and U.S. Senator Ed Brooke—but ahead of Mike Dukakis. In the face of near anarchy in the prisons, Boone resigned on June 21, 1973.

The situation was equally out of control in the welfare department. The state government had made no preparations for taking over the administration and financing of welfare from the cities and towns, which it did at the end of 1967. The state was not ready for the mountains of records, new departments and federal regulations that such a vast centralization entailed. The Sargent years were spent trying to organize a functioning bureaucracy for the administration of welfare while trying to encourage poor people to take advantage of their legal rights to the ever-expanding benefits. While the computerization of welfare was still a planner's dream, records, bills and receipts were stored in files and, literally, shoe boxes. As the local economy worsened during the Sargent years, the number of shoe boxes grew.

The reform impulse on Beacon Hill was also causing chaos in the 351 cities and towns of Massachusetts. In 1972 House Speaker Bartley led a legislative campaign that produced landmark legislation requiring each community to develop the resources to educate their "special needs" students in local schools. Few could or did challenge such a laudatory notion, one that kept children with physical, emotional and mental health problems close to home with their peers. But the legislation, while requiring communitites to offer special education, left the burden of paying for the program to town and city halls.

The enormous cost could only be guessed at until the law took effect in 1974. Special education quickly began to swallow up 15 to 20 percent of local school budgets, thereby placing a new burden on local property taxes, which were already exorbitant in many communities. That same year the program, known locally as Chapter 766, served as the model for a federal law which mandated all states to implement similar legislation. The group responsible for drafting and lobbying for the state law was the Massachusetts Advocacy Center, founded with the assistance of Michael Dukakis in 1971.

To help pay for the new programs, Governor Sargent campaigned valiantly in 1972 to remove a state constitutional prohibition to taxing higher incomes at higher levels, as the federal government does. But the Bank of Boston, the state's largest bank, whose well-paid officers understood that if the state were freed from the strictures of a flat state income tax they would be made to pay dearly for Sargent's liberal government, led the campaign to prevent a graduated income tax. Voters in November agreed with the bank and said no.

Thus, in the two years leading up to the election, no effort was made to raise taxes to cover the cost of such a liberal, disorganized and profligate government at a time of flattening tax revenues, double-digit inflation and rising unemployment. Over the Sargent years, total state spending went up 35 percent *after* adjustments for inflation, but state revenues only rose by an adjusted 20 percent. Federal revenue sharing helped, but, in a state in which deficits were constitutionally prohibited, the government of Massachusetts was, *de facto*, in an unconstitutional state.

The growing but unacknowledged deficit was an open secret which was freely discussed in the corridors of the State House throughout 1974. In August Michael Widmer, the communications director for the Executive Office of Human Services, was having lunch with a fellow administrator from the office while they were going over the latest official welfare spending figures. They were dumbstruck. "The election is not going to be worth winning!" Widmer said to his colleague. Because of the bureaucratic chaos, no one knew with any degree of certainty how far the state had gone into the red, yet everyone knew it was pretty far gone. In such a climate, the economy was a constant issue in the campaign for governor.

Sargent's basic position was that the state's economic woes were caused by forces well beyond his control, and that he was running a humane, caring and resourceful government, with nobility, for the less privileged. Consistent with the years spent by his administration trying to keep the people from learning the real cost of that government, Sargent came close to assuring voters that they could continue to afford his liberal government without paying higher taxes. At a debate before the primary, Sargent said there would be no new taxes "if I have anything to say about it."

Meanwhile, Dukakis was playing his strong suit, his perceived competence, against the personally popular Sargent's perceived weakness as a manager. Pat Caddell's polling continually showed that Dukakis was seen as strong and decisive, while Sargent was seen as weak and indecisive. Throughout the campaign, the hard-charging challenger took out after Sargent as a bad manager and a flaccid leader. Dukakis complained about the "callous dumping" of mental health patients on the streets, and about Sargent's wishy-washy attitude on special justices. Dukakis observed that Sargent had come out in support of a bill to end the practice of special justices, yet had continued to appoint them. "I will not appoint a single additional part-time judge to the courts of the Commonwealth," Dukakis said in a

TV appearance. "Special judges have no place in a modern and efficient judicial system."

Reporting on the results of the primary, the Boston *Herald American* observed that the Dukakis-Sargent matchup offered voters a choice between "a moderate" and "a liberal." It was a perceptive observation. While he was the leader of the Young Turks in the House, Dukakis earned the reputation of a liberal, a reputation which was fed by the liberal circles in which he moved and by the image of Brookline, a spirited center of social reform and anti-war activism, an ultra-liberal town. In his run against Quinn, the quintessential regular from the old guard, his reputation as a liberal grew. Certainly, in his personal rectitude, in his commitment to civil rights and civil liberties, in his reverence for culture and education, and in his belief in a government actively involved in solving problems and serving the general public, Dukakis was a liberal.

But his liberalism was not that of the New Deal, or of Lyndon Johnson's Great Society. That his ideal government would be active did not mean it would be free-spending. Quite to the contrary, the household Michael Dukakis grew up in placed high value on frugality and individual responsibility, and the government he had in mind would do the same. It wasn't that Dukakis was a cold and uncaring person. It was that Dukakis, who grew up in a household that was for the most part spared the hardships of the Great Depression, had led a life untouched by the realities of poverty.

As youngesters, while many of their friends were getting paid for doing chores, Stelian and Mike Dukakis toiled for the family without financial reward as part of an explicit oral family contract. Dukakis was suffused with the ethos of personal initiative and economic progress through individual effort. His sympathies were with the working class and the middle class, the shopkeepers, the tenants, the bus and subway riders, the clerks and the average folks who, like himself, worked hard, played by the rules, saved what they could, and planned for the future.

In the shorthand of daily newspapers, the *Herald*'s calling him a moderate was fair comment. But what Dukakis was and always had been was a reformer. He was a man who could peer into the government as it had evolved under the influences of the Democratic old guard and observe how the general interest had been subverted by special interests. He could see how the special interests, the accident lawyers, had gotten hold of the auto insurance laws and had perverted them for their profit. He could see how shadow governor Bill Callahan had callously, without concern for the general public interest, planned mile after mile of urban highway that would cut through neighborhoods and despoil the fragile city environment. Having identified the perversion of the public interest, Dukakis's professional achievements stemmed from a series of crusades to reform the government so as to eliminate the unfair advantages that had gone to the special interests and to rededicate the government to the public interest.

In his observations and judgments, Dukakis was guided by a transcendental vision of society in perfect balance and harmony, organized into a representative democracy that responds reflexively to the competing legitimate needs and desires of people and, through the governmental process, reaches fair, just, wise and honest resolutions of conflict. This idealized vision of the perfect state subsumed the traditional left/right polarity. To the reformer, to this reformer, anyway, left/right ideology was worse than an irrelevance, since the ideological lens must distort. Instead, character, skill, activism and performance were what mattered. The measure of these was best achieved on a non-ideological polarity: from high competence, high integrity and good management down to incompetence, corruption and chaos.

The reformer's final ascent to the summit of the state government in Massachusetts would be over the detritus of the most liberal government the state had ever seen. By Mike Dukakis's measure, the Sargent government did not measure up at all, although he shared many of its goals. He had supported most of the programs and the efforts to raise the revenues to pay for them. But Sargent's government was in desperate need of reform. Dukakis's task, once the politics of an election campaign were put behind him, would be to get the well-intentioned government under control.

Notwithstanding the *Herald*'s judgment, liberals were flocking to Dukakis after the primary on the assumption that he was one of them. So extreme were the defections that a group of prominent liberals, headed by Martin Peretz, a lecturer in social studies at Harvard and a leading anti-war activist, and Bill Homans, Jr., the attorney and civil libertarian who had served with Dukakis in the House in 1963-64, volunteered to publicly endorse Sargent and remind liberals who was who.

But it was of little use. "The liberals never felt close to Sargent personally," said Tom Glynn, a policy advisor to Sargent (now an aide to Dukakis). "He was a distant political figure. Liberals said to each other, 'At last I could have a governor who kisses me on the cheek when he sees me on the street. If we did well with Sargent, what will we get from one of our friends?' " Besides, most of Sargent's liberal support had come from Democrats, as well as independents who for the most part were lapsed Democrats, folks who liked Sargent's liberalism but were uncomfortable with his party label. Dukakis gave these voters a chance to go home to the Democratic party.

Certainly some of the liberals defecting from Sargent to Dukakis thought or felt that order had to be brought to the government now that the liberal programs had been passed. But many others simply assumed that Dukakis was every bit as liberal as Sargent, although there was no excuse for making that error; he had campaigned as a reformer, not as a liberal. In fact, on the day liberals Peretz and Homans were endorsing Sargent, Dukakis was picking up the endorsement of the fiscally conservative Massachusetts League of Cities and Towns and talking about a new state partnership with local governments, and property tax relief.

At a news conference on Friday, September 7, 1974, four days before the primary, Dukakis articulated his concerns about the economically troubled times. "The most dangerous byproduct of this persistent inflation is fear," he said." "The basic cause of that fear is that people will work all their lives and have less and less to show for their labor. And that intensifies class and race tensions. It forces citizens into uncompromising, selfish positions, and it makes the delicate art of democratic government even more difficult." The root problem, from the reformer's perspective, was not the economic misfortune of the citizenry, but the corrosive effect that human misfortune was having on the democracy.

With the liberals breaking for Dukakis and the regulars held in by the O'Neills, Dukakis's lead over Sargent swelled to 25 percent, 54 to 29, by mid-October, in another *Globe* poll. From the start of the general election campaign, Dukakis hammered away at the economy, trying to make Sargent responsible for its sorry state and complaining that the governor had failed to improve the business climate. In a major address before the Greater Boston Chamber of Commerce, Dukakis asserted that "...it is not Mr. Nixon nor the complexities of international monetary economics that have done us in. It is the utter failure of state government to manage itself effectively and responsibly."

By these tacts, Dukakis burdened the incumbent with the economic albatross and showed regular Democrats that he understood the need for more jobs, which was a constant theme of his campaign. The dirty secret of the budget deficit could no longer be kept, although both sides tried. At the start of a series of debates beginning in early October, Dukakis repeatedly insisted that he would be able to maintain services and, with better management methods, squeeze from the $3.6 billion state budget $100 million, an amount that a Dukakis supporter, House Taxation Committee Chairman Jack Buckley, told a Dukakis campaign aide the size the revenue shortfall would be. In making this proposal, Dukakis was careful not to acknowledge that there was a deficit; if he had, he and Sargent would have had to address the possibility of program cuts or higher taxes. The issue of management efficiencies entered the political dialogue as just meritorious efforts at productivity and frugality.

On October 15, in response to continuing outbreaks of sporadic anti-busing related violence in the streets and schools of Boston, Sargent mobilized the National Guard, a decision that threatened to turn the election around. "It was an act of leadership and strength, just what his image needed," said Joe Grandmaison. "We immediately dropped 13 points. I called a staff meeting the night I got the poll, and then I burned it. Literally, I put a match to it."

Now back in the hunt, Sargent thought he saw an opportunity in Dukakis's proposed $100 million in management savings to undermine his credibility. In a debate on October 20, a skeptical Sargent said, "Since he has promised welfare groups he won't cut welfare, promised elderly groups he won't cut Sargent programs for them, realized you can't cut police forces in times like these—he suddenly had a serious problem: where to find the $100 million to pay for those promises. Solution: make the promise now, but don't keep it...."

The next day, October 21, the Massachusetts Taxpayers Foundation, a well-respected, business-supported think tank, announced that it believed the deficit would be higher than $100 million, perhaps 50 percent higher. Out in western Massachusetts Sargent, who had turned his fiscal irresponsibility to his own advantage, was keeping the heat on. "I won't promise these cuts because I can't deliver on them, and neither can Mr. Dukakis," Sargent said. This line of attack angered

Dukakis, who denied ever proposing savings through management efficiencies; he had been talking about productivity increases, better cash management and reduced use of private consultants, he insisted.

Like most on Beacon Hill, the *Boston Globe*'s State House bureau sensed the deficit was even larger than estimated. The next day it received some new data from Sargent's budget analysts indicating that the guesses were right; the deficit would be larger by far than $100 million or $150 million. *Globe* reporters found Dukakis speaking about the budget at Suffolk University, just behind the State House. The reporters were determined to clarify his position on the deficit and new taxes. "We went to him pretty damn confident of the numbers and skeptical that he didn't know them too," said the *Globe*'s Ken Hartnett.

"Are you really, really sure about no new taxes?" Hartnett asked. "Absolutely. No new taxes," Dukakis said. "Are you willing to give that as a lead-pipe guarantee?" they persisted. "Yes," answered Dukakis. "I am making a commitment I intend to keep." Dukakis added that he had the ability to close the deficit "in the first six months and balance the budget."

Could Dukakis have had such confidence in his own abilities that he was prepared to make a lead-pipe guarantee that within six months of his inauguration he would have been able to save $100 million or more through better management? "He really did believe," said Hartnett. "You talk to him and he's so confident you think maybe he was right and maybe you were wrong. You begin to doubt your own data." Dukakis, as was his wont, had convinced himself of what he needed to believe. So great was his hubris, so disdainful was he of the Sargent administration, especially its managers, so full of waste was the government that he knew he could do it. Having never been an executive, having never had heavy management responsibilities, it was not difficult for Dukakis to imagine how easily $100 million could be saved—it was only 2.8 percent of the budget.

Little more than a week before the election, Grandmaison had less lofty economic problems to discuss with Dukakis. The campaign was next to broke, Sargent was closing in, and Grandmaison needed to spend $10,000 right away. Would Dukakis take out a personal loan? Before a campaign manager could have gotten the request out, most other candidates would have been on the way to the bank, but debt was close to a sin in the value system of Mike Dukakis. A borrower is less than fully self-sufficient; borrowing was a sign of weakness, and very much out of Dukakis's character. These were extraordinary circumstances, Grandmaison argued. The election was next week. Dukakis relented, only on the condition that the loan be repaid on election day. Grandmaison agreed.

But the bank lending officer had surprising news for Dukakis: his application had been turned down. The Democratic nominee for governor, a man who was favored to be elected governor in a matter of days, did not qualify for a loan without collateral. Later in the day, after a financially successful friend of Dukakis's co-signed the note, Grandmaison got the badly needed $10,000.

The final days of the campaign were full of hostility and bitterness. The Brahmin liberal and the Democratic reformer engaged in a brawl to the wire. Dukakis had claimed in the first debate that Sargent had increased taxes in the two previous years. Sargent produced a TV ad that all but branded Dukakis a liar for making that claim, and Dukakis appealed to the stations not to run it. The contretemps was almost a replay of the final days of the Quinn-Dukakis campaign. "We were surprised by the force of the governor's attack," said Grandmaison. Dukakis called the ad "scurrilous."

But when questions arose about Sargent's repertory of a $40,000 loan his wife had made to him for the campaign, at a news conference Dukakis said, "The attempt to cover up what appears to be a modest illegality" reminded him of "Watergate." At the same time, he again denounced Sargent for running a "scurrilous" campaign. Dukakis made that connection in an interview with an all-news radio station, insuring that it would be oft-repeated; in addition, the charge garnered headlines in the *Globe*. The next day, after Fran Meaney convinced him that Sargent had merely erred in the way he listed the loan on public documents, Dukakis told the press that the loan was a non-issue.

For the first time since he started running for office, Dukakis was on the defensive; worse still, he was losing a bit of his cherished self-control. His credibility had been effectively challenged, and the absence of a clearly stated agenda from the challenger was also beginning to hurt. Always intense and hard-driving, Dukakis was becoming strident, argumentative and self-righteous. Again, as he had done with Quinn, he elevated the standards to which he wished Sargent held, and then found him wanting. With little more than a week to go before the election, Dukakis asserted that Sargent's judicial appointees were "mediocre" and charged that fourteen of them were unqualified to sit as judges. Dukakis's political instincts were beginning to fail him. Sargent challenged Dukakis to "name names," and when Dukakis refused to do so, Sargent had won another point—and had reclaimed the moral high ground.

In politics, turnabout is fair play. On Thursday, October 31, Sargent turned Watergate back on Dukakis—in a convincing fashion. Speaking to Rotarians in a city just outside of Boston, Sargent said his opponent "has exhibited a self-righteousness and even an arrogance that are not good qualities for government.... The major thing that brought down the Nixon administration was that they were so darn sure that they were right."

On Monday, the day before the election, the *Globe* published the results of its final poll, taken during the previous week and retaken the previous day to double-check its surprising results. Dukakis's 25-point lead of mid-October had eroded. He now led Sargent by 6.4 percent, 46.8 to 40.4.

Irwin "Tubby" Harrison (now Dukakis's pollster), who took the poll for the *Globe*, explained that Sargent had been winning over undecided voters. He had been "getting his message across that he was a sincere, hard-working guy handling difficult problems, and Dukakis had not shown voters any greater ability to handle these difficult problems." Harrison said that if there was a message in the poll, it was that Dukakis "has not told us what he is going to do."

In fact, Dukakis had no specific program. Dukakis had been campaigning feverishly, first against Quinn and then against Sargent, for the better part of a year and a half. He believed that he would be able to prevent new taxes because he was Mike Dukakis. But beyond that, figuring out what to do would have to wait just a few more days.

In the meantime, with the *Globe* poll as a potent motivator, Dukakis exhorted his troops to work even harder. Well established and all by themselves in many small working-class cities, the members of the reformer's organization performed to expectations, as they had in the primary.

As the polls were closing, Michael and Kitty, their parents, Tommy and Jackie O'Neill, the Meaneys and a handful of closest friends and campaign aides paced nervously in a suite high above the ballroom at the 57 Hotel. Grandmaison arrived with enough data from key precincts to venture an extrapolation. Dukakis spotted him, and they walked toward each other until they met in the middle of the room, face to face. Dukakis wanted to know, "Did you pay back the loan?" "Yes," said Grandmaison. Then Dukakis asked, "How'm I doing?" "You've won," the campaign manager informed his boss. Dukakis and Tommy O'Neill hugged each other like little boys as they jumped up and down on a queen-sized bed.

In the end, the hard-pressed people had voted for a change. The Dukakis-O'Neill juggernaut, a unique coalition of reformers, blue-collar regulars, liberals and some conservatives removed the popular Republican governor in favor of the businesslike Democrat who knew the value of a dollar and the importance of jobs. The governor-elect had just turned forty-one. He was sweeping to victory in blue-collar cities across the state. Two-to-one margins were not uncommon, and there were even some three-to-one margins. But in liberal bastions like the town of Newton, and even in adjacent Brookline, where Dukakis was the favorite son, enthusiasm was tepid at best. Sargent carried Newton, 18,110 to 15,645. Back home in Brookline, where Dukakis had crushed Quinn, 8,825 to 1,803, in the primary, the result was almost embarrassing. Liberal Brookline gave Mike Dukakis the nod by only 1,568 votes, ll,426 to 9,858.

Rita Nason, the widow of Jack Nason, watched the unfolding Dukakis victory on television from her home in suburban Melrose, feeling alternately excited and sad. She was ecstatic for Dukakis, for whom Jack had worked so hard and who had cared so much for the Nasons in their time of tragedy. Jack had been dead almost four years, and during that time, she had not been able to bring herself to drive into Boston, the city where he was killed on election night, 1970. But as Mike Dukakis was preparing to claim his victory, Rita Nason grabbed her daughter Laurie, who was now thirteen years old, and found herself behind the wheel of her car driving into Boston, where she and Laurie joined the crowd in the ballroom of the Sheraton Boston Hotel. With his family, closest friends and top campaign aides standing behind him, Governor-elect Michael Dukakis prepared to speak.

Kitty Dukakis spotted Rita Nason in the crowd of faces and motioned for her to join the party on the podium. A security guard stopped her at the steps, but

Kitty nodded that she was invited, and Rita Nason ascended to take an honored place with the victory party.

When the counting was over the following day, Mike Dukakis had won the opportunity to fulfill his dream to be governor in a landslide, by 209,931 votes: by 11.6 percent, 55.8 percent to 44.2 percent, 992,284 to 784,353. That was the good news. The bad news was that Mike Dukakis, in less than two months, would become governor, the governor of a state whose economy was collapsing, whose liberals expected a continuation of the Sargent enlightenment, whose regulars expected to play ball with the first Democratic governor in twelve years, whose reformers expected just the opposite, and whose citizens expected that the problems of the state would be straightened out by the end of June, with no new taxes. Mike Dukakis had promised.

Chapter 12
"Lead Pipes" and "Meatcleavers"

On the morning after his great victory, the governor-elect and Kitty Dukakis took the streetcar downtown to begin the transition process. The streetcar had been Dukakis's preferred means of travel as a state rep and private citizen, and he had every intention of continuing to ride it as governor. The long black limousines with state police escorts that traditionally moved the busy governor through traffic from appointment to appointment were vestiges of the old politics. The Spartan who had just been elected by the people would ride with the people, courtesy of the Massachusetts Bay Transportation Authority, where, as Dukakis complained during the campaign, "the heating works in the summer, and the passengers ride in frigid cars in the winter." If the people were suffering on the "T," as it is known, then so would he—until he could fix it.

As he had said time and again in the campaign, he had cut no deals, made no compromises. Beholden to no one and to nothing, he would take office as a reformer pure and unadulterated. He would give the people not the vision of his idealized government, but the government itself.

He would do it as a practicing ascetic. Dukakis never tried to accumulate wealth. He was a man of simple tastes and few needs, and, even though he had never earned more than $25,000 a year despite the opportunity his Harvard Law School degree afforded him, he had no economic frustrations. He bought his clothes off the rack at discount stores, he owned his own home and had no mortgage worries. His idea of excitement was a good book; his idea of a night on the town was an evening at the symphony or dinner with friends.

Brookline, after the election, was euphoric. All over town, friends and supporters got together at parties. One such celebration was held at the house of Jacques Dronzick; he had a half dozen couples over for cocktails while the glow of Dukakis's win was still hot. Dukakis's friend Hackie Kassler and his wife were part of the small gathering.

During the evening, Michael and Kitty Dukakis dropped by to share the mood and say thanks. Dukakis asked for quiet to speak to his friends. "I want to run something by you," he said. "I think I'm going to give $10,000 of my salary back to the state. Who needs more than $30,000?"

His friends were stunned. "He wasn't kidding," said Kassler. "We all hooted and hollered. Someone said, 'You can try it, Mike, but Kitty can probably find a way to spend it.' "

The ridicule was so severe that Dukakis dropped the idea, but the thought had been serious. His father had always taught him to economize. To Dukakis, voluntarily forgoing part of his salary was leadership by inspiration, albeit of a kind most people, even his friends, were likely to find self-righteous.

Dukakis gave his friend and campaign chairman Fran Meaney overall responsibility for managing the transition. Next to the Dukakises, the victory was especially sweet for Meaney, the "boss," as Steve Kinzer described him, of all of Michael Dukakis's statewide campaigns. "He was the steady, experienced hand, someone to go to to bounce ideas off of," said Kinzer.

"The surge of excitement was enormous," recalled Meaney. "Thousands of resumes flooded in, the phones never stopped ringing. I'd never had such a busy, straight-out time in my life." Throughout the Commonwealth, the pervading sense was that a new era had dawned. The old politics was out, replaced by a new politics and, hopefully, as many Dukakis supporters assumed, a new cast of characters to staff the bureaucracy, as well. Meaney designated a small task force to search for talented leaders to staff the top ranks of the government, and Dolores Mitchell, a leader in Americans For Democratic Action and a loyal supporter, was appointed to survey the various special-interest constituencies for their ideas and to make cabinet-level hiring recommendations.

Dukakis had worked out in detail the theoretical nature of his ideal of a reform government. A fundamental component of the plan was to remove improper and undue political influence from the decision-making process of the government he was about to form. To accomplish this, Dukakis intended to transfer all policy-making responsibity from the governor's office and senior staff to the ten cabinet secretaries, an approach he had developed in an environment clouded by Watergate. John Ehrlichman and H. R. Haldeman, the strongmen of Nixon's White House, were going on trial even as Dukakis prepared his own government. Closer to home, the government of outgoing Governor Sargent had been dominated by a powerful troika, with chief policy advisor Al Kramer, who had been something of a prime minister, at the center.

Dukakis wanted to give the cabinet great latitude to do what each member thought was right in evaluating the competing needs of various agencies and departments. In theory, issues, matters of dispute, problems and initiatives would be defined and evaluated by the cabinet secretaries, who, with the advice and consent of the governor, would proceed toward action according to an approved list of priorities. The governor would see to it that cabinet initiatives were coordinated and not in conflict.

To insure that the cabinet was free from political influence from the governor's senior staff, Dukakis determined that the senior staff would be the junior staff. As he had promised in the campaign, Dukakis halved the size of the governor's staff and, for the most part, filled the few positions that were left with young pro-

teges whose job it would be to serve the cabinet, coordinate its inter-office communications, administer the appointments that would be made, answer correspondence, schedule the governor, and deal with the press.

One member of the emasculated senior staff was not going to be the hard-driving
campaign manager, Joe Grandmaison, the architect of the victory. During the heat
of the campaign, Dukakis had raised the issue of Grandmaison's staying on after
the victory as chief secretary, but Grandmaison told Dukakis he did not think they
should be discussing staffing questions until the election had been won. Grandmaison never heard another word on the subject from Dukakis, either before or
after the election. Instead, Fran Meaney approached Grandmaison the day after
the election to tell him how much Dukakis appreciated all he had done for the
campaign, and that his job now was to close down the campaign. He would be
paid for a number of weeks more and he would be bonused, but that was it.

Grandmaison was shocked. The staff at headquarters, which Grandmaison had
pushed until it was ready to drop, was devastated, for its members had come to
have a deep affection for their 31-year-old leader. But Grandmaison did not fit
into Dukakis's schema. At one level, it was impossible to envision the cocky and
peripatetic political technician as deferential either to the cabinet or to Dukakis;
at another, the decision not to hire Grandmaison was based on Dukakis's "false
sense of patronage," said Meaney.

In assigning Dolores Mitchell to search for talent for the cabinet, Dukakis had
specific criteria. Publicly, he informed her that he wanted his cabinet officials to
have management ability and political skills, and to be compassionate. He wanted
generalists, and he wanted to be sure that each cabinet post was filled by someone
who did not have ties to the constituency groups active in the part of society the
cabinet office served. The logic behind this approach was clear: in Dukakis's
idealized government, there was no place for an advocate for any special interest.
Each cabinet official, in order to reach correct conclusions, must be free from emotional involvements and historical relationships that might color his or her reasoning.

At the first post-election news conference, a reporter asked the governor-elect
how many women he planned to appoint to his all-important cabinet. Dukakis
paused to consider the question. While he was thinking, Kitty Dukakis piped up,
"I think there ought to be four," she said. "I'll pick four," Dukakis agreed.

Dukakis had a theoretical model for his perfect government, but he had not
given much thought to practical issues. He had assigned no one to monitor the
Ways and Means Committee budget hearing for fiscal 1976, which in Massachusetts,
began on July 1, 1975. If anyone from the transition team had been present at
the hearings, they would have heard requests for ever-higher budgets just to hold
the line on existing programs. Agencies were trying valiantly to keep pace with
the double-digit inflation that was driving up the cost of government.

The deepening Massachusetts recession promised a winter of discontent for the
incoming governor and hard times for the commonwealth. The final Sargent budget,
which covered the state through June 30, 1975, committed the state to spending

approximately 25 percent more than the previous year. Welfare spending was on a track for a 30-percent hike, as unemployment raced upward from 7.2.

The chairman of the Senate Ways and Means Committee set the deficit at $220 million on the day after the election. The following day, Dukakis met with Sargent and later with legislative leaders, David Bartley, the House speaker, and Kevin Harrington, the Senate president. The legislative leaders urged Dukakis to face reality and abandon his no-new-tax pledge. They proposed that he take dramatic action soon after the inauguration: go on TV, announce that Sargent had hidden a huge deficit which was discovered only after the books came into his hands and, taking advantage of the honeymoon period, propose a tax hike that would clear up the crisis and allow him go forward into the new administration unburdened by the deficit.

The proposal had merit. Certainly it would have placed blame where it legitimately was deserved. In addition, if taxes were raised quickly, the rate of increase—and the total to be raised—could be kept down. But Dukakis balked at the idea. For one thing, no one knew how large the deficit was. Without hard data, there was no way of knowing what to ask for. It was possible to ask for too little and be compelled to go back to the legislature for a second hike, a politically untenable situation. Dukakis, the reformer, took a long and structural view of problems. He would not act until he had the facts on which to base a plan of action. And Mike Dukakis was not one to go back on his word, not unless he had no other choice. He was not ready to concede that good management and austerity could not close down the deficit. Finally, Dukakis refused to lay the blame on anybody else.

If he blamed Sargent for the deficit and then raised taxes to pay for it, the root causes of the profligacy—inefficiency and underproductivity—would not be attacked and expunged. To Dukakis, the idea Bartley and Harrington had proposed was facile politically, but it lacked the purgation, the answering for the sins of deficit spending. Here was the reformer as Cotton Mather.

Bartley, who entered the House with Dukakis in 1963, was surprised, but Harrington, who knew Dukakis less well than Bartley, was flabbergasted that the governor-elect, offered an easy way out of a difficult bind, had turned it down flat. Following the summit conference, Dukakis was asked about his no-new-tax pledge and the deficit. "We have made a commitment and we have the will" to keep it, he told reporters. But he allowed that he did not yet have a way to do so.

The press corps was nearly unanimous in the opinion that Dukakis was waiting for what he considered the propitious moment to abandon his lead-pipe guarantee and take the course of least resistance, a course in which everyone benefited, everyone except the outgoing Republican governor. The next morning, Friday, the editorial page of the *Globe* contained a Paul Szep cartoon that showed Dukakis, trying to hide behind a pair of sunglasses, sitting on a trolley bench, surrounded by three subway riders who were reading that morning's *Globe*. The headline screamed: "Dukakis Hints of $150 Million in New Taxes." The cutline read: "You just can't believe the *Globe* these days! I voted for Mike Dukakis and I know damned well he promised no new taxes."

Dukakis had the worst of all worlds. He was getting criticized on the assumption that he was preparing to break a campaign promise even while the principled and uncompromising governor-elect was rededicating himself, against sagacious political counsel, to keeping that promise. So unusual was Mike Dukakis, so different from all previous governors, that no one was reading him very well in the first few days after his victory. He was coming on the scene just as the times were demanding extreme austerity and sacrifice. No one could remember a governor who was inspired by such a challenge, but austerity and sacrifice were strangely appealing to Mike Dukakis.

Dukakis, who neither smoked nor drank alcoholic beverages except for a glass of wine now and then, saw clothing as a utilitarian necessity; he had been shopping for many years at Filene's Basement, the bustling discount section of a landmark downtown department store. And when the Arab oil embargo kicked off double-digit inflation in the Boston area, Dukakis rose to the challenge by planting a vegetable garden in his front yard. "Personally, Michael's always been extremely tight," Allan Sidd, Dukakis's close friend, explained to an inquiring reporter at the time. "And he thinks everybody—and every entity—ought to live that way.

"He believes very strongly in the Protestant work ethic. He doesn't go around saying that, but frugality has been a way of life for him. His family used to save old clothes and send them back to Greece. When he first ran for state rep, he had only a [motor]cycle, no car. And he went to Swarthmore where the Quakers, I think, reenforced that Horatio Alger 'strive and save' philosophy. He always had a paper route and his son has a part-time job. Welfare fraud? That would drive Michael right out of his mind."

He was always careful to keep himself in top physical condition by running, which continued throughout his campaign for governor. Now the time had come for the fat and out-of-shape government, left unhealthy and exhausted by self-indulgent liberals, to be thinned down, exercised, disciplined and strengthened. Dukakis would lead the way. But the leadership he intended to provide was moral and ethical, not political. As part of the austerity drive, Dukakis ordered that no new gold-embossed stationery be ordered. Instead, he and his staff would use leftover Sargent letterheads, with Sargent's name crossed out and Dukakis's name hand-stamped on.

The first cabinet officer Dukakis named was State Representative John R. Buckley, a member of the Young Turks who had always maintained good relations with Bartley; in fact, Bartley had planned to name Buckley to be chairman of the House Ways and Means Committee if Dukakis had not made the call. Buckley was given the cabinet position of secretary of administration and finance, responsible for organizing a balanced budget.

A few days later, Dukakis announced his second cabinet selection, Lucy Wilson Benson, to take the giant cabinet post of human services. In Benson, Dukakis had a model for his vision of the reform government. She was a past president of the League of Women Voters and thus had both political and management experience.

In addition, she was smart and decent, and—which was critically important—she had no strong ties or relationships with the community of human services providers or recipients. Nor, as it turned out, did Benson have ties to the Dukakis campaign. When she was introduced to the public at a press conference, she was asked how she intended to meet Dukakis's 5-percent productivity increase he had promised during the campaign. Benson said that she was not aware that such a pledge had ever been made.

By November 11, little more than a week after the election, the deficit was tabbed at as much as $321 million, according to the fiscal affairs commissioner of the Sargent administration, economist Edward Moscovitch. Immediately after the election, Moscovitch had drafted a memo explaining the causes of the huge and growing deficit for Buckley. At a news conference four days later, Dukakis repeated his "hopes" for no new taxes, but when reporters asked how he was going to balance the budget, he said, "That's a good question." The next day Michael and Kitty Dukakis took off for Bermuda and a well-deserved, if untimely, week's vacation.

On November 9, while Dukakis was away, Buckley got his first look at hard numbers in a meeting with his outgoing counterpart and announced that he thought the deficit would be $316 million. But two weeks later, at a budget hearing, Sargent's outgoing welfare commissioner shocked the Ways and Means Committee by testifying that his agency alone was running a deficit of $213 million. If that was the case, then the overall state deficit could be as high as half a billion dollars—or more. The deficit seemed to be running up about as quickly as Dukakis's standing on Beacon Hill was running down.

Two days later, on December 5, Dukakis held a press briefing at his Tremont Street headquarters. The deficit had been more or less officially tabbed at $400 million and rising. Did Dukakis think he would have to take a scalpel to his human services programs? a reporter wanted to know. "He's generous when he talks about a scalpel," Dukakis answered. "It might be a meatcleaver."

A "lead-pipe" guarantee of no new taxes, and now a "meatcleaver" to social welfare programs? What was going on here? Liberals, especially those who had abandoned Sargent for the "equally liberal" Dukakis, were beside themselves with fury that Dukakis would penalize the poor before he went for new taxes. Richard Rowland, a leading social welfare activist and the director of the Public Welfare Council, reacted harshly. "The meatcleaver approach to slashing human services is not 'creative leadership,' " he said. "I hope that the governor-elect would show greater sensitivities to human services and not punish the poor for being poor, and the sick for being sick."

The architect and designer of the idealized democratic state responded that the state had been living beyond its means. "Look," Dukakis told the press, "we've got lots of serious problems and no one has all the answers, least of all Michael Dukakis." Throughout the growing crisis, given his overarching self-confidence, that comment was the most dramatic sign of how bad things really were. On the same day it was announced that the number of new unemployment claims for the last week in November—during the Christmas shopping season—was 26,742, double the number from a year before.

Just before Christmas Dukakis, as part of a $200 million cut in welfare spending, proposed shifting recipients of general relief, which was paid entirely by the state, into two programs, nearly 50 percent of the costs of which were reimbursed by the federal government. The outgoing welfare commissioner explained that the general-relief recipients were ineligible for the federal programs. That was why the general-relief program existed, to provide cash assistance and medical benefits to poor people who could not get federally reimbursed coverage. Dukakis, it was obvious, was groping like a blind man in the dark. His "senior" staff of glorified paper-pushers was of no help. Lucy Benson, the secretary of human services, had no experience with welfare and had no idea whatsoever of how the agencies and departments that she managed had spent $1.7 billion that fiscal year. The welfare commissioner was a lame duck who was considered one of the prime culprits for the red ink.

It was eight weeks since Dukakis had won the election. He had put most of his cabinet in place but had suggested no plan to raise revenues, nor any timetable for the announcement of such a plan. As far as anyone knew, there were no plans. Senate President Harrington, who had observed the inaction of the governor-elect with growing alarm, was the same practical scholar of the political art who had offered the proposition that Mike Dukakis would either be the best governor the state had ever had or the worst. He was beginning to fear that it would be the latter.

As the pace slowed for the Christmas and New Year's holidays, Michael Dukakis prepared to deal with the grave economic crisis, which was also a political crisis. The state would demand more and provide less. Who would pay more and who would get less were issues that would sorely test even the greatest of political leaders.

Dukakis approached the gauntlet not as a political leader but as the giver of a government, the great reform government he had been planning and thinking about for years. He was rejecting and casting off the accouterments of the office— the state troopers, the big black car—demystifying the office of governor so that the logic of debate in the new reform democracy could be heard without distraction. As he had said repeatedly in the campaign and afterward, "There will be no exchanges of jobs for favors," and he added that he would "neither threaten, nor cajole" the legislature. His intent had always been to rely on reason to win them to his side. Thus it was that Dukakis prepared to come to office not with a carrot and a stick, the time-tested tools of political leadership, but with a lead pipe and a meatcleaver; these were symbols for two ill-conceived promises that seemed to have frozen him in inaction as if each had nailed one of his feet to the floor.

Consciously disengaging himself from the political process and insistent that his minions do the same, Dukakis designed a government that minimized the technical and policy staff support he desperately needed in order, so he thought, to develop a better understanding of the vast and often irrational bureaucracy. The role of his central office would be to keep the cabinet secretaries disengaged from the excessive political influence of those over whom the secretaries would minister. But what was excessive influence? How was it to be known? What was to be done? The fiscal crisis called for leadership. Dukakis was dishing out naive management theory and courting disaster. A honeymoon? That was part of the old politics: giving the new governor what he wanted without his having been made to demonstrate its value. Dukakis did not want a honeymoon, and he was not going to get one.

New Year's Day, 1975, began at 85 Perry Street with Dukakis reading the morning papers. He read that unemployment was up again. There were 222,000 jobless in his state, when the 33,000 newly unemployed from November were added in. That was 50,000 more than a year ago, and predictions for the new year were dire. He read about the two additional women he had named to the cabinet the previous day, making the quota of four that he and Kitty had agreed to back in November. He read that H. R. Haldeman and John Ehrlichmen, Nixon's top staffers, had been convicted of Watergate-related crimes on the last day of the old year, and he read an editorial in the *Globe* urging him to raise taxes.

The paper, which had endorsed his opponent in the November election, cited a recent state supreme court ruling that struck down the practice of taxing commercial property at a higher rate than residential property as yet another reason why tax reform was needed. "Mr. Dukakis almost certainly will have to raise taxes to ensure adequate social services," the *Globe* said. The liberal newspaper recommended that the new governor "explore selective increases in the sales tax, especially on luxury items."

On Inauguration Day, January 2, 1975, Mike Dukakis was up before six, reading the papers. The household was decidedly low key but full of restrained excitment. The only dramatic sign that the day was special was the rented Chrysler station wagon that sat outside ready to take the governor-elect to the State House to be sworn in as governor. Dukakis left at 10:30 a.m. for Boston.

One-hundred and eighty years, six months and two days after Governor Samuel Adams, assisted by Paul Revere, grandmaster of the Order of Masons, laid the cornerstone for Bulfinch's State House, Michael Dukakis stood in the great hall of flags quietly going over his inaugural address while the corridors buzzed with the excitement of a historic rite of passage. Six hundred invited guests swelled the traffic in the marble-floored corridors as old pols mixed with the new. Much of the formality of the day had been removed at Dukakis's request. Formal attire was not to be found, and no nineteen-gun salute would echo from Boston Common, just across Beacon Street, to mark the new beginning.

The inaugural address was delivered with a sharp self-confidence. Dukakis called it a homecoming, and he reminded the audience that he had served in the House for eight years "as an eager but occasionally brash young legislator." It was in the House, Governor Dukakis continued, that he had learned that "one does not necessarily achieve one's goals overnight or transform society in a month's time, but where, together, in less than a decade, we forged the most sweeping record of achievement in the history of the Commonwealth."

Now a former member of the House had been elected governor. He hoped that his election would serve as an inspiration to his colleagues in the legislature. He said he understood the legislative process, and that he intended to involve the legislators "deeply and actively" in the work of his administration. To the liberals so upset about the meatcleaver comment, he nodded. Balancing the budget was not an end in itself, but "a means to social justice." The state's fiscal crisis had to be stabilized, Dukakis seemed to be saying, before he could get on with the business of providing care for those in need. And, he said, the sale of cat food was up 12 percent "because the senior citizens who are consuming it don't have even one nutritious meal each day in a senior citizens' center or school cafeteria."

He talked about his belief that political power had to be diffused throughout the political system. He reiterated his determination to eliminate "a patronage system that has plagued the state for decades." And he quoted one of his inspirations, Sam Adams, whose portrait Dukakis had chosen to hang on the wall behind the governor's desk. Why Sam Adams? Dukakis asked rhetorically. "Because Sam Adams reflects what was and is best about this Commonwealth of ours. He was a simple man. His frugality was almost legendary. But to me, Sam Adams was more than a man who understood the value of a simple, uncluttered life. He was an inspired and inspiring leader." Never moreso, Dukakis continued, than when he addressed the Continental Congress during the worst days of the Revolutionary War. " 'Gentlemen,' he said, 'Your spirits appear oppressed with the weight of public calamities. Your sadness of countenance reveals your disquietude. Our affairs, it is said, are desperate.'

" 'Let us awaken then and evince a different spirit—a spirit that shall inspire the people with confidence in themselves and in us, a spirit that will encourage them to persevere in this glorious struggle....' "

That was it: leadership through inspiration. Personal frugality to inspire a government to become frugal. Personal optimism and confidence to inspire a government and a society to become optimistic and confident of the future. Enlightenment and rationality in the government to inspire a political culture to change hundred-year-old habits.

The legislative leaders and the liberals wondered. This was Dukakis's day. No new taxes, a lead-pipe guarantee? A meatcleaver to social programs? The economy was as bad as it had been since the Great Depression. The man responsible for solving the economic and political crisis was not one of them. An uneasiness hung over the celebration. Governor Dukakis's inaugural address was interrupted for applause only three times.

Chapter 13
The Reformer Immobilized

It was 10:00 on the morning of the first full work day of the new administration, and Dolores Mitchell, the cabinet coordinator for the new governor, could not believe what she was hearing. She had gathered the nine cabinet officers who had already been appointed to an initial meeting in the cabinet room just across the corridor from Governor Michael Dukakis's "corner office."

The governor was sitting in a high-backed chair as the room filled with members of the cabinet, the men and women he had designated to be the policy-making body of his new administration. Reporters and photographers milled about. "I want to welcome you all to the first public cabinet meeting of this administration," Dukakis said. "This and all the cabinet meetings of this administration will be open to the public." The idea had never been discussed with Mitchell or the senior staff. Presenting them with the public cabinet meeting policy as a fait accompli was a clear signal that Dukakis really did intend his staff to serve as functionaries for the cabinet. It also implied that he felt he did not need their advice and counsel. If the cabinet was to be the body of primacy in the Dukakis administration, Mitchell wondered, how did he expect the cabinet to formulate policy and struggle with difficult issues and personalities with anything approaching candor while reporters wandered about taking notes and TV cameras preserved the deliberations for posterity?

Over the next few days, additional elements of the reform administration were revealed, and they began to highlight the importance Dukakis placed on creating a government that was open and accessible to the public. These reforms also underscored Dukakis's commitment to depoliticize government. The cabinet officials were told that the decades-old practice of hiring lobbyists to represent the interests of different departments and agencies with the legislature was to end; department heads or cabinet officers henceforth would do their own testifying and conduct their own legislative relations. The cabinet officials were also told that they and their agency heads could testify in favor of bills that the administration did not support so long as they made it clear that their testimony was personal and not meant to represent official positions.

On taking office, Dukakis's first official act was to sign an executive order establishing an eleven-member Judicial Nominating Commission. Under the order, the commission was responsible for sending Dukakis a list of three well-qualified candidates for each vacancy on the bench. In the event Dukakis found the three unacceptable, the nominating commission would send him a second list. Under the executive order, Dukakis was limiting himself to selecting his nominee from one of the two lists.

There was no question about the independence of the Judicial Nominating Commission Dukakis named on February 13. The racially, ethnically and geographically diverse group, which claimed four women among its eleven members, included a leader of the Hispanic community who had worked in the Sargent administration, the wife of Sargent's campaign treasurer, and a law school dean who had fought with Dukakis over no-fault auto insurance years before and had been active in Bob Quinn's primary campaign against Dukakis just months before.

As the administration began to settle in, the cabinet was told that it was expected to work hard at affirmative action in order to bring qualified minorities and women into the government as quickly as was practical. This was the kind of liberal government Dukakis had always dreamed of heading: open, rational, honest and efficient. On January 11 Dukakis predicted that the legislative session would be among the shortest in memory. He said he was aiming for adjournment by Labor Day.

"Good government is the best politics," he was fond of saying, and he had every intention of convincing the legislature of that aphorism. In one of his debates with Sargent, Dukakis was asked how he would respond if a legislative leader demanded some favor in return for his support for an important bill. "I'm confident that when those kinds of very new guidelines and methods of procedure are made clear to members of the legislature, that they will accept it, there there will be no such calls and that we can then begin to go about the business of legislating in the public interest without jobs or favors," Dukakis said. He added that he would neither "threaten nor cajole" the legislature, but would rely on reason to win them to his side.

Toward that end, Dukakis made it a habit of meeting on a weekly basis with the legislative leadership. He also began weekly meetings with a dozen or so state representatives from the Democratic Study Group, the group that had evolved from the Young Turks, the reformers Dukakis led during the sixties while he was in the House. The new leader of the DSG was Barney Frank, who came into Massachusetts politics as executive secretary to the DSG and went on to serve as a top aide to Mayor Kevin White in his first term at the end of the sixties. Frank, who first entered the House in 1973, was a wise-cracking, cigar-chomping, Harvard-educated liberal. Under his leadership the DSG became less concerned with reform and more concerned with economic and social justice than it had been when Dukakis was setting the agenda.

State Representative Phil Johnston, a social reformer who had helped organize the South Shore for Dukakis in 1974 while running a successful campaign to enter the legislature himself, was called by the governor's secretary and asked to gather the DSG in Dukakis's office for lunch on a Wednesday near the start of the term. More than a dozen of Dukakis's closest allies arrived at the corner office; they listened as he lectured for close to a half hour about various problems and programs in which he was interested. The reps were starting to get hungry when an aide entered the room and handed a brown paper bag to the governor. Dukakis took a sandwich and a soft drink from the bag and proceeded to eat his lunch. From then on, Wednesday "lunch with the governor" was understood to mean "bring your own."

As he had promised in the campaign, Dukakis abolished the patronage office, replacing it with an appointments office that served a pure tracking function to determine where vacancies existed, and he turned hiring over to the cabinet secretaries. "He had a very rigid standard for any normal human being to meet," said David Liederman, a social liberal who had been a Young Turk in the House with Dukakis and had organized and headed up the state Office for Children, an agency created during Sargent's term. Dukakis had picked Liederman to be his chief secretary after Fran Meaney had turned down the job but had declined to delegate to him any real authority. "If you were even close to Mike, it ruled you out for so many things," groaned Liederman. "No patronage, no appearance of patronage—God, it was so hard to meet." So rigorous, so squeaky clean was the anti-patronage mandate that the vaunted political organization that had always been Dukakis's hidden strength was becoming frustrated as its members found themselves shut out of government service and treated like strangers. Core organizers, many of whom had attended meetings at 93 Perry Street back in 1971 and 1972 and who had toiled selflessly and idealistically for Dukakis in hopes of one day entering government service, were told to send in resumes and wait to be contacted.

Across the Commonwealth, loyal and dedicated ward and town coordinators were treated as impersonally as was Bill Geary, an early fixture at headquarters, and they were becoming angry. To the vanguard of the Dukakis campaign, even more infuriating were announcements in local papers that neighbors who had not been active for Dukakis were getting hired to join the administration. In a number of cases, members of Sargent or Quinn's campaign actually got tapped for important state jobs for which qualified Dukakis campaign workers were turned down. When Red Ouellette, a well-known Sargent coordinator, was given a long-term reappointment to a quasi-judicial regulatory board, Dukakis loyalists screamed long and loud, but this kind of appointment was evidence that Dukakis would not loosen his rigid policy, not even a little.

Geary, who had joined the campaign as a volunteer in 1971, before Dukakis had even decided for which office he was going to run, did advance work and at times drove for Dukakis during the campaign. Shortly after the election Dukakis called Geary to his office and asked him if he would like a place in the administration. Geary was thrilled. The governor-elect asked where he wanted to work. "I want to work with you. I want to be on the governor's staff," Geary told Dukakis. Dukakis reminded him that the action would be in the cabinet; he left Geary with the impression that something would be worked out, and the meeting ended.

By the end of December, nothing had been worked out, and the 28-year-old Geary, who was married and had three children, went to Chief Secretary Liederman. "We've got experts from experienced search firms doing hiring," Liederman explained. Finally, after the new administration took office, Geary was called to interview with a search firm. Dukakis's aide with a master's degree in government told the experts his goal was to run the state's tourism office. He was sent to interview with the belatedly appointed secretary of economic affairs, who decided not to offer him a position. In desperation, Geary went to Dukakis to remind him of their conversation; Dukakis reminded Geary of the non-political screening and selection process. Soon Geary got called to another interview, this time with the secretary of consumer affairs. She offered Geary a job, and in February of 1975, he finally began his career in government, as assistant secretary of consumer affairs. "I'd wanted to work for the governor," said Geary. "I was crestfallen."

In other breaks with tradition, Dukakis ordered all summer jobs filled by an elaborate lottery system and an end to the practice of printing and distributing low-number and special-issue license plates to reward political cronies and campaign workers. At the same time, in response to the need for austerity, he mandated that state automobiles used by Boston-based state bureaucrats be centralized in a motor pool and returned at the end of the day to eliminate their improper use for private purposes and to make better use of the vehicles. He also eliminated chauffeurs for high-level state employees and out-of-state travel (except to Washington to seek federal grants), and instituted a no-hire, no-fire policy and the prohibition of overtime for state workers.

But these kinds of symbolic gestures were like band-aids for the economically depressed Commonwealth. Despite constant pressure from the legislative leadership—House Speaker David Bartley and Senate President Kevin Harrington— and the DSG, who each saw new taxes as inevitable and wanted to get them passed immediately to minimize the social, financial and political disruptions, Dukakis resisted. He had been elected to reform the government, not patch it up. Dukakis told the legislative leaders that he would deal with the fiscal crisis when he was ready.

This approach left regulars and liberals alike increasingly angry, frustrated and fearful. With expenditures far in excess of revenues, every day of delay meant a larger deficit and a larger tax hike down the road. The liberals worried that it might also mean more chops from Dukakis's cleaver. It had not registered with the governor how onerous that was as a symbol. A souvenir replica of one was given to Dukakis by a jokester; he put it on display in his office. Barney Frank and the DSG were hoping Dukakis would take advantage of the crisis to embark on a Roosevelt-like "hundred days" of reform that would leave Sargent's social programs intact while yielding a more progressive tax system. But Dukakis would not be hurried. He scrapped the proposed budget for fiscal 1976 left him by the Sargent administration and ordered a new one built from the ground up, demanding that every program and every job be justified.

To meet a legal requirement, he filed a skeletal budget—a rough estimate with no details—on January 22. Dukakis said he would call for new taxes only after "I make a Herculean effort to reduce expenditures, to eliminate waste, to reexamine old programs. . . . If, and only if, we cannot balance our budget after taking every step humanly possible to do so, I will then be compelled to ask for additional revenue." Going through such a process, said Dukakis, was "the best kind of self-discipline for the executive branch." But the effort was hopeless in a degenerating economy. On February 14 Dukakis learned that the caseload for general relief recipients, people who received a small stipend and who had their medical bills paid by the state because they did not qualify for the federally reimbursed Aid to Families with Dependent Children (AFDC) program, was up 33.4 percent in the first half of the fiscal year, July 1 through December 31, while AFDC was up 10.8 percent.

Justifying the worst fears of Barney Frank, Phil Johnston and the rest of the DSG, Dukakis announced on February 28 that he was barring previously scheduled cost-of-living increases for welfare recipients and state employees. Keyed to the rise in the consumer price index, the raises for 1975 were to have been 11 percent. Predictably, labor leaders fumed at the decision. Frank called it "morally despicable." Friends and supporters felt stabbed in the back; they could not believe that Mike Dukakis was really going to try to balance the budget, in part, on the backs of society's poorest members. Dukakis responded with a cool detachment to his friends and allies. The administration in general seemed callous and detached. Jack Buckley, the secretary of administration and finance, was widely regarded as hostile toward welfare spending, and his welfare commissioner, selected principally for his reputed managerial skills, was an investment banker.

In his dedication to all the people equally, those who opposed him as well as those who supported him, Dukakis was fast losing his ultimate State House political base, the DSG. "You don't mess with your base," observed chief secretary David Liederman. Dukakis refused to countenance discussion of the political fallout from the course he had set, and Liederman, a social liberal with values very much like Frank's, had no success appealing to Dukakis's sense of social justice. "Human services wasn't his special area of interest in the legislature," Liederman said. "On good-government issues, I'd come in to the [House] chamber and say to Dukakis, 'What's my vote?' On human services issues, he'd come into the chamber and say to me, 'What's my vote?' "

On March 7 a discouraged Dukakis fended off badgering reporters with blunt language. "Look, we're broke. We're dead broke," he said. "And when you're broke you can do two things. You can go to the taxpayers—who aren't doing very well themselves—and ask them to cough up some more, or you can cut. We will go that second route as hard as we can until we find as a matter of judgment or policy that we can't cut any more."

In a meeting with Administration and Finance Secretary Jack Buckley and Chief Secretary Dave Liederman on April 14, Dukakis finally had no choice but to face reality. He was looking at an operating budget deficit of $450 million for the current fiscal year, which would end on July 1, with no way to pay for it, and an even larger deficit looming in fiscal 1976. All the belt-tightening Dukakis was able to demand and inspire, all the productivity increases he was able to catalyze, were, in the short run, like spitting in the ocean. "No new taxes" would become two

new tax hikes: one to cover the fiscal 1975 deficit inherited from the Sargent administration, and one to give the state the revenue to cover costs for the upcoming
year.

Acting on the recommendation of Buckley, who had gotten the idea from a
banker, Dukakis decided to close the deficit by floating a bond issue and paying
it off over time. Bonds had never before been used to pay for operating costs in
Massachusetts, and it would be an expensive approach, but this was crisis management; it was unthinkable to ask the legislature to vote and the people to pay for
a $450 million tax increase for fiscal 1975 and an even larger increase within months
to reduce the shortfall for fiscal 1976. By bonding the deficit, the tax increase could
be kept to a minimum. Dukakis decided to raise what was needed, about $110
million, through a five-cent increase in the cigarette tax and a four-cent increase
in the gas tax for the five years necessary to pay off the bonds.

The next day Dukakis moved with steely resolve to take a bite out of the runaway
costs of the welfare budget as he anticipated trying to convince the legislature and
the people to accept two major tax hikes. He proposed $311 million in cuts in welfare
for the coming fiscal year. One element in the program was to strike from the general
relief roles anyone under forty years of age deemed employable, even though
unemployment was by then over 10 percent and still rising, and even though many
general relief recipients had chronic physical, mental health or alcohol-related problems. For a savings of approximately $20 million, approximately fifteen thousand
general relief recipients would lose their cash assistance.

This proposal marked the breaking point for Barney Frank, whose anger at his
old friend had become personal. "The good thing about Michael is that he takes
the 'T' to work," noted Frank. "The bad thing is that he gets off at the State
House." He never again went to a Wednesday lunch session in the corner office,
where attendence gradually dropped.

Not that Dukakis was indecisive in the least about what he needed to do, but
in the following week the welfare commissioner and his assistant were looking
through files in the department when they came upon an unexplored cabinet. Inside, they found forgotten bills from vendors totaling roughly $50 million; they
had never been submitted for payment. A week later, on May 2, Dukakis formally
abandoned his lead-pipe guarantee and called for $131 million in new taxes on
cigarettes, liquor and gasoline, the so-called "sin taxes," to finance the $450 million
bond issue to cover the fiscal 1975 deficit.

In mid-June the legislature finally sent Dukakis the bond and sin-tax package;
within days Dukakis announced on statewide television, in his first appearance since
taking office, his proposed tax hikes for fiscal 1976. They totaled $687 million and
would just cover spending if the legislature resisted liberals' efforts to restore the
close to $500 million in cuts Dukakis had made in cabinet requests, including the
abandoned cost-of-living increases for welfare recipients and state workers and the
trimming of "employables" from the general relief role. Legislative leadership and
liberal opposition to cuts was intense.

With the filing of his massive tax bill—a hiking of the sales and income taxes—Dukakis and the Commonwealth had reached a strategic impasse. On one hand, he was determined to remake the government in his own image, righteous and severe, cleansed of the bargaining and trading that customarily lubricated the political process. On the other hand, he was asking the legislature to approve the type of bill that in the past had required the give-and-take he found distasteful and improper. Harrington simply could not muster votes in the Senate for the budget-tax package. Over in the House the bitter liberals in the DSG and the smug I-told-you-so regulars argued over who hated Dukakis more. In the midst of the crisis, House Speaker David Bartley resigned to become president of a state college, and the members elected his floor leader, Thomas W. "Tommy" McGee, a recovering alcholic and former U.S. Marine, to succeed him. McGee was a protege of the late speaker, John "The Iron Duke" Thompson; like his mentor, McGee's politics were personal, emotional and anti-rational, yet simultaneously New Deal liberal. Needless to say, he was contemptuous of his former colleague, the governor.

As a political force on Beacon Hill, Dukakis had "become irrelevant," as Barney Frank observed. "Michael has reduced the power of the governor to the formal legal powers. He can submit. He can veto. He can appoint. But he cannot influence." Yet the feeling was that Dukakis still enjoyed great general popularity, much to the frustration of the legislators whom he had treated so disdainfully. Supporting this view was the publication in the *Boston Herald American* of the results of a poll taken immediately after Dukakis repudiated his lead-pipe guarantee. According to the poll, the governor had an approval rating of 60 percent, with 31 percent disapproving. Two-thirds of those polled believed his campaign pledge of no new taxes had been sincere.

But Dukakis stubbornly refused to exert leadership with the people to create the public support that Harrington and McGee needed if they were to convince enough of their members to accept the budget-tax bill. Throughout the summer and early fall, the impasse continued and the fiscal and political crisis deepened. Without a new budget when fiscal 1976 began on July 1, the state continued to use the old budget, which was badly out of balance and getting more so every day. Meanwhile, bankruptcy threatened New York City, which was in the throes of its own fiscal crisis. The thought of a similar fate for the entire Commonwealth of Massachusetts was no longer apocalyptic science fiction.

In late October, threatening and cajoling, McGee jammed a $295 million sales and income tax increase, tied to a $2.88 billion budget, through the House. The tax hikes were less than half the $687 million Dukakis had called for, and the cuts were ruthless. Whereas Dukakis proposed dropping "employables" from the general relief program, the House concurred and went further, denying medical coverage for the remaining general-relief recipients, as well.

The Senate was intractable, however. A desperate Harrington called a caucus of Democrats. At the end of four hours, a majority said that, while they understood the crisis, they would not be recorded on a roll call as voting for the budget and tax bill. Since there was an insufficient number of Republicans in the Senate to demand a roll call, Harrington herded all the Democrats into the chamber and passed the historic bill on a voice vote.

"This has to be the first time in the history of democracy that a bill opposed by the majority will become law," complained a Republican leader. Another called it "anarchy, not democracy." Harrington called it "an extraordinary procedure. Maybe the tactics were harsh. Maybe the tactics were unreasonable. But we violated no rule. We violated no constitutional provision. The responsibility thrust upon us at times is a heavy and ugly responsibility. In my judgment, we had to have this budget. Otherwise, disaster would have resulted." In hopes of convincing the public of the seriousness of the fiscal crisis, Harrington called newspaper publishers across the state to a meeting in his office the next day and attempted to justify his actions by explaining that Massachusetts was on the verge of bankruptcy. He dropped the suggestion that Governor Dukakis go on statewide television to catalyze action.

But editorials in the daily newspapers characterized Harrington as a dictator. When the governor's office, reporting in good faith but relying on outdated information, said that Harrington had overstated the magnitude of the problem, the publishers began calling the senate president a charlatan. Observers saw no little irony in Harrington's abuse of the democratic process to keep alive a budget-tax package for the pristine reformer. Harrington was furious that the governor's office appeared to have gone out of its way to inflame public opinion against him after what he had done, and that he did not seem to understand the seriousness of the crisis.

The bill that passed the House did so with the most tenuous of majorities, with liberals barely able to stomach the program cuts, and regulars and conservatives barely able to take the tax hikes. The bill that passed the Senate did so without a functioning majority and was considerably more liberal than the House version, proposing $445 million in new taxes, up $150 million from what the House approved, and $3.05 billion in spending, up $175 million from the House. The majority coalition in the legislature for the budget-tax program was fragile, to say the least. Further program cuts meant the loss of critical liberal support, and higher taxes meant the loss of necessary conservative votes. Under the circumstances, forging a viable compromise, as a House-Senate conference committee set out to do, seemed a nearly impossible task.

In this atmosphere, Dukakis and the rest of the citizens received more bad news on Wednesday, October 29. According to newly released figures, unemployment in September, after seasonal adjustments, had jumped to 14 percent; the result was a corresponding expansion of the welfare rolls. The same day Richard D. Hill, chairman of the First National Bank of Boston, the city's largest financial institution, made an unprecedented journey to Beacon Hill; he delivered a dire warning to Dukakis and the legislative leadership. If the state did not have a "credible" tax and budget package in place by November 13 at the very latest, the bank would be unable to sell a new bond issue to pay off $120 million in housing bonds that were coming due. If that occurred, Hill explained, the Commonwealth would be in a state of default, its capacity to borrow in the bond market would evaporate, and something akin to bankruptcy would follow, as Harrington had warned.

Dukakis, who had set out to detach himself and his administration from politics as usual, found himself detached from crisis politics, as well. No one on Beacon Hill cared much about his thoughts on what should be done. But he was the only political figure in the Commonwealth who had a hope of convincing the public of the need for legislative action on the tax and budget package. He was still the reform governor, and if the crisis was to be resolved, the people would have to accept the facts, as only Michael Dukakis, the politician who was trusted to tell the truth, could convincingly lay them out.

For weeks Dukakis had resisted the advice of aides to make a dramatic statewide address. He continued to believe that the legislature should work out its own problems. Furthermore, the statewide TV address had been Frank Sargent's favorite ploy, and it had grated on Dukakis. But before the weekend, the senate president presented Dukakis with an ultimatum: the conference committee would not reach a compromise until Dukakis agreed to go on statewide television to acknowledge that Harrington had been correct in his assessment of the crisis and to use his influence with the people to mitigate the political damage approving the budget-tax bill would have on rank-and-file members. Without any real choice, Dukakis agreed. A speech was drafted over the weekend, and Dukakis prepared to go on TV on Thursday night, November 6.

On November 3, the conference committee finally broke the impasse and produced a compromise budget-tax bill. The $3 billion budget bill included an increase from 3 to 5 percent in the sales tax, a 7 1/2-percent surcharge on the state personal income tax and elimination of the one-dollar exemption on the 8-percent meals tax.

On the morning of his address, Dukakis went before the Massachusetts Labor Council AFL-CIO to urge them to lobby the legislature to restore social spending to the budget. Before he could speak, about one hundred delegates walked out in protest of his having broken his no-new-tax pledge. In the afternoon he taped his mea culpa, which was telecast statewide at 7:30 p.m. a year and a day after he had been elected.

"Fiorello LaGuardia, the late great mayor of New York used to say that when he made a mistake, 'It was a beaut.' And I suppose every politician makes statements which later come back to haunt him," Dukakis said. "I'm afraid that's the case with my campaign statement about new taxes. . . . Quite clearly, I was wrong. I'm only too well aware of the deep feelings aroused by the no-new-taxes pledge. And I sincerely regret it."

Dukakis, having apologized for promising more than he could deliver, went on to defend the need for new taxes. "Some of you will say, 'Why not cut more: If you're still short, why not cut another three or four hundred million dollars?' In good conscience, we cannot do that." Already, he said, the cutting had gone too far, and he cited as examples the elimination of medical services for the working poor and those on general relief, and the elimination of dental services and drugs for the elderly.

As Dukakis spoke to the people, the conference committee released its report to the House. But the House was kept in recess until 2:30 a.m. while the membership was polled and support shored up. When the House voted, just before 4:00 a.m., the leadership was shocked. The budget-tax bill lost, 120-112. A recess was called; everywhere there was feverish lobbying to turn the vote around. Jack Buckley, the administration and finance secretary to the governor who had promised never to threaten or cajole the legislature, bluntly told five members from the city of Worcester that if they did not reverse themselves and vote yes, he would kill funding for the Worcester State Medical School hospital. Buckley issued a similar threat to members of the black caucus, who were trying to establish a state community college in the black, Roxbury section of Boston. The black representatives were so angry that one of them, Mel King, physically pushed Dave Liederman through a set of swinging doors and out of the House chamber into the corridor.

None of the black members, who were protesting the social cuts, voted ''yes'' on reconsideration, but the Worcester reps saw the light, and so did a small number of others. The DSG was almost evenly split. Angry and frustrated, Barney Frank in the end was pragmatic and voted ''yes.'' Phil Johnston, equally upset, could not bring himself to endorse the Draconian cuts and voted ''no.'' At 5:20 a.m., when the time for voting had expired, the electronic tote board showed an almost equal number of red and green lights. The speaker announced the tally. The budget-tax bill had finally passed the house, 114-110. Harrington had the Senate under control, and at 9:16 p.m., in the second night of an all-night session, a little more than twenty-four hours after Dukakis's TV address, the monstrous tax and budget package was on its way to the governor for his signature.

The legislature vindictively cut appropriations for the cabinet, which were down close to 20 percent overall. At a time of expanding welfare rolls, Medicaid funding was down $79 million to $410 million, general relief funding was down $47.5 million to $62.5 million, while AFDC and mental health were level-funded. On Saturday afternoon, November 8, ahead of the bank-imposed deadline, the governor unenthusiastically signed the budget-tax bill with hopes that ''we can put the divisions and disagreements of the past ten months behind us.'' The crisis was over.

None could remember a time when the kind of high hopes and promise that Dukakis had brought to office had been so thoroughly and completely dashed. Dukakis entered office determined to do what he thought was right, in the abstract sense, without reference to the political context. And that was the way he went through the year. In almost every instance, his dedication to an apolitical course of action yielded impolitic results. In bringing the disaster upon himself, seemingly without concern for the effect on his reform agenda, his organization, and the delicate coalition that had brought him to office in the first place, Dukakis had himself a living and isolated monument to the hubris of trying to govern on a plane above political reality.

But if Dukakis paid a heavy price for his extravagant conceit, the integrity of the effort won praise for the government. "The executive branch, to the surprise of many, has shown for the first time in memory that it is capable of tightening its own spending belt," observed Richard Manley, president of the Massachusetts Taxpayers Foundation, a business-backed state watchdog agency, on the day Dukakis signed the budget. "No one is happy about taxes. No one is happy about curtailing some state services. But every Massachusetts citizen can feel relieved that Massachusetts has finally faced a very serious financial crisis and met it."

On Monday, November 10, pre-Christmas shoppers went on a spree in an effort to buy before the sales tax jumped from 3 to 5 percent two days later. And in coffee shops all over the Commonwealth, now that the one-dollar exemption on the meals tax had been repealed, customers were reminded that the twenty-five cent cup of coffee had gone up to twenty-seven cents. "Two cents for the Duke," they were told.

Chapter 14
Achievements of a Reform Government

By the end of 1975 Mike Dukakis, who had run for governor to influence people and not necessarily to win friends, was the most disliked man on Beacon Hill; lonely, misunderstood and roundly disliked. The legislature had just experienced its first taste of reform government, and it was a bitter experience. They had been forced to live without patronage and the less harmful political amenities, such as summer jobs and low-number license plates. During this period of involuntary purification, the legislature had been forced to raise a half billion dollars in new taxes and cut deeply into humanitarian social programs to balance the books—honestly and with no tricks.

Michael Dukakis was blamed for the tortured year; legislators failed to see their own culpability as products of the old politics. Speaker Tommy McGee, the lunch-pail Democrat with big cigars and a Marine's vocabulary, thought Dukakis was a heartless snob and a political idiot. Senate President Kevin Harrington, the consummate powerbroker, was bemused that Dukakis had voluntarily surrendered political power and initiative.

But the leadership and their members were still respectful of Dukakis's glossy reputation with the public. "I was talking to a bunch of regular people," Tim Taylor, an aide to the speaker, told a reporter in the corridor of the State House at the start of the new year, 1976. "They said, 'It's about time he threw the bums and freeloaders off welfare. Let them go to work. Let them find jobs.' What he's doing is making anti-welfare policies respectable."

In recognizing a popular support for Dukakis that was not shared by the political establishment, the game plan for the Democratic legislative leadership was clear: get him in the end, but avoid the kind of public disputes they had had with Dukakis in 1975. "Victory through attrition is the idea," a legislative leader confided privately to a reporter. The ultimate goal was to be rid of Dukakis as soon as possible, which meant in the Democratic primary in September of 1978, two and a half years off. "Everything else will be subplot," the legislative leader said, "but that's the plot."

Cheerful and practical, Dave Liederman, Dukakis's chief secretary who had come out of the House, the DSG and the Sargent administration, where he had organized and run the Office for Children, had never had a more miserable and frustrating year. His many friends in the building were furious; they hated his boss and took it out on him. And Liederman had no success in reasoning with Dukakis that he had to consider the importance of legislative politics and public relations to his program. Only with great effort did he get Dukakis to agree that the senior staff had to be upgraded, that it needed the political resources which the rigid reform governor had denied it on principle in 1975.

Liederman brought in Mike Widmer, a former reporter at United Press International and a Harvard Ph.D. in Russian Studies who had worked in the executive office of human services as top advisor to the secretary during the Sargent administration; afterwards he had stayed on to help Dukakis's secretary, Lucy Benson, when the administration changed. Widmer was put in charge of communications, working with press secretary Mary Fifield. Bill Geary, who had been exiled to the executive office of consumer affairs a year before, was given responsibility for appointments to the administration and was expected to monitor selections with some political sensitivity. He was finally going to get his wish to work with the governor. When Geary mentioned his new job to Barney Frank, Frank quipped, "Yeah, [it'll be] like pimping for a nun."

Liederman, Widmer, and almost everyone around Dukakis knew and understood the depth of hard feeling he engendered with his puritanically self-righteous and uncompromising reform approach. But not Dukakis. The governor seemed genuinely oblivious of the viscerally negative response he and his policies were evoking.

On one occasion, during that horrible first year of the term, 1975, Dukakis held a "town meeting" at Southeastern Massachusetts University. The students were furious about cuts in the school's budget that had been taken during the all-out austerity drive. Two 1974 Dukakis campaign workers—a dean and a student, Andy Sutcliffe—met Dukakis and an aide, Dick Giesser, at a restaurant near campus for the ride to the school and the events of the day.

"We tried to convince him to accept that he was very unpopular," said Sutcliffe, "but he was stubborn. The walk to the auditorium from the parking lot was lined with students. They were yelling and holding signs. The auditorium was packed. There were close to two thousand people in an auditorium made to seat eight hundred.

"He talked platitudes. I don't think he ever fully realized the depth of anger. I think he felt the force of his personality and his logic would change their minds."

Sutcliffe, who went on to work closely with Dukakis for years, Widmer, and others who were close to Dukakis at this time, explained his apparent blindness to the broad-based hostility he encountered as resulting from a powerful capacity to deny. The governor's aides saw their boss in a continuing fight against the legislative establishment. But the reformer who had succeeded in reforming the political establishment in Brookline by making it over to comport with his values was planning to do the same with the entire Commonwealth. He convinced himself and acted on the belief that he was making progress with McGee and Harrington, that he was beginning to convince them of the wisdom of reform government. "Every time we wanted to attack the legislature," said Widmer, "he'd say, 'What are you talking about? We have to be friends with the legislature.' "

Dukakis's righteousness took its toll much closer to home as well. Fran Meaney, Dukakis's friend since law school, had managed the transition and had chaired a Management Task Force which produced an extraordinary report on management reforms. But he had also become a mover and a shaker, as Dukakis viewed things, and moving and shaking was decidedly not on the Dukakis reform agenda. Meaney, a partner at a Boston law firm, intervened with the state to try to find a job for the brother of R. Robert Popeo, a senior partner at his firm, after the brother was let go by one of the cabinet secretaries. Meaney was opening doors for clients of his firm, salesmen wanting to sell services to the state. Meaney had put Dukakis in a position where the absence of action to end his friend's governmental free-lancing would have been read fairly as tacit approval; but then, Dukakis had set no limits on the behavior of his friend. "Michael never talked to me about my business activities," Meaney said.

The final straw in their strained relationship was a matter of perception. State Treasurer Crane, a roguish student of the Bill Callahan/John Thompson school of help-a-friend-if-you-can politics, was a good friend of Robert Popeo and had given Popeo's firm forty thousand dollars' worth of bond-counsel work in 1976. When Dukakis heard of the deal between Crane and Meaney's firm, he was concerned about the image of his administration, thinking incorrectly that Meaney had attracted the business, and agitated enough about this contract that he called Meaney and the chairman of the firm, William Glovsky, to a meeting. Recently embarrassed by the discovery that department heads had been trading favors with legislative leaders for action on key bills, Dukakis sought to convince the attorneys that their contract with the treasurer, though he was an independently elected state official, could somehow further embarrass the "clean, clean government." The attorneys, of course, did not see it that way. "We were adamant about not letting Francis's relationship with the governor interfere with our practice of law," Glovsky said.

The law firm refused to back off. Meaney and Dukakis had a final scene in his office. "Fran stormed out: 'That's it, it's over,' he said on the way out the door," said Mike Widmer. "Michael walked out, stood in the outer reception area and said to no one in particular, 'If that's the way he wants it, so be it.' Without a hint of emotion, he turned, walked back to his office and resumed his work." If Dukakis was upset by the ending of his relationship with Meaney, his constant comrade-in-arms, alter-ego, and the chairman of his gubernatorial campaign, he gave not a hint of his feelings to his closest aides. Meaney, who the day before had submitted a letter to Dukakis resigning as chairman of the Management Task Force and as chairman of the governor's political committee—a position he had held since 1966—never heard from his friend again.

Unconcerned about his political standing and convinced that he was winning converts daily to his reform crusade, Dukakis pushed forward. There wasn't an establishment he didn't challenge, a closed club he didn't try to open. He stubbornly continued to ride the streetcars to and from work, not because he liked the subway rides but because he believed it was the right thing to do. As he crammed onto the antiquated cars each morning and evening, standing next to people who would have loved to have been anywhere else, he was convinced he was right, and not just about riding the "T." He believed he had a mandate to reform the government.

Systematically, he set out to do that. He sought and obtained a stronger, more independent public utilities commission, one that treated the phone company and electric utilities as adversaries of the government rather than the friends they had become through deft lobbying of the legislature and past administrations.

Dukakis long had had a concern, one bordering on obsession, with billboards and the billboard industry. For years, the politically powerful industry had gotten its way in Massachusetts by softening up politicians with generous campaign contributions, free Red Sox, Bruins and Celtics tickets, and free and cut-rate billboards for political advertising. As a consequence, the Outdoor Advertising Board, which was created to regulate the placement of billboards, had become an acquiescent agency, and the state's beautiful countryside and city neighborhoods were being despoiled by outdoor advertisements, as far as Dukakis was concerned.

The advantages the billboard industry obtained through the garnering of improper influence within government produced "an offense to his sense of neatness and order," said Jim Witters, an attorney and former Dukakis Raider. Dukakis appointed Witters to be chairman of the Outdoor Advertising Board and charged him to "get the billboards out of the countryside."

Witters proceded to regulate the industry aggressively. In one instance, he demanded that a ski resort owner in western Massachusetts remove a roadside sign directing skiers to his trails. The resort owner fought the order bitterly. Finally he took down his sign, replacing it with a live cow with the directions painted on its sides penned in on land owned by the resort owner. Witters had no authority to order the cow removed, so it grazed in peace, a living monument to Dukakis's rigid regulation of billboards, until the end of the term.

An even larger and more powerful industry and special interest was made up by the state's insurance companies. Massachusetts was the corporate home of giants like the John Hancock Mutual Life Insurance Company. Overall, insurance accounted for the jobs of close to 60,000 residents. From his experience with Professors Keeton and O'Connell during the fight for no-fault auto insurance in the sixties, Dukakis had a sophisticated understanding of the field and was determined to provide better and cheaper coverage to the consumer.

For his insurance commissioner, Dukakis chose James Stone, a Ph.D. in economics from Harvard, the author of a visionary book on the future of Wall Street, and the vice-president of an insurance brokerage firm. At twenty-seven, Stone, a native New Yorker, was the youngest state insurance commissioner in the nation. His mandate was simple: to do whatever the law allowed for the consumer. "If you find something's wrong and you have the statutory power to fix it, you fix it," said Stone, summarizing his charge from the governor.

Stone found three basic problems. The first was that, in setting rates for the companies based on the relationship of expenses to revenues, the state had been considering only income from premiums, not investment income as revenues. As a result, companies were realizing excessive profits, which were reaching windfall levels in the mid-seventies, as interest rates soared. A second problem was the way in which policies were written: in something akin to a foreign language for any layperson. And the third big problem was that auto insurance rates were based on a driver's age, sex, marital status and residence, rather than on his or her driving record.

Dukakis gave Stone full support in his effort to find solutions to these problems. For years the industry had been talking about making policies more easily understood, but as yet nothing had gotten done. "I told Mike I can write a readable policy, and I can do it in three weeks. Shall I do it?" Stone said. "He said, 'Of course.' So I did. It was a scary precedent for the companies."

Point by point the companies challenged the legality and/or constitutionality of the reform insurance program, but the Supreme Judicial Court upheld the administration. This made for more bitter feelings. "Mike Dukakis was an interior decorator who came into people's homes and told them how to rearrange the furniture," said Stone. "It wasn't whether or not his ideas were right. It was that we were arrogating to the state the decision where the couch would go. And it was their furniture."

No regulator in the reform government of Mike Dukakis was more aggressive than Carol Greenwald, the banking commissioner. At thirty-one, Greenwald, a New Yorker and a brilliant economist who had been working at the Federal Reserve Bank of Boston, could have been Jim Stone's big sister. Almost immediately after taking office in 1975, she took up a crusade of neighborhood activists to expose and end the industry-wide practice of writing off for the purpose of mortgage-lending entire sections of Boston that were considered bad risks. This policy, known as "red-lining," for the circles that critics claimed banks used to define the areas in which they would not do mortgage business, discriminated against minorities who were concentrated in poor urban neighborhoods. Furthermore, red-lining was a self-fulfilling prophecy. Using a red marker to define a neighborhood as a poor investment insured that it stay that way.

Community activists, pouring over thousands of deeds, had discovered a pattern of urban disinvestment in which banks' mortgage-lending policies were encouraging the trend toward suburban development at the expense of the host city. But the data was sketchy and inconclusive. Greenwald wanted the facts and announced new regulations; she ordered all state-chartered banks to disclose where they got their deposits and where they invested them. This information had always been closely held, and the banks were furious at what they saw as an invasion of their private affairs.

In February 1976 the banks got another request for information from Greenwald. The nineteen-page questionnaire on bank personnel policy not only requested the facts about minorities and women, but it inquired about the ethnic and religious backgrounds of bank workers, and whether the banks had memberships in any clubs or organizations that were discriminatory towards women or minorities. These were areas unexplored by the most demanding affirmative action programs of the federal government. When Greenwald called public hearings on these matters, the bankers felt demeaned and insulted to even discuss "this kind of crap," as one of Greenwald's bank president-witnesses described the questioning. The bankers begged Dukakis to call off his crusading reformer; the governor turned them down cold and encouraged Greenwald to continue her work.

Inside the government Dukakis was equally aggressive in attacking the old-boy patronage network which he had been fighting since his first days as a state representative. Many agencies that had carefully insulated themselves from the civil service law over the years and were havens for patronage were found throughout the bureaucracy. Bloated with relatives and friends of pols, these agencies, filled with artifacts from a bygone era—elderly white men, for the most part—were a reflection of how badly the government was in need of reform. The most encrusted agencies—the department of public works and the turnpike authority—were almost entirely male and white-skinned above the level of secretaries, typists and clerks.

In the Dukakis administration, these two agencies came under the authority of Fred Salvucci, the secretary of transportation and construction. Salvucci hired Kay Gibbs, a black political activist from Boston, as an assistant secretary of transportation and construction, and set her to the task of integrating the agencies, which together had seventeen thousand employees. "We had all the agencies up," said Gibbs. "They told us to stick it in our ears. Then we told them what they had to do." But institutional resistance was formidable, having been well practiced over the years.

Over at the turnpike authority, Director John Driscoll "was very slick," said Gibbs. "Soon as we started, there was a revolution in toll-takers." Minorities and women soon were hired for those most visible of jobs. "But they were only 10 percent of the work force. The rest of the turnpike was kept white and male." Dukakis had a political and personnel problem with Driscoll. To carry through with his commitment to breaking up the old-boy network, Driscoll, one of its most entrenched legates, had to go. But Driscoll was a friend of Tip O'Neill's, and O'Neill strongly supported Driscoll. Dukakis attempted to beg the issue; he declined to reappoint Driscoll, but he did not replace him, leaving him in charge of the turnpike but in limbo. It was a solution that satisfied no one and left the impression that Dukakis talked like a good reformer but, when confronted with a tough political choice, he ducked.

After 1975 the economic hard times of the Commonwealth began to loosen up. The unemployment rate, which peaked at 11.2 percent in 1975, was down to 9.5 percent in 1976 and continued dropping throughout Dukakis's term to 6.1 percent in the 1978 election year. By the start of the campaign, roughly seventy-five thousand fewer people were unemployed than when Dukakis took office, and the number of employed had increased by about the same number during that time. Massachusetts' recovery reflected the national comeback from the recessions of

1973-75. Even before the downturn, the state's economy had been largely dependent on high technology, both military and non-military, but that dependence had increased during the downturn as some of the few remaining old industries of the mill cities failed to come back. A full third of all the state's manufacturing jobs were in high tech during this time. And that meant the suburbs.

It was in the cities where the transition from the Industrial Revolution to the Information Age was most costly and painful. In 1975 unemployment in Haverhill, where Euterpe Dukakis's family had settled, reached 15.7. The situation was almost as bad in Lowell, in Lawrence, where Dukakis's father settled, and in Brockton and Pittsfield.

Dukakis had campaigned for office promising economic growth. Back in November 1975, when he signed the record tax and budget bill to prevent default, Dukakis knew what the long-term goal had to be. "In the last analysis," he said, "it will be economic growth that will produce the revenue we need to provide services for our people. That is the job that lies ahead." Committed to economic development, the administration was mindful of where that development was needed most—in the old factory towns and cities which, coincidentally, provided many of the votes that had brought Dukakis to office.

Dukakis created a development cabinet, headed by Frank Keefe, a fast-thinking dealmaker who had been the planning director of the city of Lowell. Keefe became the senior staff exception to the rule: the policy advisor with substantial responsibilities. Dukakis had first met Keefe during the 1974 campaign as he and Alden Raine, his campaign's advisor on local development issues, were putting together their thoughts on the state economy. "We were talking about Urban revitilization all during the campaign," Raine said, "and we were trying to figure out what that meant." One day Raine read a newspaper account of Governor Sargent's rejection of an invitation from Keefe to discuss his concept for an urban Heritage Park for Lowell; Sargent, the environmentalist, thought state parks were meant for rural areas. Afterwards, Raine wrangled an invitation for Dukakis to meet Keefe. At the conclusion of Keefe's briefing, Dukakis turned to Raine and said, "This is exactly what I've been talking about."

The development cabinet included the secretaries of economic affairs, environment, transportation, and communities and development, plus the lieutenant governor, Tom O'Neill, who was given responsibility for managing federal-state relations. Taking advantage of the fact that his father was the most powerful Democrat in Congress, O'Neill helped many projects clear hurdles in Washington. Unlike the cabinet as a whole, which continued to meet in public, accomplishing very little in the process, the development cabinet was run quite differently by Keefe and his deputy Al Raine—out of the glare of the spotlight where they were extremely effective.

Keefe's primary goal was to fashion a growth policy for the Commonwealth, an action agenda that would rationalize and encourage development in city and town centers while at the same time discouraging the proliferation of suburban industrial parks and commercial malls. In 1977 a planning document, "City and Town

Centers: A Program for Growth,'' was produced by Keefe and his staff. In it, the Dukakis approach to revitalization—anti-sprawl and urban-focused, catalyzed by new, quasi-independent, low interest rate bonding authorities for a variety of development needs—became a top policy priority for the remainder of the term.

"We weren't into shopping malls on marshes with fourteen-screen cinemas and a MacDonald's,'' said Raine. Raine and Keefe were constantly looking to abandoned inner-city areas and old mill towns to encourage redevelopment. Frank Keefe, the master planner of Lowell, made certain that his former employer, the city of Lowell, received a healthy dose of state attention. A ten-million-dollar investment in the innovative Urban Heritage Park which he had worked to develop paved the way for forty million dollars in federal funds brought in by Congressman Paul Tsongas of Lowell. And when Dr. An Wang, founder of the computer company that bears his name, chose Lowell for his corporate home, the state provided partial funding with a five-million-dollar, low-income construction loan as a form of thank-you.

The western Massachusetts city of Pittsfield, located in long-neglected Berkshire county, near the New York border, also came in for a disproportionate share of attention. A parcel of land in the city's downtown section had lain barren for years, the victim of an earlier era's urban renewal bulldozer. A series of city-designated developers had failed to come up with a workable plan for the plot. When Keefe learned that a large mall developer was running into difficulties with his plan to construct a mall on Route 7 in the neighboring town of Lenox—the summer home of the Boston Symphony Orchestra—Dukakis and Keefe's Office of State Planning sprung into action.

The Dukakis administration did everything it could to thwart the developer's plans to build in Lenox, encouraging the company instead to consider building in Pittsfield; the state would not approve sidewalk curb-cuts, and it refused to put traffic lights on the state highway where the mall was planned. Lenox zoning officials eventually told the developer to look elsewhere—and Michael Dukakis told the company to look to Pittsfield. It did, and with the encouragement of public-opinion leaders throughout hard-pressed Berkshire county, the developer signed an agreement with the city to develop the unused inner-city parcel. If Dukakis had eschewed the carrot and the stick in the political arena, he had no problem wielding both in the pursuit of urban-oriented economic development.

Michael Dukakis took special pleasure in the unfolding story in Pittsfield. On several occasions he visited the city, which was at the opposite end of the state, more than a two-hour drive away. He was there to announce his opposition to the Lenox mall, and he returned to stand with the mall developer when they announced their agreement to build in the city. After three tortured years in office, the warm welcome he invariably received in Pittsfield was proof that his remedy for relieving poverty—the fostering of strong local economies built around thriving central municipalities, not increasingly expensive benefits paid to those out of work—was proving itself in Pittsfield.

To encourage this regional development, Dukakis decided early in his term to get involved in the public sector venture capital business. As a state representative in the mid-sixties, he had served on a gubernatorially appointed commission charged with devising ways to spur the growth of affordable housing. A product of the deliberations was the Massachusetts Housing Finance Agency, which made low-interest loans to finance housing developments that included subsidized and lower-than-market-rate units. Direct state intervention was not in favor in the mid-seventies, but the MHFA proved so successful that Dukakis seemed, in his first term, to want new development agencies to meet each need he could identify. The Community Development Finance Corporation was developed in 1975 to invest in community-controlled business enterprises and housing developments. Later, just two years after signing the largest tax increase in state history into law, Dukakis agreed to a lowering of taxes on state-chartered insurance companies in return for their creating a $100 million pool of money, administered by the industry, to provide loans to firms that were unable to secure comparable financing elsewhere. The five-million-dollar Wang loan came out of this Massachusetts Capital Resource Company fund.

These were preludes to what was to come in 1978, the fourth year of Dukakis's term. A package of bills designed to foster his revitalization plans were enacted and signed into law. The centerpiece was the Massachusetts Industrial Finance Agency, a central clearinghouse for the issuance of industrial development bonds. Another, capitalized at a lower level, provided funds for start-up high tech firms; the Massachusetts Technology Development Corporation became the first state-controlled venture capital firm in the nation. One more law enabled the state to use federally tax-exempt industrial revenue bonds for urban commercial projects. And still another provided technical assistance to non-profit community development corporations who were expanding their efforts into generating business ventures and low-cost housing.

But this impressive litany of pro-growth authorities, backed by liberal planners and proponents of community-controlled development, developers, construction trade unions and others, only served to drive a wedge between Dukakis and the chief executive officers of several of the state's emerging high-technology companies. They wanted taxes cut and the government out of the marketplace; instead, Dukakis was a pro-growth activist who wanted to have a major say in their expansion and locational decision-making. In 1977 high-tech firms, impatient with the slow pace and the willingness of existing business groups to compromise their core beliefs, formed their own lobbying group, the Massachusetts High Technology Council. By banding together, the CEOs of some of the fastest growing firms in the state set out to prove that the governor was wrong in his prescription for a healthy state economy.

In 1976 Dukakis set his sights on the most elaborate reform of all, that of the chaotic and Balkanized court system of Massachusetts. Like the other elements in the government, the courts of Massachusetts reflected the politics that had created them: they were decentralized, unorganized and highly politicized. The courts of Massachusetts ran on 417 separate budgets, each subject to the patronage and back-scratching that had given Massachusetts such a bad name in the fifties and sixties.

Within the byzantine judiciary were six of the twelve most congested county court systems in the country. With Jack Nason's death, Dukakis had witnessed the horrors of his state's system of justice. He recruited Harvard professor Archibald Cox, who had been a hero in Massachusetts since being fired as special prosecutor by Solicitor General Robert Bork at President Nixon's insistence during the Watergate investigation, to devise a system-wide reorganization.

For months, in 1976, the Cox Commission studied and analyzed the courts before presenting Dukakis with a masterplan for reform which he made the centerpiece of his legislative program for 1977. In his annual message to the legislature, Dukakis stated that without court reform the people would "turn away, cynical and alienated" from the courts, leaving "our democracy" endangered. It took until early 1978 before such a sweeping reform package moved through the legislature, withstanding a withering attack from judges and clerks whose autonomy was threatened. Dukakis got his court reform. The 417 separate budgets, representing little judicial fiefdoms, were consolidated into a single, state-funded budget, removing the cost of the lower courts from the counties, which had been using property taxes to support them. In addition, the trial courts were consolidated under an administrative judge, freeing resources, judges and other personnel to be assigned where they were needed.

On the human services front, Dukakis refused to back down from his initial assault on the poor. In 1976, in secret, in the office of Administration and Finance Secretary Jack Buckley, he began to develop a make-work program for welfare recipients. This "workfare" plan, initially designed for all welfare recipients including single mothers with young children, eventually was applied only to the fathers on AFDC who were living with their wives; a refusal on the part of the father to participate would result in the cancellation of his share of the family AFDC grant. Dukakis proceeded with his plan in the face of intense political opposition by welfare rights activists, their allies in the legislature, the media, his cabinet and his senior staff.

"He is a bootstrapper," said Communications Director Mike Widmer. Presented with the near-unanimous opinion from his top aides that workfare was a bad idea, Dukakis persisted. "We went around and around, and nobody could convince him it made no sense. He insisted, 'It's got to be mandatory.' "

Ultimately, the Carter administration granted Dukakis the necessary federal waiver he sought for his workfare proposal, but not because it believed in workfare; federal officials were looking for a failure to convince conservative U.S. senators that such punitive measures could not be effectively implemented at a time when Carter was trying to win passage of a less draconian national welfare reform bill. Combined with the depressing stories of the effect of the welfare cuts on the poor during the early days of the administration, the governor's intransigence on workfare during the second half of the term cemented the impression that he was a heartless technocrat. Workfare ensured him the continued enmity of most liberals.

As the term dragged on, as the Massachusetts economy recovered, and as the state began to enjoy large budget surpluses, Dukakis refused to restore the welfare cuts of his first year. His only notable effort on behalf of the poor was his controversial and courageous veto late in the term of a bill co-sponsored by State Representative Ray Flynn (now the mayor of Boston) to deny Medicaid funds for abortion services.

As Mike Dukakis strode to the microphone to deliver his annual address at the start of the 1978 election year, he considered how far the state had come since the fall of 1975, when he had had to apologize to the people for a promise he had not been able to keep—had not even come close to keeping. He ticked off the reforms in insurance, banking, utilities, and his commission against discrimination. He talked about the community-based corrections and mental health facilities that had opened, although much of the increased spending in those areas had come from the legislature over Dukakis's objections. He talked about the recovery of the economy, the two hundred thousand new jobs that had been created and the four hundred plant expansions. And he emphasized economic development as the root to a progressive society, noting that "the most important social program in America is full employment."

But he made sure to mention other social programs, some of which were victimized early on by his cleaver. He emphasized the elderly and physically or emotionally abused children. He highlighted his urban policy, the only comprehensive one in the nation. "Abandoned mills and schools are being converted for housing and new industry. Older downtowns are competing, and competing successfully, with suburban malls. Urban industrial parks are filling up with new businesses and jobs." He reminded the legislature of the new housing that had been financed by the administration, and of the coastline which had, for the first time, come under the protection of the administration through a comprehensive management program.

The irrepressibly optimistic Dukakis had many reasons to be hopeful of winning a second term. From the rubble of 1975, a solid mass of accomplishments grew— as he had proudly recounted in his address to the legislature. Furthermore, as he failed to note, it was done, for the most part, without playing games, without trading jobs for favors.

Each month the polls brought in by young Pat Caddell showed a positive trend: a slight inclination of voters to think better of Dukakis as the disasters of 1975 slipped farther into the past—although close to a third of those polled continued to give Dukakis bad marks, month after month. Still, the talk on the street was that Dukakis would win a second term.

Then came the blizzard of 1978, the worst winter storm that anyone in Massachusetts had ever seen. It began as a steady snow and strong winds on Monday morning, February 6; six inches was predicted. The surprise nor'easter began to peak Monday night on a flood tide. Driven by hundred-mile-an-hour winds, the tide destroyed houses up and down the coast and flooded low-lying communities. Motorists were stranded on highways all over New England. Late Monday Governor Dukakis called out the National Guard. On Tuesday, a massive power failure left many Bostonians without heat. Late Tuesday, President Carter declared Massachusetts a disaster area. By the storm's end Wednesday morning, twenty-seven inches buried Boston.

Governor Dukakis closed all the state roads in eastern Massachusetts. While citizens were snowed in with nothing to do but watch the hundreds of big and little dramas unfold on television, the governor was firmly at the helm, day and night, issuing orders, explaining developments, letting the people know he was in charge and that things were being done to bring relief. For the better part of a week, Dukakis was a ubiquitous presence, in slacks and a sweater, the uniform of the hour, governing Massachusetts smartly and effectively through a natural disaster.

''When I saw the blizzard, I said, 'Here's the intervention of the Good Lord,' '' said Bill Geary, the governor's appointments secretary, who instinctively thought of the political ramifications of every event. Michael Goldman, a communications specialist in the administration who was at Dukakis's side for the duration of the storm, said Dukakis thrived on the management of the crisis. ''He was cool and mellow, not at all hyper. He gave the aura and the appearance of control. The blizzard gave people the opportunity to evaluate him as a leader.'' A more dazzling and memorable kickoff for the campaign for reelection could hardly have been imagined.

(above) January 4, 1979: Congratulating his successor, Ed King, on Inauguration Day. (photo © Michael Grecco)

(left) 1982: Running against Ed King. (Sean Kardon photo courtesy *Brookline Chronicle Citizen*)

1982: ''Big Chief Brain-in-Face'' on the comeback trail. (photo © Michael Romanos)

September 14, 1982: Evening the score with Ed King, with daughters Kara (left) and Andrea. (photo © Michael Grecco)

Primary election aftermath, 1982: Receiving the endorsement of Ed King and out-going Lieutenant Governor-elect John Kerry (right). (photo © Phyllis Graber Jensen)

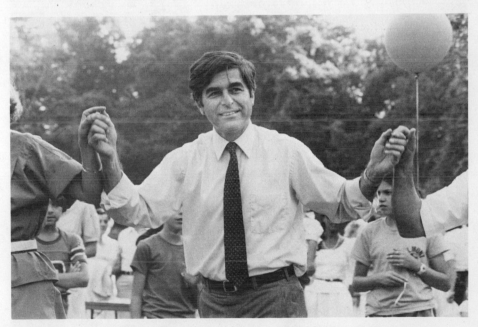

1982: Dancing at a primary election victory party. (photo © Michael Romanos)

November 2, 1982: Elected governor again, with his father-in-law, conductor Harry Ellis Dickson, and Lieutenant Governor-elect John Kerry (right). (photo © Michael Romanos)

Dukakis fundraiser Bob Farmer, with 1984 Democratic presidential nominee Walter Mondale. (courtesy Bob Farmer)

Announcing for president, with his mother, Euterpe. (photo © Richard Sobel)

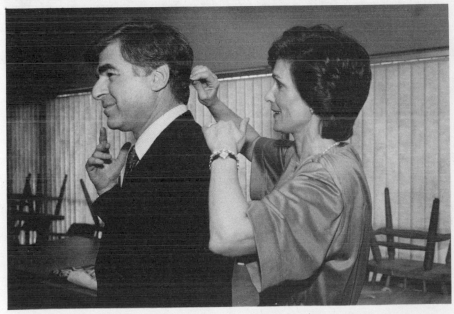

Kitty gets her husband ready for an early Iowa speech. (photo © Richard Sobel)

Blowing his horn, with father-in-law Harry Ellis Dickson conducting, at a Boston fundraiser, October 1987. (photo © Richard Sobel)

John Sasso, standing outside his State House office, in 1986. (photo © John Nordell)

Chapter 15
Politics Denied, Virtue Unrewarded

The top advisors of Mike Dukakis viewed the blizzard as an omen that the governor would be reelected. In the subsequent weeks and months of the spring of 1978, citizens treated Dukakis like a hero when they saw him on the street. Although some staff members let down their guard in the aftermath of the storm, becoming overly optimistic, Dukakis himself took nothing for granted and planned to campaign vigorously for renomination and reelection. And as he had sought to insulate his administration from improper political influences, so too did Dukakis try to keep his staff and cabinet out of the campaign.

He repeatedly told the frustrated members of his senior staff and cabinet that "the best way to be reelected is to be a good governor. The best way to help me get reelected is to do your jobs well and stay away from the campaign." After more than three years in the governor's office, Dukakis continued to believe that in politics, virtue was rewarded. Only Chief Secretary David Liederman and Communications Director Michael Widmer from the administration were allowed to enter campaign headquarters.

Bill Geary, who had been so helpful during the 1974 campaign, was excluded completely. His one service to the campaign involved comparing lists of contributors' names sent over from headquarters to lists of those Dukakis had appointed to important posts in agencies and on boards and commissions. Geary guarded his list carefully, lest a reporter see it and conclude that the squeaky-clean governor was dunning appointees, when in fact he was doing just the opposite; Geary was responsible for ensuring that the campaign did not accept contributions from anyone working in the government on appointment from Dukakis, his cabinet and department heads, or from anyone who was an applicant for appointment. When he found a name on both of his lists, he informed the campaign and the contribution was returned. In all, Geary was successful in cleansing close to twenty thousand dollars from the contributors' list.

To be campaign manager, Dukakis chose Dick Giesser, the assistant secretary of economic affairs who had met Dukakis in 1968 and become a friend. A successful businessman who had owned a company that made heels for ladies' shoes, Giesser was introduced to politics during the 1970 Dukakis campaign for lieutenant governor; in 1974 he served as Dukakis's link to the business community. He had raised some money for Dukakis, but unlike his predecessor, Joe Grandmaison, Giesser—as he freely conceded—had no idea how to organize a statewide gubernatorial campaign. Indeed, in choosing Giesser, Dukakis insured that he himself would be in charge of the campaign, literally managing things through his deferential campaign manager. Giesser picked as the campaign's press secretary a young man from his cabinet office who only recently had moved to Massachusetts from out of state. He had few contacts in the press and little knowledge of the history of the Dukakis administration.

Dukakis had two opponents, neither of whom seemed to represent much of a threat. The more serious of the two was Edward J. King, an anti-intellectual businessman and former football star at Boston College, where he had gotten close to Bob Quinn, who was running for office to settle a grudge. As the executive director of the quasi-independent Massachusetts Port Authority in the late sixties and early seventies, he had expanded Boston's Logan Airport aggressively, without concern for the well being of the residents in nearby neighborhoods. King was finally ousted from Massport by a slim majority of neighborhood-oriented board of directors in 1974 during the transition between outgoing Governor Sargent and incoming Mike Dukakis. A majority on the Massport board had wanted to fire King earlier, but they hesitated for fear of embarrassing Frank Sargent during his campaign for reelection. When the dismissal letter arrived, King refused to clear out his office; instead of leaving, he sued the board and continued to show up for work. The matter was eventually resolved when transition chairman Frank Meaney brokered a compromise: King would drop his suit and resign in return for a letter of commendation from the board and a hefty severance payment.

Ed King saw the Machiavellian hand of Fred Salvucci on his demise. It had been Salvucci, working with community activists Mike Dukakis and Al Kramer, Sargent's top aide, who managed to bring the anti-highway campaign to victory in 1970. King viewed this as a disaster and believed correctly that he had been sacked by the same coalition of anti-development activists. So he felt he had two scores to settle: one with Salvucci and one with Salvucci's boss, Mike Dukakis. Motivating himself for the campaign, King repeatedly said, "Can you imagine that little Greek firing me, Eddie King?" Few people thought King had much of a chance. He had never run for office before, was unknown throughout much of the state, and was decidedly ham-fisted on the stump.

The other candidate was Barbara Ackermann, the liberal mayor of Cambridge. She was running to protest the illiberalism, the sellout that she felt was Dukakis's legacy. Her candidacy gave Barney Frank and the liberals an outlet for their anger at Dukakis—for the welfare cuts, for workfare and for his casually signing a House-redistricting bill in 1977 that eroded the electoral bases of many members of the liberal Democrat Study Group. The arrogant reformer had climbed above the fray and insisted upon remaining there—aloof and distant—and it was time to teach him a lesson.

In April Frank wrote a scathing critique on Dukakis in the progressive weekly newspaper, *The Real Paper*. In the lengthy piece he established the rationale for liberals to support Ackerman: "[T]he Massachusetts gubernatorial election this year should be an event of fundamental moral importance, a test of the proposition that government has a duty to provide a decent minimum standard of living for those unable to share in our general affluence. With a progressive opponent for the governor, it will also be a test of the willingness of middle-class liberals to be wooed away from an alliance with the poor by a clever politician who puts his entire emphasis on helping people who are already living well to improve the quality of their own lives." Despite support from Frank and other members of the DSG, Ackermann was not expected to beat Dukakis by coming at him from the left.

It was Dukakis's decision, announced by Giesser, that the campaign would spend nothing on media advertising in the primary. This was not complacency on Dukakis's part; he simply wanted to squirrel away all he could for the general election. Besides, he recalled that in the 1974 primary against Attorney General Bob Quinn, he had won by spending only $29,000 on media advertising. As an incumbent anticipating a lesser challenge than Quinn, Dukakis saw no need to mount a media campaign.

Geary, Liederman, Widmer and other aides and advisors were aghast at this decision. Giesser, the buffer to Dukakis, was in no position to have a strong opinion one way or another, and the more political governmental advisors were being kept away from the campaign. Fran Meaney had not been around for more than a year, and Dukakis's dear friend, Allan Sidd, had died in surgery in 1977, so for the first time Dukakis had no one who could grab him by the lapels and tell him that he was wrong, dead wrong, in the way he was setting up for the election.

If the reelection effort had no planned media campaign, neither did it have any particular message or thrust. Having wrought havoc with virtually every establishment in the state, Dukakis had an impressive list of enemies and opponents, and could easily have crafted a campaign—based on the facts—that described him as a courageous reformer, consumer advocate and populist, someone with the guts to challenge the powers that be in Massachusetts. Instead, Dukakis simply catalogued his total record for voters. The one piece of campaign-planned advertising was a newspaper ad into which was crammed notes on every accomplishment of his career. "The print was so small, the elderly couldn't read it," Geary said.

The organization, or what was left of it, was mobilized but dispirited. In August Dukakis held a fundraiser for supporters from the south of Boston at a restaurant on the South Shore. The parking lot was filled, but when Bill Geary arrived, he noticed that few of the cars had Dukakis bumper stickers, which was curious since Dukakis adored bumper stickers and had positioned two aides at the entrance with piles of them. The young aides told Geary that the people did not want them. "They'd come and shake his hand, and maybe vote for him," said Geary, "but they weren't bragging about it. It was superficial support."

As the summer wore on, Dukakis grew worried. Something just did not feel right. Lieutenant Governor Tom O'Neill gave voice to the feeling when he told friends, "I know Michael's going to win. I just don't know anybody who's voting for him." As his concerns increased, Dukakis relented and authorized some TV spots to be made, but it was only weeks before the primary. Working with another friend of Dukakis, who worked for an advertising agency, Widmer and Paul Brountas struggled to cut three spots, one focusing on the blizzard, one attempting to make Dukakis seem softer and more human, and one reminding viewers of the governor's commitment to economic development. The agency had never done political advertising, and as none of the advisors had any experience in political media, the rushed ads were not very effective.

Dukakis also made an eleventh-hour effort to get some political mileage from a massive increase in local school aid which the administration had distributed to the cities and towns; the money came from a state surplus that was amassed by the frugal Dukakis as the economy picked up. Liberals saw the surplus as a final sign that Dukakis had sold out the poor for the middle class, and in the municipalities Dukakis got little political mileage from the state's largess. In eschewing a tax cut for individuals, something that voters might have remembered and appreciated, Dukakis acted responsibly, he felt, and non-politically. Now, experiencing a degree of political desperation, he personally called Boston mayor Kevin White to ask if he would lower taxes in response to the infusion of local aid Boston had received. White turned him down; the state elections were in 1978, but the municipal elections were the next year.

Dukakis himself campaigned feverishly all through the summer. "I saw him come back from the beaches, where he loved to campaign, with his hands bleeding from all the hands he'd shaken," said Dick Giesser.

Andy Sutcliffe did much of the driving for Dukakis in the campaign. Dukakis, Sutcliffe said, restored his flagging energy with short, fifteen-minute catnaps he would fall into "at the push of a button.

"I hated the trips because I couldn't smoke—unless Kitty was along," said Sutcliffe. Michael and Kitty Dukakis seem to have sublimated their differences— his cool, even, controlled personality as opposed to her hot, mercurial temperament, his serious nature and her conviviality, his aversion to cigarette smoke and her tobacco habit—into a yin/yang of banter and mutual acceptance of each other as they are. When Kitty traveled with her husband, Andy Sutcliffe could smoke. Kitty made sure of that. "He'd get into the front seat with me, and Kitty'd get into the back. We'd drive off. She'd light up. He'd sniff the air. He'd crunch his shoulders and give her the body language. He'd say 'Cath-er-ine....' She'd say, 'Forget it, Michael, I'm going to smoke.' "

The tete-a-tete over cigarettes was stylized, so often had they had the same exchange over the years, and it was, at bottom, comical and full of affection. But Sutcliffe felt the weight of the stress-filled years on Dukakis at times as they drove long hours across the state. "Sometimes we'd talk about nothing. Sometimes we'd talk about sports. He didn't know what was happening, he was so busy, and I was the sports nut," Sutcliffe said. He wanted to know what was happening so that he'd appear knowledgeable."

From time to time, Dukakis would muse about the good old days—before he was governor. "It used to be great going to Fenway [Park], sitting in the bleachers," a nostalgic Dukakis told his young aide. "Now it's a drag. Everybody's looking at you, so you've got to stay for a while. Hey, I've got better things to do. I've got a state to run."

In the tension of the campaign Dukakis began to show the streak of glib arrogance that had gotten him in trouble in 1974 and 1975. After California voters in the spring had shocked the nation by voting for Proposition 13, a radical tax-cutting law, a reporter asked Dukakis how he thought the voters of Massachusetts might react to such a proposition. Dukakis quipped that the voters of Massachusetts were too smart to fall for a gimmick like that.

In August, at an important appearance before the state's new High Technology Council, a body that represented the state's most talked about industry, Dukakis bombed, coming across as patronizing and didactic. It was a damaging performance, since his top aides from the business community had worked hard to obtain the speaking invitation with the idea that high tech would love Dukakis if it really got to know him. To try to undo some of the damage, Howard Smith, the secretary of economic affairs, sent a letter to Ray Stata, the founder of Analog Devices and the chairman of the High Tech Council, describing in some detail the many pro-development achievements of Mike Dukakis that had failed to excite the high-tech CEOs when they were initially proposed.

The only debate of the campaign took place on August 31. Watching the debate in the control room of the TV station, Dukakis aides were "dying a thousand deaths," as one put it. Smugly detached, Dukakis was letting Ed King walk all over him. No matter what the question was from the panel of journalists, King hammered at his five-point limited agenda. He wanted massive tax cuts, like Prop 13 in California, the return of capital punishment, mandatory sentencing for drug pushers and burglars, a return to the twenty-one year old drinking age, and an end to state-funded abortions for Medicaid recipients.

Dukakis held well-known positions that were antithetical to King's. In fact, the legislative leadership, led by his old nemesis, Kevin Harrington, made Dukakis hold up approval of the fiscal 1978 budget while he vetoed and fought a rider banning Medicaid-funded abortions. And during the election campaign, with much media attention, Dukakis vetoed a bill to raise the drinking age just one year, up to nineteen; in his view, teenage drinking was a sign of parental failure, a problem that did not require state intervention.

Ackermann also disagreed with Ed King's positions, but she derided Dukakis as a suburban liberal who cut services to the needy. "I'm a bread-and-butter Democrat," she said, as if to distinguish herself from Dukakis. Dukakis, who looked annoyed and tried to correct what he considered to be errors in his opponents' description of his record, did little to change the terms of the debate—which were all King's.

What Dukakis's aides in the control room had not seen was a sucker punch administered—intentionally or not—to Dukakis just before the debate began. Instead of counting to three for his microphone check, one of the panel of questioners, a TV anchorman named Tony Pepper, spoke mockingly into his microphone: "My name is Mike Dukakis, and I promised no new. . . ." Pepper did not need to say "taxes"; it was already on everyone's mind. Dukakis reacted to the jibe as if he had just taken a blow to the solar plexus. Minutes later, Ed King started pounding on him, and Dukakis stoically took it.

When the debate was over, Dukakis was visibly angry and left for home in a foul mood. King's campaign strategy was brilliant. All polling data indicated that Dukakis was much more popular than King, but the data also showed that the people were desperate for tax cuts, furious about crime and desirous of a higher drinking age. Dukakis had misread the public. King felt he could sew together a victorious crazy quilt of single-issue zealots with an array of special interests—the banking industry, the insurance industry, the high tech industry, the outdoor advertising industry, and the like—who Dukakis had offended in pressing his reform agenda. With the help of the old-boy political network based at the State House, Dukakis would not have a chance, especially with Ackermann attracting liberals to her protest candidacy. The combination of Dukakis's guileless optimism that the public would recognize his achievements and act accordingly and the proscription of much of his best political talent from the campaign would cause King to be correct.

The public's post-Watergate hope for honest politicians which had helped carry Dukakis into office four years before had, since the election of Jimmy Carter in 1976, turned decidedly bitter and angry toward elected officials. Part of the anger was caused by the feeling that the nation was leaderless; part was due to runaway inflation which was eroding honest effort day by day. Journalist and social critic Andrew Kopkind, writing in *The Real Paper* three weeks before the September 1978 primary, noted the decline of idealism and the sour mood of the electorate. "Not too many years ago, citizens fought to make themselves heard in political campaigns. They organized movements, interest groups and bases of support. There were 'peace campaigns,' 'civil rights campaigns' and 'new politics' campaigns—in which the candidates were encouraged to speak for issues larger than their own employment prospects.

"At length," Kopkind wrote, "the voting public lost that sixties sense of commitment and high-energy participation. The mood shifted to post-Watergate apathy and alienation; it was open season on incumbents of any stripe. Now, quite suddenly according to the political clock, there has been a deepening of boredom into bitterness and resentment. 'It's not that people are apolitical,' a senatorial candidate said recently, 'they're antipolitical—up to and including the point of rage.' "

Mike Dukakis, ever the optimist, found out on primary day that good works and honest effort were not enough. He got his comeuppance from a darkly pessimistic electorate. The sad news came from a TV reporter and friend, Jack Cole, who had developed an elaborate computer program for extrapolating from fragmentary returns, using historical voting patterns. Kitty Dukakis, more than Mike, had been following Cole's polling data over the final weeks of the campaign, as it tracked King's surge. In the afternoon of primary day, September 19, Cole called Dukakis at home to tell the Dukakises that Mike had lost, and lost badly. Kitty answered the phone. She understood and accepted the bad news—she had felt it coming. But when Cole gave the same news to the candidate, he said, "Michael wasn't buying it. 'No, no, no, wait till Pittsfield comes in. I'd had this terrific project in Pittsfield. They'll come out for me.'

" 'Look, Mike, there are only so many registered voters in Pittsfield. It's just all over!'" Cole told him. A few hours later, in the small and crowded ballroom of the 57 Hotel, loyalists wandered about around in a daze. "He followed policies that he thought were good for the Commonwealth, not what was politically expedient, and no one would argue with that," a loyal campaign worker said in a monotone, as if hypnotized. Long-time Dukakis aide Lanny Johnson could only say, over and over, "He hasn't made people like him."

Over at Ed King's victory party, thrown at Anthony's Pier 4 restaurant on the waterfront, campaign worker Angelo Berlandi was ebulliently candid in stating a third explanation for the turn of events: "We put all the hate groups in one big pot and let it boil."

King got 51 percent of the vote to Dukakis's 42. Jack Cole had been right; King's victory margin was substantial, about 70,000 votes. Ackermann received only 58,220 votes, but her candidacy reminded liberals of Dukakis's sinful past and undoubtedly encouraged many liberals to skip the Democratic races and take a Republican ballot in order to help save U.S. Senator Ed Brooke from a virulent conservative challenger.

Mike Dukakis had arrogantly and naively thought he knew it all; instead, he found he had a lot to learn. So the reformer would go, but what about the reforms he would leave behind? In his brash manner, Dukakis had pushed hard against almost every closed club he could find in building his meritocracy. The excessive purity and rigidity of his approach—the pursuit of political goals by an anti-political construct—insured an impermanence to the reform experiment. And as the Dukakis administration wrapped up its affairs, an experiment is what it had seemed to be, a noble but misguided experiment.

Chapter 16
The Out-of-office Campaign

Mike Dukakis had been a lame duck for less than twenty-four hours on September 20 when he met with his senior staff in Room 360, the governor's office that would be his for another three and a half depressing months. He was somber, hurt and distraught about what had happened. But he was functioning, and, after thanking his staff for their efforts, he urged them to use the final weeks to produce a smooth transition for the next governor, whether it would be his conqueror Ed King or the Republican nominee, the House minority leader. As Dukakis spoke to his staff, men and women broke down and cried.

In defeat—the first important defeat in a life that had been marked by a string of carefully planned triumphs—Dukakis was not angry. He did not seek scapegoats. He blamed himself and began to analyze where his plan had been wrong. At home, he hardly slept. Only his need for so little sleep allowed Dukakis to continue functioning.

Sixteen-year-old John Dukakis, who had voluntarily assumed his father's surname, flew to Boston from Los Angeles where he had been pursuing an acting career. John did not leave Michael's side for days after the primary. Kitty Dukakis, the emotionally aggressive one, struck out at the liberals who had abandoned her husband, and provided the family's energy during the first dark days of defeat.

Dukakis withdrew to recall and examine four years in the progression of a career built on lofty, if not faulty, assumptions that had led to failure. His self-confidence was destroyed. All his assumptions—about human nature, about the rewarding of virtue, about the way to lead a democracy—had been shattered. How wrong he had been about so many basic things. His hubris gone, he was humbled. He stopped Mike Widmer after the primary. "Am I really that awful? Am I really that cold? Am I really that bad?"

If Dukakis did not understand why he had been turned out of office, the people who had been guilty of the deed could not believe what they had done. Across the state, liberals, moderates, voters and non-voters alike reacted to King's upset of Dukakis with shock. It was as if they had not meant to kill off the government but had simply wanted to teach the governor a lesson, and things had gotten out of control and gone too far.

By Thursday, the governor's switchboard was lighting up as it never had before, and letters and cards were pouring in. "The deluge was incredible," said Bill Geary. "The letters were expressing shock and dismay; many were confessions of guilt that they had not voted because they didn't think he was in trouble, or that they had been upset at something he'd done—or admissions that they'd voted for Acker-mann." It was the talk of the office. Everyone was getting the same reaction. Wherever Dukakis went, people came up to him to express their condolences for his loss. Dukakis told his State House staff and his crew at headquarters to record the name, address and telephone number of every person who expressed regrets at the turn of events. He wanted to respond personally to each of them, he explained.

"Michael didn't think he had a political future," said campaign manager Dick Giesser. "He thought he'd blown it. I asked him about the future. He said, 'You're crazy, Dick. If Ed King is a halfway decent governor, he's got two terms.' For a long time after he lost, he did nothing but think about where he screwed up; he was not in a political mode." Instead, said Giesser, he was thinking about his future. Soon after the primary, feelers from President Jimmy Carter's White House suggested he could have a high postition in Washington, perhaps in the Cabinet, if he wished. But Dukakis was not attracted to the possibilities. The thought of pulling up stakes and throwing himself into another dislocating challenge was too much to take while dealing with such a devastating defeat.

As the administration was wrapping up its affairs, Giesser and other friends convinced Dukakis of the wisdom of maintaining a skeleton political operation, if for no other reason than to get on with the business of thanking the thousands of people who had expressed their sympathies at his premature political demise and, of course, to have an on-going political committee in order to legally accept the thousands of dollars—much of it guilt money—that was coming in. Dukakis had refused to allow Giesser to permit the campaign to go into debt in the effort to fend off King and Ackermann, but by primary day the campaign had spent all it had. Within days, however, the Dukakis Committee was in the black and getting blacker.

Geary's assistant, Andy Sutcliffe, wanted to remain with Dukakis, and was hired to manage the office; space was rented on Beacon Street a few doors down from the State House even as the administration wound up its business. The office consisted of one large room, in the center of which stood a large table where Sutcliffe neatly concentrated a number of boxes. In the boxes were thousands of three-by-five index cards with the names, addresses and phone numbers of the mourners. Every day Sutcliffe dutifully made out additional cards. If events proved fortuitous and Dukakis did decide to run again, Sutcliffe was working on the base of a new, emotionally dedicated political organization, one that would not take Dukakis's success for granted.

With the help of Barney Frank and a majority of the liberal wing of the Democratic Party, which was appalled and remorseful that they had helped deliver the nomination into the hands of a tax-cutting businessman and social reactionary, the moderate Brahmin Republican Frank Hatch made a race of the run-off. However, the Democrats, led by the old-boy political network and a plea for party unity, were too numerous. Ed King was lifted into the governor's office by a comfortable margin in November with no help from Dukakis, who refused to endorse the party's nominee.

At noon on January 4, 1979, Edward J. King and his entourage strode down the aisle of the House chamber in the State House, where the governor-elect was to take the oath of office as the Commonwealth's sixty-sixth governor. Four armed and jodhpured state troopers—an honor guard of two in front and two in back, their spit-polished boots gleaming in the TV klieg lights—accompanied King. Their presence bespoke the change in state leadership far more eloquently than the new governor ever could: King marched to the speaker's dais with his own Praetorian guard. It was a scene reminiscent of Huey Long's Louisiana—and it could not have been further removed from Michael Dukakis's Massachusetts.

King's inaugural address, delivered with the new governor's curiously clipped, one-beat-off-the-metronome cadence, stated the goals of his administration with vigor, if not eloquence. He called for a cut in state taxes, "not gradually, but now—in this session and in a single act." And he declared, "It is time to eliminate unnecessary regulation—not only that which is obsolete but that which serves no public purpose." Most of all, he took aim at the button-down, good-government legacy the vanquished Dukakis and his ilk had forced on a State House filled with plaid sports jackets and memories of the palmy days of the Iron Duke, John F. Thompson. "The era of anti-politics is over," Ed King declared. For the legislators gathered in the House chamber, that was the best news of the day.

But if the men and very few women of the legislature thought they had found a soulmate in Ed King, they could not have been more wrong. It was all well and good to attack the "anti-politics" of the reform crowd, that refusal to bargain and dispense patronage that had struck so many as priggishly self-righteous, but what King offered in its place was hardly more to their liking. Though nominally Democratic and undeniably Irish, King's newly acquired taste for "politics" was suspect. The fact is that King had little interest in the essential flip side of politics: government.

Like his true soulmate, Ronald Reagan, King was convinced that government was not the solution but the problem—like Reagan, he was determined to play the game of politics only as a means to securing power, power he could use to neuter all but the most basic public-safety agencies of government. In appearances, King was seductively familiar to those who saw in him a political reincarnation of Bob Quinn, a sort of Bourbon Restoration for the old-line Irish. The son of a subway toll-taker, King had the blue-collar roots, the street-corner accent and the degree, as did Quinn, from Boston College. A former offensive guard who had played with the Baltimore Colts, he had the barroom appeal of the ex-jock. He did not stand on ceremony; Dukakis may have insisted on "Michael" among his friends, but King was "Eddie" to everyone. He could unbutton in a way that the oh-so-serious reform crowd would not.

But King lacked the essential psychic ingredient of any successful Boston Irish pol: he did not love the game. Indeed, he seemed at times to disdain it. He liked to remind audiences that he had not spent his career running for things—he had run them. He was an accountant and an administrator, a man who during his tenure as executive director of the Massachusetts Port Authority was once described by a close friend as "a happy civil servant," albeit one who relished his ready access to helicopters and limousines. While at Massport King had pressed relentlessly for the expansion of Logan Airport into the surrounding community of East Boston with an arrogantly impolitic disregard for the attendant howls of protest. He ignored the criticism because it was not his job to worry about the public—not even his hometown public. He just worried about his bottom line. And King was good enough at what he did that, had he not been forced out of the Massport post, he would never have had any reason to think about running for the corner office.

When he finally did run, King did not campaign as a clone of Bob Quinn, even if some of his backers dearly hoped he was. He was undeniably a conservative, opposing abortion and favoring the death penalty, preaching government frugality and damning drunken teenagers, but King's conservatism was of a piece with what he was—a business-oriented prophet of growth. His slogan said it all: he was the "Can-Do" candidate—not "Can-Govern," simply "Can-Do."

From the onset, it was obvious that Ed King, the political amateur, could not do. Even more quickly than Dukakis's image had eroded four years earlier, King's began to fall apart to sniggers from the cynical press and from politicians who had just seen a different kind of outsider-governor come and go. His initial problems were with his appointments. King's secretary of elder affairs resigned within two weeks of his appointment after the press reported that he had embellished his educational background; he claimed non-existent degrees from the University of Heidelberg in Germany and Cambridge University in England.

Less than a month later, King's replacement for Jim Stone, Dukakis's brilliant reform insurance commissioner, was forced to resign. The appointee, it turned out, knew next to nothing about insurance; he had been hand-picked to be commissioner for that very reason by the Commercial Union Insurance Company, which had chafed under the regulation of Dukakis's reform administration. To help convince Ed King to see things their way, Commercial Union executives and directors had delivered thousands of dollars in contributions to King the day before the election—after his victory was a foregone conclusion. In a press interview King explained that he had selected the industry's choice for the position because he was "amenable to the 'Can-Do.' "

Next to go was an old friend of King's who had always wanted to run the Metropolitan District Commission, the state agency that administers parkland and some roadways and reservoirs near Boston, as well as a large police force. It did not take long for the press to discover that, in one of his first acts, the new head of the MDC had brought in as an associate commissioner a friend of his who had been named in congressional hearings as an associate of reputed New England Mafia boss Raymond Patriarca. By the time this third personnel scandal had unfolded in March, only weeks after the inauguration, the new governor was reeling.

As time passed, King found it progressively harder to attract quality people to work for him. Some were kept away by the air of near-buffoonery that attached itself to the King administration, others by the certainty of intense press scrutiny made inevitable by the embarrassments of the first three months. As a result, King had to rely increasingly on the people Dukakis had brought into state government, people he did not fully trust, and with good reason. The mental health commissioner, the welfare commissioner and the director of the State Office for Children, key administrators in the executive office of human services, all were veterans of the Dukakis administration.

"What drove King crazy was the constant frustration of his will," said a former aide. "The Dukakis people, the holdovers, would continually oppose him." For instance, King would attempt to pave the way for some private economic development project, only to find the project held up because of environmental concerns or bureaucratic foot-dragging. For the "Can-Do" governor, it was infuriating to be told that he could not do what he wanted—and to be told so, he was certain, by people who were loyal to Michael Dukakis.

King's solution to the problem was to adopt a highly personalized management style. The governor kept a card file of the names of people in the various state agencies, whom he felt were loyal to him. When a problem arose, often in the form of a complaint from a businessman facing difficulty with the state bureaucracy, King would call his contact—usually not a cabinet secretary or agency commissioner—outline the problem, and demand a solution within a week. Each morning, King's secretary would type a list of return phone calls, each call representing a problem to be solved, that King expected to receive that day. As the day progressed, King would personally call the bureaucrats who had not checked back with their solutions. The scenario was bizarre: it was the governor as ombudsman, the complaint department for businessmen who had a beef with a state agency. The process was enormously time-consuming and inefficient. It was also the only way that Ed King, the Can-Do governor, could get anything done. "That's how he made policy," said a former associate.

It certainly was not the way most governors conducted their business, but King, having painted himself into a corner with his early failures, had little choice. The cascade of early embarrassments established King in the public mind as a sort of unlovable Rodney Dangerfield. Newsweek magazine summed up the early King disasters with a story in the spring of 1979 headlined "Amateur Hour," and subsequent pieces in such national media outlets as the Washington Post only intensified the ridicule. "It was something from which he never recovered," admitted one King associate, "the perception that he was unfit to be governor."

The perception was not fully justified. King was, according to most accounts, an eminently decent man who fit all the comfortable stereotypes of the successful, self-made Irish-American businessman: a regular churchgoer whose personal honesty should have been above question, an Old World thinker who was instinctively courteous, if chauvinistic, to the women in his administration, and a sincere believer in the gospel of American success.

For the most part, King did not bring pols in to run his government; he brought in businessmen who were so alike in their views and backgrounds as to be virtually indistinguishable. Of King's first ten cabinet appointments, nine were white, nine were male, and five boasted some affiliation with Boston College. "This isn't an administration," observed Barney Frank, "It's a twentieth reunion."

King went through the same sort of ordeal that had faced Michael Dukakis during his first year. Both men were outsiders, entering the corner office with strong ideas about how state government should be run—or, in King's case, not run—and both men tried to implement those ideas without regard for the prevailing realities of politics and government. Not surprisingly, both men became political cripples within a year. The only real difference was that, in the process, King ended up looking much sillier than Dukakis had.

The next few months did not improve matters. A hostile press, embarrassed that it had allowed King to sneak up on them in the previous year's election and determined not to allow him to get away with anything, seized every opportunity to blast King, playing on the symbolic in a way that hinted at the sinister. Reporters wrote ominously of King's state-trooper escorts, who led gubernatorial motorcades with sirens screaming and stood ostentatiously on guard by the entrance to the corner office; of his penchant for taking helicopter rides to any and every ribbon-cutting held in the state; of his fat black touring car, which provided such a jarring contrast to Dukakis's once-celebrated daily commutes on the subway.

The coup de grace came with a disquisition on the governor's dining habits. King, Boston papers revealed, had a habit of billing the state for lobster-salad lunches, sent to his office from a restaurant near the State House, for himself and his bodyguards. The *Globe* ran the story alongside an enormous, above-the-fold photo of one of the tasty crustaceans and a photostat of a bill from Dini's Sea Grill that listed meals-to-go in September and a balance due of $1,209.66. The headline of the story was: "Lobster To Go...And Other King Expenses."

The working press had some help in its investigations, from the Dukakis political office, all two of it: Andy Sutcliffe, its director and sole paid staffer, and his boss, the former governor. "He made it clear in November that he didn't know what the future would hold, that he was going to give King two years," said Sutcliffe. "It was clear to me, though, that the office should take the position that there was going to be a race in '82."

Within six months, Sutcliffe—with Dukakis's full knowledge and approval—settled into a routine befitting a full-fledged campaign manager. As such, he began leaking information to the press about goings-on in the King administration. The information would typically be passed on to Sutcliffe by the Dukakis holdovers still working all throughout the King administration. Dukakis could, of course, claim deniability for the leaks, but the work of this "shadow government," as Sutcliffe called it, was extraordinarily effective. It produced stories on a regular basis that embarrassed King, stories that only served to reinforce the public image of King as a clown in a pinstriped suit. It was Sutcliffe who helped get out the story of how King's registrar of motor vehicles planned to reclassify his employees with job titles more befitting an army than a bureaucracy—and the story about King's lust for lobsters.

When King took over the administration of state government, he tried to replace as many of Dukakis's appointees as soon as he could. In the governor's office, he cleaned house with one important exception; for some reason, King did not replace a clerical employee whom Dukakis had appointed. A functionary and not a political operative, the aide felt nervous as a lonely holdover. "I got a very concerned call one day," Sutcliffe said. The caller had a pile of bills from King which were considered improper. "I was told about all these bills—lobster lunches, dry cleaning, security systems"—that King had accumulated. Sutcliffe's associate told him, "This is the type of stuff that they want me to pay. But I'm not going to pay for this. I don't think that this is right."

Sutcliffe's associate told him, "This should be public, but I don't want to lose my job over this." Sutcliffe told his source, who was planning to leave the government soon, to take no action and to continue accumulating the bills.

Sutcliffe in turn told Dukakis what he had. "We talked about it at length, frequently," Sutcliffe said. "He had a two-fold response: it was a confirmation of everything he thought of King, and it was unbelievable that King would be this bad.

" 'Can you use it?' Dukakis wanted to know. We discussed who our source was, how we want to protect our source." Sutcliffe contacted Walter Robinson, the *Boston Globe*'s State House bureau chief, who had earned a reputation as the premier political investigative reporter in the state.

At a meeting Sutcliffe set up, he introduced Robinson to his source, who gave to Robinson copies of the accumulated documents. Robinson agreed not to publish his piece until his source had left the government. He also agreed to obtain another set of documents using the Freedom of Information Act to further protect his and Sutcliffe's source.

Based on the dates indicated on the copies, Robinson filed a Freedom of Information Act request that the government give him receipts for specific days on which King had filed his bills. At the end of the ten days state law allowed a government agency to delay before responding to a FOIA request, King's chief legal counsel made Robinson refile the request, claiming that there was a technical defect in the original request.

At the end of the second ten-day period, King, who hated the *Globe* for its liberal position on issues and its staunchly anti-King editorial and reportorial record, decided he would get even and had the bills and receipts leaked to the conservative *Boston Herald*—even as his staff delivered the material, as the law required, to the *Globe*. In doing so, King bought himself a double dose of bad publicity, but at least the *Globe* had lost its exclusive exposé.

To Dukakis, "Ed King was a buffoon," said Sutcliffe. "He was not good for the people. We were bringing out material that was evidence of that. If the governor was allowing the public to pay for his dry cleaning and restaurant bills, the public should know about it."

The leaks served their purpose, as did repeated efforts on the part of other Dukakis holdovers to thwart King administration policy objectives. "Regardless of what

Michael's ultimate decision would be [on running in 1982]," said Sutcliffe, "there were certain things we had to do. King could have done things to make Michael yesterday's news. We did what we could to make sure that didn't happen. But we didn't really have to do too much; King was self-destructing."

It did not really matter that many of King's purported excesses were neither sinister nor particularly outre. Most governors of most states often ride in limousines, state police bodyguards are hardly unheard-of, and the governor of Massachusetts, who unlike most governors does not live in a state-provided residence, would have good reason to ask the state to provide a security system for his home. And if King spent a lot of time jaunting about the state in helicopters, attending plant openings and ground-breakings—so much so, in fact, that the management consulting firm of Coopers & Lybrand concluded in a state-requested study that the governor was seriously mismanaging his time—it simply reflected King's conception of his office. Ed King was not, after all, so much a political leader as chairman of the board of Massachusetts, Inc. Like most chairmen, he drove around in a fancy car, spent a lot of time pressing the flesh with his employees, and usually ate lunch and dinner on the run, rather than at home. With this in mind, the lifestyle could hardly be seen as extravagant, but because it contrasted so sharply with the torturously frugal example set by Dukakis, it inevitably opened King up to ridicule.

King perhaps rightly resented the media's scrutiny of his manner of conducting business. As a close aide put it, King's attitude was "Hey, I'm governor—I'm entitled. Dukakis was a fraud with all his I-take-the-T stuff." Unwilling to cut back on helicopter flights or take a form of mass transportation to work, King became a prisoner of his own self-image, an image that was easily transmutable into one more sinister.

The spring of 1980 brought yet another round of scandal, this time in the form of public hearings by a blue-ribbon commission into the practice of bribery and extortion in the awarding of hundreds of millions of dollars in state and county building contracts. Although the investigation focused on events that antedated the King administration, it did involve Ed King's administration of the Massachusetts Port Authority and the concentration of architectural design work that went to a firm owned by one of King's best friends.

It also involved as a central figure William Masiello, the former co-owner of an architectural firm who had become the linchpin for New York design consultants and various politicians in the late sixties and early seventies. At the time, the New York consultants were supervising construction of a state university campus in Boston. Costing more than $250 million, it was the biggest construction job for which the state had ever contracted. By the time the commission opened its hearings, two state senators had been convicted of extortion; in their trials, it was alleged in FBI documents that a fundraiser for Republican Governors Volpe and Sargent had shaken down the firm for many thousands of dollars. Masiello's role had been to facilitate the various transactions.

The scandal broke while Dukakis was governor. When he discovered that Jack Buckley, his secretary of administration and finance, had extended contracts which the state had had with Masiello, a furious Dukakis ordered Buckley to terminate the relationship immediately. Ironically, in his campaign for attorney general back in 1966, when Dukakis accused various architectural firms receiving work from the Volpe administration after making contributions to Governor Volpe's reelection effort, he had identified Masiello and King's friend as prime examples of the way in which money talked in the corrupt environment of old-style Massachusetts politics.

Though no evidence against King was presented to the commission, the public, nonetheless, found it easy to associate these tales of the "old politics" with their new disciple, Ed King. The connection was made explicit by the commission's star witness, the cheerfully amoral businessman and political fixer, Billy Masiello. After testifying under a grant of immunity about corruption in the administrations of four of the five most recent gubernatorial administrations, Masiello made an impromptu closing statement: "I hate to give him an endorsement because, if any one man destroyed me, it was Governor Dukakis," Masiello said. "When he came in there were no open hands. And the game was over.

"And you had four good years. And what did Dukakis get for it? He got kicked out. All right, the people of Massachusetts deserve what they get."

The audience that had listened for most of the spring to tales of how the Commonwealth was for sale burst into applause. It was becoming obvious to everyone that the cards Andy Sutcliffe had been accumulating and filing were going to come in handy, after all.

Chapter 17
Learning to Do the Politics Right

While the anti-intellectual Ed King was busy embarrassing the Commonwealth, Mike Dukakis ensconced himself across the river in Cambridge. The best student at Brookline High and at Swarthmore College went back to school to learn what he had done wrong, so that if and when he ran again—or, if fortunate, governed again—he would do it right.

On January 21, 1979, Dukakis began work as a lecturer in public policy and as director of intergovernmental studies at Harvard's John F. Kennedy School of Government. The career move was not a radical one; Frank Sargent had spent time as a fellow of the school's Institute of Politics after his loss to Dukakis in 1974. But Dukakis's move was at least a bit out of the ordinary. Unlike Sargent, he would not be an Institute fellow, auditing courses and appearing as window-dressing at the occasional seminar or cocktail party. He would actually teach and assume a lead role in redirecting the focus of the school.

The previous October the school had finally moved from its old quarters on the other side of Cambridge Common, in Harvard Square, to a huge, $11-million brick edifice on the banks of the Charles River. The new building was an architectural monument to openness, a building specifically laid out to encourage what social scientists are fond of calling "positive interaction." Offering classes to as many as five hundred graduate students pursuing master's and doctoral degrees in public policy, as well as dozens of career state and local government bureaucrats and elected officials who were about to embark on a new three-week summer program in how to be better public officials, the Kennedy School was just then beginning to pride itself on a modern, pragmatic and decidedly non-stuffy approach to government and politics.

Unlike the dusty warren of cubicles and narrow hallways of its old home, the Kennedy School virtually forced its denizens to see each other, to drop into each other's offices, to converse and to listen. Designed around a massive atrium-like auditorium, the building arrayed its offices and classrooms in tiers which circled the central open space, making the academic's customary retreat into a secluded, isolated office all but impossible. Classrooms were horseshoe-shaped with the intent of fostering eye contact and interaction. At the Kennedy School, Michael

Dukakis, who had found it so hard to deal with people one-on-one, would have to do just that.

Though the former governor had seemed a logical candidate for a fellowship since his defeat on primary day, he had made it clear that he wanted a substantive teaching post and the opportunity to work alongside a man he had come to respect for his prowess as a public sector manager and teacher, Gordon Chase. Just before his loss to King, Dukakis convinced Chase, who had distinguished himself in the fields of public health and human services, to take charge of human services in Massachusetts. After the defeat, Chase left the administration immediately to return to the dual appointments he had held at the Kennedy School and at Brandeis University's Heller School of social welfare graduate studies. Quickly, he accepted a tenured position at Brandeis.

In the Kennedy School's search for a successor to Chase, Dukakis quickly emerged as a strong contender, but his candidacy was not without problems. Said Kennedy School professor Laurence Lynn Jr., who conducted the search for a successor to Chase, "The issue that arose was, were we avoiding reality by picking up a defeated candidate from our own backyard?"

Dukakis's candidacy fed into an on-going debate at the Kennedy School over whether courses in public policy should be taught by traditional academics schooled in analytic studies—areas such as decision analysis, modeling, micro-economic theory, statistics and econometrics—or by experienced professional policy-makers. Until Dukakis's arrival, the basic message of the Kennedy School had been that the problem in government was the lack of careful analysis at the top; that better analysis resulting in optimum results was the way to power and influence; that through analysis one would find the answers to why cities were in flames, why the United States was in Vietnam. "It seems ridiculous in retrospect," said one school administrator. Gordon Chase's legacy to the Kennedy School had been to convince school officials that they should begin to articulate a *theory* of public management and abandon the single-minded focus on bringing rational, analytical choices to federal policy-makers. "He advocated for a focus on real people in the real world making real choices," said Betsy Reveal, who, prior to becoming administrative dean of the Kennedy School, had been a Chase and Dukakis student.

The debate was particularly sharp in the late seventies as the school, seeking to widen its market of tuition-paying students, had expanded its executive programs, training sessions for top-level elective and appointive officials looking for both the practical knowledge and the Harvard cachet that would help advance their careers. A summer program for federal officials—predominantly generals and admirals with a national security focus—had been instituted the summer before Dukakis's arrival on campus. Having initially concentrated their focus on federal officials, school officials decided to add a similar program for state and local policy-makers, a program that would be ideally suited to Dukakis's skills but one whose initiation, with its focus on real-world practitioners, was seen by some traditional academics as a dilution of the school's scholarly mission.

Some faculty members raised concerns over the Dukakis candidacy in confidential discussions with Lynn, but their objections were limited and their concerns were confined to issues of process, which was not surprising at a school noted for its fascination with proper procedure. "Dukakis wasn't a totally different animal," Lynn recalls. "What made him different was his visibility, and his earlier success as an elected official." Lynn conducted routine checks with some of Dukakis's law school professors—whoever got the job would, after all, have to have the basic skills needed to present cases and grade student papers—and the responses were unqualifiedly positive. So strong was Dukakis's candidacy that Lynn never interviewed another applicant.

Lynn knew when he hired Dukakis that his man would stay on the job no longer than four years, and probably less. "We knew he was taking a four-year sabbatical from politics," said Lynn, "but we also knew that he would adopt the mindset of a Kennedy School faculty member." If Dukakis even then was looking down the road to a rematch with Ed King, his well-known devotion to the job at hand allayed any fears that he might ignore his academic duties in favor of planning a comeback.

Dukakis's aide Andy Sutcliffe, who talked regularly with the press, commented to a reporter that the Kennedy School was but a weigh station for Dukakis as he recharged his batteries for another campaign against King. Dukakis was not pleased, Sutcliffe said. "The next day [after the story appeared] he told me, 'This is not a weigh station. I'm taking this very seriously.' "

"You didn't see lots of people from the *Boston Globe* or from political circles running around his office," said Kennedy School economics professor Richard Zechhauser. "He was very conscientious."

According to Edith Stokey, a public policy lecturer and school administrator, Dukakis did all the "grubby" things that endeared him to faculty, administrators and students. While working to get the program for state and local executives off the ground, carrying a half-time teaching load of such graduate-level courses as "Institutional Leadership and the Agency Manager," he also found time for faculty meetings, for helping out with curriculum development, for advising students on both their studies and their futures, and for eating lunch with students in the school's cafeteria. Simply put, he spent time that he was not paid to spend. As he had back in Brookline High, Swarthmore and Harvard Law, Dukakis once again became a big man on campus.

But he also had a lot to learn. Professor Lynn sat in on a few of Dukakis's early classes and saw that the transition from chief executive to junior faculty member did not come easily. "He had some tendency to browbeat people in a class," Lynn recalled. "He would tend to be a bit overbearing, and he was caught up a bit short by some of the older students." Dukakis was not dealing with callow undergraduates, whether they were masters candidates or summer program participants. Candidates for a masters degree in public policy were generally in their late twenties or early thirties, frequently pursuing that degree in conjunction with studies at the Law School; students in the program for state and local executives were older, more seasoned, professional bureaucrats. Dukakis's very first summer class of thirty-five pupils included the speaker of the Wisconsin House of Representatives, Minnesota's secretary of state, a Louisiana mayor, and a half dozen state cabinet officials from around the country. Serious policy-makers in their own right, these people were not about to permit a failed chief executive to tell them how they should go about their business after he had so clearly demonstrated his own inability to run a successful administration.

"He was pretty didactic," said Reveal, who took time away from her position with the municipal government of the District of Columbia to attend the summer program, Dukakis's first at the Kennedy School. "At first, he did not brook other people's opinions very well." Of the ten or so faculty members who participated in that first series of classes, Dukakis was ranked third from the bottom in terms of classroom appeal based on student evaluations. The two who scored lower than Dukakis were dismissed, one before the three-week session ended. "His rating was 'respectful,' " said a school administrator, who added that Dukakis would probably have ranked lower had he not been a former governor. The imperious, self-convinced reformer who operated with a disdain for the opinions of others—legislators, lobbyists, utility company executives, social-service advocates—the governor who routinely failed to heed the advice even of his own kitchen cabinet suddenly found himself preaching the virtues of listening. More importantly, he began to listen a bit himself. Recalled Reveal, "He became like a kid in a candy store, always bouncing ideas off people, testing every idea and fact he ever had about government. He began to sublimate his own opinions."

It was during his second year of teaching at the Kennedy School that the pall from the loss to King lifted. About this time the struggling teacher began to ask questions and stopped preaching; the lecturer with a penchant for bombast and hyperbole adopted the Socratic method. Dukakis was unwinding for the first time in years. "He began to be happy again in the second year at the Kennedy School," said his friend, Richard Giesser.

The upbeat Kennedy School years did not spare Dukakis yet another tragedy; this one took the life of his close friend and associate, Gordon Chase. Within months of leaving the Kennedy School for Brandeis, Chase was killed in an automobile accident while returning home late one night from work. With Fran Meaney out of the picture and Allan Sidd dead, Chase had emerged as the only person who could approach Dukakis as a peer, not as a former governor. Ever since Dukakis's primary election loss to Ed King, Chase had hammered home the point that Dukakis had taken his eye off the prize, that good government was not enough, that to be a good governor one had to be a good politician.

In an expression of love for the late Gordon Chase, his friend and mentor, Dukakis saw to it that a book Chase had been preparing at the time of his death found its way into print. Initially he approached Chase's widow, Naomi Feigelson Chase, a former contributing writer to *The Village Voice*, the author of books on sixties' counterculture and child abuse, and an in-house editor of an early draft of her late husband's work in progress. When she told Dukakis that she was not emotionally prepared to finish the work, he called Betsy Reveal, who, after completing her summer program in Cambridge, had returned to resume her public sector career in the office of the mayor of the District of Columbia. Reveal agreed to help finish the book. She returned to Cambridge, where she spent the next two years completing the manuscript, entitled *How to Manage in the Public Sector,* co-authored with Gordon Chase. The book became something of a bible to modern public-sector managers.

In the prologue to the book, written by Michael Dukakis, the former governor expressed his fondness for his colleague and mentor. "Gordon's greatest strength as a public manager was his understanding of the complicated political environment within which a public manager has to operate and the importance of mastering that environment. . . ." As though penning not merely a memorium to his late friend but a post-mortem on his first term as well, Dukakis wrote, "The political environment that too often stopped managers in their tracks was, for Gordon, the real thing. What kind of mayor, governor, or president are you working for? How do you handle chiefs and their staffs? What about the 'overhead' agencies—budget, personnel, general services? Advocacy groups and community activists? The political 'talkers'?...What do you do when four hundred community activists blockade the entrance to your office? How do you deal with the press and make them an ally, not an adversary?

"It all seems so obvious now."

Not all of Mike Dukakis's listening was confined to the Kennedy School. As he had done during his earlier time out of office, Dukakis kept himself informed on public issues: the kitchen at 85 Perry Street became a regular gathering place for policy experts to talk through the most abstruse points of government. Moving hard-core unemployed welfare recipients into the workplace, using government transfer payments as salary supplements for the poor (something Dukakis had refused to do during the first term when the opportunity was offered by the Carter administration as an alternative to his workfare program), youth employment, criminal justice, economic development—these were the topics of the evening in the Dukakis household.

Ed Lashman, a gruff-talking political pragmatist who was employed by Harvard University as a development specialist, began to coordinate the issue-briefings in the middle of 1980. Just as his Raiders had helped keep Dukakis up to date on what was going on in the Sargent administration in the early seventies, this collection of issues activists kept him informed of the goings-on of the King administration.

Dukakis appeared to be most interested in the issue of job creation. Throughout his time at Harvard he was absorbed with economic development studies. He sought and received a contract from the federal Department of Housing and Urban Development to write case studies and develop curricula on economic development at the state and local level, and to provide fellowships for local economic development officials. He incorporated business-development case studies into the classes he taught at the Kennedy School, and he discussed development issues incessantly with his colleagues, both academic and political. Although he had always considered economic development to be a key to social and political reform, as governor Dukakis had come off as an an excessive regulator. At the Kennedy School, he adjusted the balance in favor of development and became an unabashed apostle of growth.

A fundraiser he held in June 1980 at Boston's Quincy Market, a vast collection of trendy and upscale shops and restaurants in a formerly decrepit section of Boston near the waterfront which symbolized Boston's economic comeback, marked Dukakis's political reemergence. The celebratory crowd was huge; twenty-four hundred people came to be with the Dukakises. Many of his once-alienated friends, members of a broad liberal coalition now shut out of influence by Governor King, came by to renew commitments. Dukakis was notably warmer and more outgoing than he had ever been as governor as he buried the cleaver once and for all. Two years before the next election, the evening had the feel of a campaign rally. The crowd represented a government in exile, and Dukakis was *their* governor.

While working at the Kennedy School, Dukakis also managed to return for a full season as moderator of "The Advocates," the public-television public affairs program that had helped him enhance his reputation during the early seventies. In addition, Dukakis taped introductions and closings for a special, twenty-episode series of shortened, previously aired "Advocates" segments distributed to public schools across the country. After the show had finally run its course as a regularly scheduled program, he returned yet again in the fall of 1980, as moderator of a special five-part "Advocates" series devoted solely to that year's presidential election.

During the course of that series, which was taped at the Kennedy School, Dukakis wound up sharing the television screen with the likes of Ed Meese, Alexander Haig, Caspar Weinberger and David Stockman, although as moderator he did not engage the Reagan advocates—nor the backers of Jimmy Carter and John Anderson, who also appeared on each show—in debate. Nonetheless, he prepared himself exhaustively on the national issues to be discussed, to such an extent that the show's staff, which routinely gossiped about Dukakis's plans to run for another term as governor, found itself discussing the chance that their boss quite possibly had ambitions for national office, as well.

As Michael Dukakis began to leave the devastation of his 1978 defeat behind him, Ed King had reason to feel hopeful as well. Despite the spectacular failures of his first year, King had persevered in his routine of relentless corporate boosterism, to the evident satisfaction of the state's business community, and the official economic performance indicators continued to improve. By 1980 the state's unemployment rate, 5.6 percent, had dipped below the national average, reflecting a surge of new development, especially in the high-tech sector. King had also acquired what amounted to a gubernatorial trademark: in 1979 the state's Commerce Department initiated a series of phenomenally popular promotional ads, keyed to the slogan "Make It in Massachusetts" and featuring the stylized logo of a disembodied fist forming a confident, thumbs-up sign. The slogan, the logo, and the improved state economy quickly became identified with King.

Businessmen loved Ed King, and for good reason. He was one of them. After four years of perceived hostility from Dukakis, businessmen discovered that, in the words of Howard Foley, the president of the High Technology Council, "You didn't have to apologize if you came in talking about creating a good job in the private sector.'' The governor was receptive to ideas from any source, as long as they were pro-business. ''We started with an advantage. People felt there was a comfort factor [in the corner office],'' Foley said. ''This was true for any businessman: high-tech, low-tech, no-tech, a jockey at Suffolk Downs who had an idea.''

King was always trying to be helpful. After the owners of the ski resort had painted directions on the side of a cow to protest the Dukakis administration's refusal to allow for a billboard on their land, King relieved the cow of advertising duty by allowing a conventional sign to be restored. Similarly, Edson DeCastro, founder of Data General Corporation and a founding member of the High Tech Council, had long lobbied for the installation of a traffic light on a state road near one of his facilities to ease the flow of traffic entering and leaving the area: a simple matter, really, nothing that the chief of a major manufacturing company should have to worry about—except in Michael Dukakis's Massachusetts. Dukakis's people had repeatedly refused to grant the request. In Ed King's Massachusetts, DeCastro got his traffic light.

The little things kept adding up for Ed King, but it was on the big things that he truly rounded into form as the governor who could *not* deliver. Since its inception in 1977 the High Technology Council, along with its lobbying partner, the Associated Industries of Massachusetts, which represents a broader range of manufacturing firms, had worked feverishly for tax reductions. The groups called for elimination of the 1975 surtax on personal income and a drastic cut in state and local property taxes, the latter of which, by the late seventies, had risen to extraordinary heights.

In most Massachusetts cities and towns, real property was assessed for tax purposes only when it was sold; if a home or parcel of land had not been sold for a few years, its assessed value, the base against which property-tax bills were figured, was lower, perhaps considerably lower, than the property's actual worth. Thus, though Massachusetts property owners paid a very high rate of tax, many enjoyed such artificially low ''official'' property values that their total tax bills were not as exorbitant as the tax rates might have suggested.

Still, the tax-rate numbers had shock value, and they caused genuine hardship for those who had purchased property in the last few years. Recent buyers, including newly recruited scientists and engineers of expanding and emerging high-tech plants around Route 128, were likely to have had their property assessed at near market value; for them, typical tax rates of around 20 percent, applied to the actual value of their property, meant yearly tax bills of staggering proportions. The word was going out to recent engineering school graduates and others that Massachusetts was an extrememly costly place in which to settle, a fact that unsettled the CEOs of the High Tech Council.

Also, the state's Supreme Judicial Court had earlier ordered that all taxable property in the state eventually be reassessed at full market value. Although the court clearly assumed that each city and town would reduce its property-tax rate once revaluation had greatly increased its tax base, there was no way to insure that this would happen. The prospect of revaluation, therefore, terrified many property owners—especially the elderly, who in general had owned their property for a long time at such artificially low valuations that they faced the prospect of dramatic tax-bill increases once the court-ordered revaluation took effect.

King had promised tax reduction, and now he had to deliver. His first attempt was to fulfill a campaign promise of reducing local property taxes by $500 million in his first year in office. To accomplish this goal he proposed a freeze on state spending, passage of a law calling for a zero-percent cap on local property-tax increases during 1979, plus other cutbacks and savings measures that he would introduce—all to create a $500 million state surplus that would be spent to lower property taxes. The problem was, the legislature would not go along with the spending freeze, and his zero-percent property tax cap became a 4-percent cap. Even as he tried to cajole legislators by playing the traditional politics of log-rolling and patronage, King failed to realize that the social programs he wanted to cut—the "government" side of politics—were just as important to many legislators as the governor's promise to find jobs for all of their relatives.

King's next move was the so-called Social Contract; it was an "implicit agreement" between the High Tech Council and the governor calling for the creation of sixty thousand new high-tech jobs in Massachusetts over the next four years, in return for a $1.2 billion reduction in state and local taxes over the same period. King signed a symbolic contract to that effect in February 1979, creating a lot of symbolic good will among businessmen, but little of substance. From the outset, the Social Contract was not a contract at all; the industry's own projections showed that high-tech in Massachusetts would expand to create 60,043 new jobs during the next four years, regardless of any reductions in state and local taxes. As for King's side of the bargain, for starters, no governor could directly control local property tax rates, although he could hold down their increase by doling out massive amounts of new local aid to the 351 municipalities. And state tax rates were the purview of the legislature, a body over which King had already demonstrated that he had little influence.

By 1980, neither King nor the High Tech Council had persuaded the legislature to do what they wanted about state taxes. Local property-tax reductions amounted to $36 million in 1979, a far cry from the $500 million in savings that King had promised as a candidate in 1978. In July 1980 the legislature adjourned without taking action on a proposed constitutional amendment, offered by the Council and a grassroots anti-tax lobbying group called Citizens for Limited Taxation, that would have mandated a sharp reduction in state and local property taxes. When the legislature was called back into session in September to address the issue of the proposed amendment, they replaced the Council/CLT language with less restrictive wording of their own. Outraged, Howard Foley and CLT director Gregory Hyatt, a lawyer from the town of North Andover, organized a massive petition drive to place a statutory tax-cutting referendum focused on local property taxes on the November ballot. The result was Proposition 2½.

Prop 2½, initially suggested in a column by the *Boston Herald*'s Warren Brookes, immediately became an issue that would be as hotly debated in Massachusetts as the upcoming presidential election. If approved by the voters, Prop 2½ would make it a state law that cities and towns would have to reduce their local tax rates to 2½ percent of full and fair market value within five years. The 2½ percent figure ($25 per $1000, compared to the $200 or even $300 of assessed value that many homeowners were currently paying) was alluring. So too was a separate proposal tacked on to the bill to entice voters who rented their homes and therefore had little reason to care about property-tax rates; Prop 2½ would allow renters to deduct half their yearly rent on their state income-tax returns. A further inducement to lower auto excise taxes was also added on.

High Tech CEOs loved Prop 2½; public-employee unions, who knew that such a drastic cut in local property-tax revenue would result in massive layoffs, predictably hated it. The liberal Dukakis wing of the party lobbied hard against the referendum while King's supporters pushed hard for it—with one notable exception. To the consternation of his closest advisors, Ed King waffled repeatedly on the subject of Prop 2½; despite all his promises to slash taxes, the governor would not take a public stand in favor of the largest tax-cutting proposal in the state's history. The ideologues around King thought Prop 2½ was a good idea; the pragmatists, who were aware that the public employee unions were against it, as well as most of the legislative leadership, counseled King to stay on the sidelines.

What he did governmentally, however, was probably more than enough to insure the referendum's passage. Earlier in the year King, determined to make a show of holding back state spending, had refused the pleas of countless local officials for a large increase in state aid to cities and towns. King kept the local aid figure, a critical component of every municipal budget in the state, at virtually the same figure as the previous year. The results of that move were predictable; faced with rising costs and no additional funds from the state, most cities and towns were forced to raise their property-tax rates. By October 1980, on the eve of the Prop 2½ referendum, more than 80 percent of the Commonwealth's 351 cities and towns had announced property-tax increases after first voting to override the 4-percent property tax cap, which was due to expire soon anyway. It was the largest *local* tax increase in the state's history, and it made for an equally predictable result at the polls: on November 4, voters overwhelmingly passed Proposition 2½.

Prop 2½ proved enormously popular with the voters. Time and again in 1981, in referenda provided for in the new tax-cutting law, local voters rejected proposals to delay the effects of the new law. The voters wanted their tax cuts, and in all but a few isolated instances they got them on schedule.

Ed King did his best to make sure voters knew exactly who had gotten them those cuts. Despite his public waffling before the 1980 referendum, King in 1981 repeatedly identified himself with the new law, touting it as one of the great successes of his new administration—which, in a way, it was: King's miserly allotment of local aid in 1980 had forced the local tax hikes that had made passage of Prop 2½ a foregone conclusion.

Largely as a result of a high-tech boom which seemed all but unstoppable, 1981 was a good year for the Massachusetts economy. Even as the rest of the country went into recession, the state's unemployment rate remained below the national average, with the predicted expansion of jobs in the high-tech sector more than absorbing the continuing loss of traditional manufacturing jobs. King should have had plenty of reason to look forward to the election year of 1982 with optimism.

But for all the good economic news, 1981 was another bad year for King's public persona, and for his reputation as a judge of personnel. Barry Locke, the secretary of transportation and construction who had become a trusted advisor to King, was arrested and indicted on bribery charges.

The Locke scandal broke open in a decidedly mundane manner; the general manager of the public transportation system accidently opened an envelope on his desk one day that had been addressed to Locke. In the envelope were ten $100 bills. The general manager took the envelope and the money to the state attorney general, and another sordid tale of political corruption in Massachusetts began to unfold near the very center of the King administration. A bumper sticker soon appeared, which King loyalists attributed to the Dukakis shadow government; the sticker contained a likeness of Locke, thumb up in the "Make It In Massachusetts" style, with dollar bills spilling from Locke's up-stretched thumb. "Barry Locke Made It In Massachusetts," it read.

In December 1981 King's newfound reputation as a bungling manager was dramatically reinforced when the governor allowed a labor dispute at the "T" to get out of control. A strike ensued, the result of which was a temporary shutdown of public transportation in Boston at the height of the Christmas shopping season. This development did not endear the governor to the very merchants and businessmen who were supposed to form the core of his constituency.

Public opinion polls reflected these strains. People generally liked Ed King, but a majority did not like him as governor. It seemed that each failure from the King administration reminded the public of a strength in the previous administration. When the subways ground to a halt just before Christmas, Dukakis's commitment to public transportation and simple dependability were recalled. In the publicity surrounding Barry Locke's arrest, it was hard not to recall the ex-governor who had been a paradigm of integrity.

During this time Dukakis had scrupulously avoided utterances about his successor. He had been true to his word to Andy Sutcliffe that he would give King two years before beginning to consider whether or not to plunge back into elective politics. But it was becoming obvious to all interested observers that the once and present leaders of the Democratic Party were headed for a climactic confrontation.

Dukakis and King were simultaneously competing leaders of the two long-basic blood lines of the Democratic Party in Massachusetts: reform and regular. In 1974, in his victory over the regular Democrat Robert Quinn and his conquest of the Brahmin Republican Frank Sargent, Dukakis initially appeared to have had the opportunity to affect a permanent political realignment. As had occurred on a smaller scale in Brookline after he had engineered the takeover of the Democratic town committee, it seemed possible that Dukakis and the reformers would become ensconced as the new Democratic establishment across Massachusetts.

But Dukakis had lost sight of the need to plant his reform movement in the terra firma of Massachusetts. The regulars and the reformers had coexisted uneasily for four tension-filled years before the reform movement was uprooted in what amounted to a political and cultural counter-revolution, headed by Ed King. At the mid-point of King's term, the Democratic party began to split into two hostile camps, each preparing for a final battle to determine the fate of the party. Almost two years before the 1982 primary election, the impending Dukakis-King confrontation already had a name. It was called "The Rematch."

Chapter 18
Making Amends

When Phil Johnston and Mike Dukakis bumped into one and other on an Amtrak train to New York in the summer of 1980, the pair of once close friends and political allies had not spoken since before Dukakis's loss to Ed King in the primary, back in September 1978. Johnston, like almost all of the liberals in the legislature, had broken with Dukakis over his human-service spending cuts combined with his know-it-all arrogance. Johnston, however, unlike Barney Frank, the leader of the liberal Democratic Study Group, had not personalized the split. In fact, Johnston had sent Dukakis a letter on the day he left office telling him how badly he felt about the way things had turned out. The letter was never answered.

Before the break, Johnston admired Dukakis; he had looked up to him. In 1974, during his own campaign to win a seat in the State House, Johnston organized the suburbs south of Boston for Mike Dukakis. Entering the legislature the same year that Dukakis became governor, he soon emerged as a leading voice in the DSG. Johnston was born in working-class Chelsea, just north of Boston, and grew up in the western suburbs of Natick and Wellesley, in a family of modest means. He had been a foster-care worker before he entered electoral politics and had served as executive director of the Robert F. Kennedy Action Corps, a children's services agency.

Johnston had earned a reputation for courage and independence after he and a Republican colleague had almost single-handedly prodded an extremely unwilling legislature to impanel a blue-ribbon commission, known as the Ward Commission, after its chairman, John William Ward, then president of Amherst College, to hunt for political corruption; it was, in fact, while testifying before this commission that fixer Billy Masiello had given Dukakis the most flattering of backhanded compliments: that his incorruptability had put Masiello out of business.

Johnston was a reformer who believed in honest, effective government, but above all else, he believed in people. To him, politics and government shared the same purpose: to focus society's resources where the need was greatest. When Dukakis in 1975 began cutting social welfare programs—without a hint of regret—Johnston was disillusioned and angry. Ironically, when the tax hikes and spendings cuts package came to a climactic vote in the House in November 1975, Barney Frank,

who had made a personal issue of his dispute with Dukakis, pragmatically voted
for the package; Johnston could not bring himself to endorse such a toll on the
poor and voted no.

It was not coincidental that Johnston and Dukakis happened to meet on a train
to New York. The train was filled with delegates, the press, and the entourage
from the Massachusetts delegation to the Democratic National Convention. Both
Johnston and Dukakis were delegates pledged to Ted Kennedy in his doomed effort to beat President Jimmy Carter for the Democratic party's nomination. During the four-and-a-half hour ride to New York, Dukakis and Johnston began to
talk out their differences.

Dukakis said that Ed King's workfare program, more comprehensive than
Dukakis's own, particularly offended him; he told Johnston that if he were elected
governor again, he would structure his welfare policies along the lines of a
demonstration project that was underway in the city of Lowell. During his first
term, Dukakis had worked to help revitalize the decaying and neglected mill city
where his father had settled after emigrating from Asia Minor. Among the many
programs already underway in the city was a job training program for welfare recipients that had the backing not only of the political establishment but also of the
business and academic communities.

For Johnston, who had opposed both King's and Dukakis's workfare policies,
these were encouraging words—but they were only words. He was skeptical. Dukakis
did not ask Johnston for any commitment, but instead suggested that they get
together again in Cambridge after the convention.

As Dukakis geared up for 1982, he knew that he would have to to have the support of liberals like Johnston if he was to have any chance of success. What Johnston
would do politically, however, was not yet clear. He was close to Lieutenant Governor
Tom O'Neill, who had not exchanged a civil word with King since O'Neill had
found himself matched with King after his great upset of Dukakis in 1978. After
King had gone out of his way to isolate and demean him, O'Neill planned to run
for governor himself. O'Neill, like his father, was a real, traditional liberal, as
Dukakis had shown himself not to be. Johnston had a couple of options: Dukakis
or the younger O'Neill.

While on the convention floor with the Massachusetts delegation, Dukakis caught
sight of John Sasso, a political operative who had helped organize Iowa for Kennedy during the winter and who now was managing the New Jersey delegation
for Kennedy at the convention. Dukakis had met Sasso once before, early on the
Saturday morning after he had been beaten by Ed King, at South Station, one
of the two railway stations in Boston. A fierce competitor since his childhood in
New Jersey, Sasso, who had earned a degree in government at Boston University,
was busy organizing a whistle-stop tour across Massachusetts to drum up support
for a voter referendum campaign; its purpose was to amend the state constitution
to allow municipalities to tax commercial and industrial property at a higher rate
than residential property.

The campaign was mounted by progressive groups—organized labor, human services advocates, municipal officials—all the component parts of the New Deal coalition, after the Supreme Judicial Court had issued a landmark decision requiring that all property, whatever its use, be taxed at the same rate. If fully enforced, the ruling would have had the effect of shifting hundreds of millions of dollars in taxes from commercial real estate to residential property, a development which would be catastrophic for homeowners. The Massachusetts Municipal Association had hired Sasso, a political staffer and field organizer for liberal Congressman Gerry Studds, to manage the campaign. He in turn invited Dukakis to join the whistle-stop tour weeks before the September primary.

After Dukakis lost to Ed King, Sasso did not press him to participate; under the circumstances, he felt the lame-duck governor would not have the stomach for more campaigning. But Sasso had underestimated Mike Dukakis, as he soon discovered when a willing, if dispirited, Dukakis arrived at the platform ready to do his part for the so-called classification campaign. Sasso told Dukakis how badly he felt about his loss and added, "You didn't have to do this." Not at all, Dukakis told him. He felt classification was "a very important campaign" and he was happy to help.

Thanks to Sasso's organizational skills, leaders of almost every group in the old Democratic coalition showed up—groups that had abandoned Dukakis in his recent campaign. The train left on time, and because of Sasso's coalition, classification won a smashing victory in November. The voters had elected a conservative governor, but John Sasso celebrated the success of his effort to add a liberal and progressive tax reform amendment to the state constitution.

During the many lulls in the Democratic National Convention, Dukakis and Sasso talked. It was not lost on either of them that Sasso had organized the coalition that Dukakis would have needed to beat Ed King. As with Johnston, Dukakis's conversation with Sasso was casual enough on the surface; never once did he mention the Massachusetts gubernatorial contest that was slightly more than two years down the road. However, Dukakis did ask Sasso, as he had Johnston a day earlier, to come over to Harvard to see him when they both returned home. Sasso was not at all convinced that Dukakis was going to run again for governor, but he was impressed with how centered and content Dukakis appeared that day, in contrast to Dukakis's muttering and obvious pain on the occasion of their first meeting, four days after the 1978 state primary.

In the spring of 1980 a decision made in Rome gave Dukakis the opportunity to achieve complete rapprochement with his former close friend, Barney Frank, the state's leading liberal. Frank and Dukakis, the former allies who had become bitter enemies during the days of Dukakis's meatcleaver, had resumed talking after the election of Ed King in November of 1978. "He asked me to come see him," said Frank. "He told me one of his regrets was his failure to show me how much we had in common, taking much of the blame on himself. He was very gracious." The two continued to speak casually off and on during 1979 and 1980; Dukakis was moving toward a decision to challenge Ed King, and Frank, stuck in the State

House at a decidedly illiberal time, was growing edgy and impatient for new challenges. The Vatican decision was a shock to the Massachusetts political establishment: Pope John Paul II issued an order that clergymen in the Roman Catholic Church could not hold elective office.

While the order was general in its phraseology, it was specific in its effect. Father Robert F. Drinan, a former dean at Boston College Law School who had held a congressional seat representing a district west and north of Boston since 1971, would have to vacate his office. His election in 1970 was a historical event in Massachusetts politics: not only did voters send a priest to Congress, but more importantly they sent an explicit anti-war candidate to help stop the war in Vietnam. Around Drinan had coalesced a powerful grassroots coalition of doves.

Drinan and Jerome Grossman, a wealthy businessman who helped found and fund the Drinan campaign, were devastated by the news from Rome. "I found a message on my answering machine," said Grossman. "It said, 'Call Drinan, ASAP.' He told me about the Pope. We're sitting there at his place like a wake, all his Irish relatives and me. The first person I thought of calling was Mike Dukakis."

Though Dukakis was not an active participant of the anti-war movement, he shared its goals. In 1972, while he was out of office, Dukakis campaigned for Drinan, whom he liked very much, outside an elementary school in Brookline until the polls closed. "I called Mike and told him I was calling for Drinan," said Grossman. "I told him the news in case he wanted to gather the signatures to run for the seat Drinan was giving up. He said, 'Thank you very much, but I'm not interested in being a legislator. I'm interested in being an executive.' "

With Dukakis having stepped aside, John Kerry, a leader of Vietnam Veterans Against the War, Barney Frank, another liberal state representative from Newton, and the more moderate mayor of Waltham, a factory city, all announced their intentions of running for the Democratic nomination to succeed Drinan.

Quickly, Kerry abandoned the race to support Frank's bid, and by the September primary the state representative had dropped out also, leaving Frank and the mayor of Waltham to fight for the nomination. The mayor had supported Dukakis in 1978, while Frank had not, although he had said repeatedly in public that he regretted his decision. Frank asked Dukakis whether he was planning on taking sides. Dukakis said he would not, adding, "I think you'd be a good member of Congress."

"He could have snuffed me out," said Frank. "There's no question about that." After the primary, Dukakis campaigned with Frank in the cities in the westernmost parts of the district, "where he was more popular than I was," said Frank, who won his seat in Congress over a staunch conservative in November and moved on to Washington with a new sense of respect and appreciation for Mike Dukakis.

In November, after Ronald Reagan's victory over Jimmy Carter and the victory of Proposition 2½, Dukakis asked John Sasso to manage his 1982 campaign. But there was a problem: Ted Kennedy was also courting Sasso to manage his reelection campaign to the U.S. Senate, also in 1982. Dukakis was not going to take no for an answer. "Look," he told Sasso, "Kennedy's going to win and I'm going to help him. I need you more than he does."

Sasso did not need much convincing. "Right from the first, Dukakis had a fix on what he had to do," said Sasso. "He told me in November that he was going to run 'because everything I've tried to do in the first term, [King] is trying to tear down.' He said it was a flashback to twenty years ago, that he had to put back together the Democratic coalition and keep it together, that he had to say to the people of Massachusetts that he had made mistakes, and that he would have to raise a lot of money."

This last area—the raising of a lot of money—was something with which Dukakis had no experience. As is the fate, traditionally, of good government reform candidates, Dukakis had been forced to run both his campaigns for governor on a veritable shoestring. Dukakis had not really minded; he had always been uncomfortable with the big-money people who make up the typical campaign finance committee. He did mind losing, however, and, in the transition from idealist to pragmatic reformer while at the Kennedy School, Dukakis came to understand the importance of paid media. At the start of 1981, he still had no idea how he was going to raise the more than one million dollars he figured he would need to beat Ed King.

The answer in two words was "Bob Farmer." Farmer, like Dukakis, lived in Brookline, although they had never met. A tall, jovial man, Farmer was a hard-driving businessman who had made a small fortune as a publisher. His entrepreneurial success began when, on leave from Harvard Law School, he got a job in the international tax law department of a New York accounting firm in the early sixties. Along with some volunteer work for Richard Nixon—the former vice president at the time was living in New York and practicing law in an office near Farmer's—Farmer began publishing analyses of the tax laws of foreign nations. These were quite popular with firms with international business dealings, and his business began to prosper.

In 1980 Farmer was attracted to the Republican presidential campaign of Illinois Congressman John B. Anderson. Farmer began raising money for Anderson from his wealthy friends and joined the congressman's national finance committee. When Anderson bolted from the Republican party to run at the head of the "Anderson Coalition," Farmer went with him—along with 382,539 fellow Massachusetts residents. With his strength concentrated in pockets of upper-middle-class, suburban, reform-oriented voters, Anderson scored most impressively in Massachusetts.

It was not much of a shift from Anderson's dry Midwestern reform appeal to Dukakis's technocratic integrity. Farmer, bitten by the political bug, by the end of 1980 was prepared to set his business aside and immerse himself in campaign fundraising. To this end he approached a friend from his Harvard days, Richard Zeckhauser (now a political economist on the faculty of the Kennedy School of Government); Zeckhauser introduced Farmer to Dukakis. The three went for lunch late in November, and Dukakis and Farmer hit it off immediately. Dukakis agreed to let Farmer host and organize a series of fundraisers. "I met the craziest guy today," Michael Dukakis told his wife that evening. "He raises money and he loves it." For a guy who had nickled and dimed his way to the governor's office seven years earlier, the prospect of raising at least one million dollars with Farmer at the helm of his fundraising operation now seemed plausible.

Dukakis announced his candidacy at the end of the year. In a Christmas-season newsletter mailed to his supporters, coupled with a request for contributions, Dukakis told loyalists what they wanted to hear. ''We worked hard to bring integrity and competence to state government,'' the former governor wrote. ''But during the past two years, you and I have seen that progress slowed, stymied and reversed by the present state administration. It is essential that confidence in government be restored. It is essential that this state have competent and effective leadership. It is essential that there be a new direction in 1982.

''For all these reasons, and with your continued support and encouragement, I intend to be a candidate for Governor in 1982.''

The newsletter also contained the comments of Dukakis's three children. John Dukakis, then twenty-two, expressed the feelings not only of the Dukakis family but of many who were, by the end of 1980, willing to give the former governor a second chance: ''There are some real pressures and they don't disappear when you walk in your front door—which means we all shared them to some degree. My father made some unpopular decisions, and there was a lot of anger directed at him—and sometimes at us. If I felt it, I know he and Mother must have felt it a hundred times more. So I've thought about that—the price you pay.

''But we've all grown through those experiences, and learning to understand them and deal with them brought us all very close together. I'm really proud of my father. I'm proud of both my parents. And I'm glad the campaign is on.''

Both Dukakis and Sasso, now firmly in charge, stepped up the effort, which Dukakis had already begun, to court Phil Johnston, the person who could best put a compassionate—and forgiving—face on the campaign. Dukakis invited Johnston to tour the Lowell job training site about which they had spoken on the train ride to New York in 1980. They met with welfare recipients, welfare department social workers and business leaders. Dukakis asked about what had worked and what had not, and what his and King's policies had meant to them. Johnston was impressed. This was not the Michael Dukakis he had known from 1975 to 1978.

When the liberal state representative received the commitments that he had been seeking—including an absolute guarantee that Dukakis would not reintroduce a punitive workfare program, and that he would provide adequate funding for AFDC recipients—and when Dukakis offered him the position of campaign human services policy advisor, Johnston signed on in April 1981.

''Phil was a perfect symbol of the difference between '78 and '82,'' said Tom Glynn, a key issues and communications advisor to Dukakis during the rematch campaign. The recruitment of Johnston ''said that there were going to be changes.'' New blood was coming in to the campaign—most notably Sasso and Farmer—and many old hands from earlier campaigns were again signing on, but nobody came in from as far out in the cold to as close to the campaign braintrust as Johnston.

Once committed, Johnston set up scores of meetings with Dukakis and local activists. ''It was brutal,'' said Johnston. ''Like me, people had to get their anger off their chests." At one such meeting, in the Jamaica Plain section of Boston, a hotbed of political sophistication and organization, the initial response at meeting the former governor for the first time was antagonistic. "It was awful," recalled Johnston. "Somebody called him a liar, and there were a lot of raised voices." When they left the encounter session, Johnston told Dukakis that he did not have to take that kind of abuse. "Oh, yes I do," Dukakis responded.

But as with the other meetings, even this one turned out a surprising amount of support for Dukakis. "Tommy [O'Neill] wasn't getting anybody," Johnston said. The strategy of meeting with liberal activists, of explaining the errors of his first term, of soliciting people's feelings and their support, was already producing big dividends.

The first public test for Johnston came in late November of 1981. Two of the state's best known liberal organizations, Americans for Democratic Action and Citizens for Participation in Political Action (CPPAX), held a joint endorsement convention. More than three hundred of the state's most ardent liberal activists gathered at a church in the western suburb of Arlington to declare their preference for governor.

It was an important test for O'Neill, who was trying to stake a claim as the third viable candidate in what was beginning to take shape as a Dukakis-King rematch. According to Dukakis polls, Ed King, despite his many problems, enjoyed a solid 40 percent of support among likely primary voters. His favorability ratings on tax and spending policies and on public safety issues measured in the 70-percent range. However, King never went beyond 50 percent of voter support, no matter how the survey questions were asked, because his "negatives"—the measure of unfavorable responses on issues such as job performance—also registered on the high side. What this told Dukakis was that, while King could not win in a two-way race, he could squeeze out a victory in a three-person field. The ADA/CPPAX convention was an opportunity to deny O'Neill viability by demonstrating that Dukakis had recaptured the support of liberals.

Johnston worked the ADA/CPPAX crowd hard, along with Jack Corrigan, Sasso's campaign field director, and Susan Estrich, a key member of the campaign staff hierarchy. The outcome was not even close. Dukakis hit the magic number of two-thirds of the votes cast to earn the significant CPPAX nod—the larger and more influential of the two groups. The ADA board also voted to give Dukakis their support.

O'Neill just barely beat out the Socialist Workers Party candidate in the CPPAX polling. The result of the balloting indicated that among liberal activists, at least, it was a rematch that they wanted; more than anything else, these chastened liberals wanted the King era to end as quickly as possible. Their choice was made all the easier by the new, more liberal Michael Dukakis for whom they voted for that day.

To insert himself into the race, O'Neill hired New York media specialist David Sawyer to produce a TV spot mocking the rematch. Two animated boxers slugged it out in the middle of a boxing ring: two tired old faces, or so the ad would have viewers believe. It was the earliest date in memory—nearly a full year before primary election day—that a campaign had purchased costly air time. After the ads had run, O'Neill began an ambitious telephone survey of registered Democrats—as many as ten thousand calls were made each night with the goal of reaching one hundred thousand voters. On the very first night, O'Neill learned of the extent to which voters wanted a rematch. No more than 8 percent of the respondents to the O'Neill poll indicated that they would support him. Night after night, similar results poured in. "They were two natural bangers," said O'Neill field director and pollster Lou DiNatale of King and Dukakis. "There simply wasn't room for anyone else in the field."

Despite the bad news, O'Neill hung in the race, hoping to pull off a miracle in the February caucuses, where delegates to the state convention would be elected. The convention had been abandoned in the early seventies by Democratic leaders who believed the internecine fighting that the conventions brought out left the party vulnerable to popular Republicans like Volpe and Sargent. In 1981 the Democrats reinstituted the convention, thereby recreating an event that played into Dukakis's strengths.

As he demonstrated in the early sixties, when he was getting his reform movement off the ground through COD, and again in 1970, when he organized himself into the convention endorsement for lieutenant governor, Dukakis had an organizational talent that was second to none. He also had the desire and the energy to criss-cross the state, meeting delegates and winning them over one by one, and he had the near photographic memory that allowed him to turn each delegate into an acquaintance instead of just a name.

Ed King's strategy in this phase of the race was, of necessity, heavily media oriented. Never much of an organizational man, King prepared for the February caucuses by calling his allies to what turned out to be an unfocused meeting at his favorite eatery, Anthony's Pier 4 restaurant, across the harbor and in sight of Logan Airport, the anchor of the Massachusetts Port Authority that he had once controlled. His only hope for a respectable showing at the caucuses was a $350 thousand TV ad campaign that began airing in January 1982. The ads were intended to shift the focus of the campaign from character, Dukakis's strong suit, to issues, the source of King's strength in 1982 as in 1978. With O'Neill and King both on television by February, the most costly race in Massachusetts history was beginning to take shape.

Motivated by the desire bordering on an obsession to even the score with King, Dukakis rolled to victory in the caucuses. O'Neill was the choice of no more than 8 percent of the delegates, as his polls had correctly predicted, and King was the favorite of no more than 30 percent. The rest favored Dukakis. Months before the state primary, it was obvious that Mike Dukakis had already won back control of the party. With the caucus results in, O'Neill closed down his campaign office and laid off his paid staff. He was a candidate in name only.

John Sasso came under pressure to start spending some of the bounty Farmer was amassing. Michael Dukakis had always used his political operation to raise money—in part as a test of their organizational skills, in part because he did not have many big donors to call upon—but for the rematch, the technique was elevated to a degree of artfulness that lent character to the 1982 rematch election even as Farmer was pulling in big donors never before partial to Dukakis. Early in 1981, Boston-based political consultant John Marttila, who had come to prominence in Father Drinan's 1970 anti-war campaign, proposed that the Dukakis campaign adopt a low-dollar fundraising model. It was Marttila's contention that the typical small contributor would be willing to do more than merely write a check to help Dukakis take the state back from archvillain Ed King.

He called his model contributor/worker the "donor-activist," someone who would contribute twenty-five to fifty dollars and who could then be called upon to staff a telephone for a night of in-house polling, or hold a placard at a busy intersection. All the organizing, beginning at mid-year 1981, was focused on fundraising.

Throughout the summer, Michael Dukakis attended two or three fundraisers each night and as many as four more on Saturday. By the end of the year, he had added the names of ten thousand small donors, who contributed $525,000, all their names, addresses and phone numbers had been added to Dukakis's computerized data base. Sasso meanwhile resisted the temptation to respond in kind to King's media attacks. He anticipated that Ed King would launch a massive paid media campaign three weeks before the election; the idea was to match King dollar for dollar in the climactic final days.

On April 20 Dukakis and King squared off in a debate, the first such meeting between the rivals since the lone debate of the 1978 campaign and Dukakis's shaken reaction to Tony Pepper's aside during the microphone check. As was the case four years before when Barbara Ackermann represented the liberal position to the left of Dukakis, Tom O'Neill, still technically in the race and running to Dukakis's left, made it a three-way affair.

Dukakis had two aims in the debate: he wanted to attract supporters of the doomed O'Neill candidacy, and he wanted to rattle King during the sound check prior to going on the air. Each candidate was asked to speak into his microphone. "Testing, one-two-three," said O'Neill. King's words were not audible. When it was Dukakis's turn, he spat out: "Under Ed King, violent crime has increased 30 percent in Massachusetts." The attack, discussed by Dukakis with his aides prior to the debate, withered King. Nixon-like, he began to sweat and squirm even before the first question was directed to him.

The debate proceeded, with candidates allowed to question each other in turn. At one point, Dukakis asked O'Neill, "Tom, whose lieutenant governor would you rather be remembered as being? His or mine?"

Toward the end of the debate, Dukakis lit into King. "Your secretary of transportation, Barry Locke, was convicted and jailed for stealing public funds. Your commissioner of insurance was a front man for the industry and had to resign after one week. Three other officials in your administration were forced to resign because they lied or were unfit for public office. The Ward Commission documented that corruption is costing each taxpayer in Massachusetts three thousand dollars per capita

that goes directly into the pockets of corrupt public officials and never gets spent
on public services. That adds up to six billion dollars. And you say that 'Taxachusetts'
is dead. With your record of bad judgment and bad appointments, what can you
say to us tonight to convince us you've changed, and that we can expect anything
better over the next four years?''

As "Do you still beat your wife?'' questions go, it was perfect. King lost his
composure completely for a moment. His eyes seemed to glaze over as he responded,
"I would urge everyone listening to disregard your totally absurd, without foundation, statements.''

Dukakis was merciless in his destruction of Ed King. The automaton had
metamorphosed into an emotional human being. All the frustrations from 1978,
the anger of his years in exile, his disdain for his rival, his passionate desire to reim-
pose his reform agenda, and his determination to replace King seemed to well up,
express itself and then recede as the debate came to an end. The passive, unen-
gaged and unpolitical Mike Dukakis who had walked like a lamb to slaughter four
years before seemed very far away indeed on this night of rhetorical blood-letting.

A month later, convention delegates assembled in Springfield to endorse Michael
Dukakis, the overwhelming winner of the delegate selection caucuses held three
months earlier. King had been advised to boycott the event, but having already
refused the advice of his kitchen cabinet to run as an independent in November,
he was committed to playing out the game. State party rules required candidates
for statewide office to receive at least 15 percent of state convention delegate votes
in order to have their names placed on the September primary ballot. If King refused
to appear, he risked alienating just enough of his estimated 30 percent of the
delegates to be denied ballot access. So King decided to attend.

When Dukakis entered the Springfield Civic Center, he was greeted by
thunderous applause. When King entered, he was met with a smattering of boos.

In what was effectively an acceptance speech, Dukakis could not mask his glee
at having, for the moment at least, defeated Ed King. After reminding the three
thousand delegates gathered before him that they were witnessing a new Michael
Dukakis ("We brought a message and an appeal. We listened and we learned''),
he proceeded to savage King without ever once mentioning his name throughout
the reading of his 21-page speech. Of King's special relationship with President
Reagan—understandably, King was one Democrat the President held up as a role
model—Dukakis said, "I can promise you that, if we win this election, Mike Dukakis
won't be Ronald Reagan's favorite governor!'' Of King's tough talk on crime, he
said, "We do not have to listen to endless lectures on the subject of crime from
the governor's office while violent crime in Massachusetts goes up, and up, and
up.'' Of King's reputation as the pro-business, Can-Do governor, Dukakis said,
"We need a blueprint for the economy in this state—not more slogans and bumper
stickers.'' And of the plethora of scandals that had given color to King's three and
a half years in office, he concluded, "We must make state government an honest
agent for the public interest—a state government that we can be proud of once
again.

"That means cabinet secretaries that can't be bought. Contracts that can't be wired. And state agencies that represent the consumer—and not just the industries they are supposed to regulate."

When the balloting was complete, Dukakis had defeated the incumbent governor by a two-to-one margin. As a testament to the success of the donor-activist organizing that had begun in mid-1981, fully one-half of the delegates who had voted for Michael Dukakis had also contributed to him, according to records kept by the campaign.

More than halfway through the rematch, Dukakis was ahead on points in the opinion of almost all the judges. But while Dukakis had staggered King a number of times, he had yet to put him down, and in any fight, the final rounds are the most dangerous—especially in a grudge match.

Chapter 19

The Rematch

A poll commissioned by Governor Ed King at the start of the election year showed that he and former governor Mike Dukakis were known by almost everyone in the state. The poll also showed him trailing Dukakis by fifty-seven percentage points. King was unquestionably the least popular sitting governor in the country, but what he learned from his polling was that the people agreed with his core positions: in favor of the death penalty, against drunk driving, for cutting taxes. If he could somehow get voters to concentrate on his *issues*—reduced, in simplest terms, to taxes and crime—if he could just get voters to concentrate on the cards rather than the players, he might have a chance.

To manage the steep climb back to the top, King turned his fortunes over to his chief policy advisor, Ed Reilly, a political strategist not unlike Dukakis's campaign manager, John Sasso: tough, smart, resourceful, energetic, competitive, and New Jersey bred. Barry Kaplovitz, a young pollster and strategist for a New York-based political consulting firm, and Tony Schwartz, a New York-based advertising specialist, completed the governor's creative brain trust. Schwartz had earned the reputation as the master of the negative spot, largely for an ad he had made for Lyndon Johnson in 1964. In it, a girl picks petals from a daisy as the voice-over completes a countdown to a nuclear explosion. Used against Barry Goldwater and telecast only once, the ad was credited for a 10-percentage-point shift in votes. Not only was Schwartz good, but no one in the business worked faster.

The Reilly-Kaplovitz approach was to develop the anti-tax, anti-crime campaign by making news and having Schwartz turn the news into ads. "We want the voters to decide on the issues," Kaplovitz explained during the campaign, "not on King-Dukakis." The focus of this effort was what King continued to call the "Dukakis surtax," never mind that the surtax on the state income tax, which had been put on the books in 1975 as part of the massive budget-tax package, had been a consensus choice of the legislative leadership which happened to be supporting King. In the election year King proposed that the Dukakis surtax be repealed, and, as planned, King's advisors had Schwartz make up ads backing the repeal.

After more than $350 thousand were spent on this media campaign, a minor tax which few citizens had even known about was turned into a bona fide public issue. In early June a *Globe* poll found that nearly three quarters of those questioned who were likely to vote in the primary wanted to see the surtax abolished.

The 57-point deficit began to shrink to a manageable gap as King's team deftly used the power of incumbency to focus public attention on its issues. Momentum was in King's favor; so were the more conservative times. "We'll never out-tough Ed King on the rhetoric," said John Sasso, "but crime is very much an issue of competence. Despite all the tough talk over there, people perceive there is a lack of competence."

That was it: competence, one of Dukakis's talismans, one, he hoped, that was imbued with the power to ward off a stampede toward the candidate promising to cut taxes and crime. Dukakis had a second amulet: integrity, his fulsome dose of it, and the impression of voters that the King administration was corrupt. In the escalating struggle for the nomination during the hot summer months, Dukakis and King were like gladiators, armed with different weapons, each capable of overwhelming the other.

If King's strengths were the creative capacity and speed of his media communicators, Dukakis's strength was Sasso's organizational genius. His presence, along with that of his field coordinator, Jack Corrigan, a brash young pol whom Sasso had met during Ted Kennedy's 1980 presidential campaign in Iowa and who idolized Sasso, gave Dukakis the advantage in the trenches. Early in the campaign, Sasso reasoned that with a minimal field organization, Dukakis could beat King by four to five percentage points; with an exceptional field, the margin could go as high as eight points. A campaign based on an organizational pull would be least susceptible to media manipulation. Sasso and Corrigan knew who their supporters were, and, unlike 1978, they were not going to take them for granted. Thanks to Bob Farmer, Dukakis was able to stay competitive with King's fundraising intake. Neither campaign wanted for money.

Dukakis did what he could to neutralize King's appeal to voters on the issues. He reminded them that "My only brother was struck down in the town of Brookline and left to die of irreversible brain injuries" by a hit-and-run driver Dukakis believed to be drunk at the time. (The driver of the vehicle that hit Stelian Dukakis while he was riding his bicycle in March of 1973 was never apprehended.) Dukakis also repeatedly called for larger and better trained police forces in the cities and towns. However, he had no good rejoinder to King's demand for tax cuts, and with as much as a twenty-point lead in the polls as the summer began, Dukakis had no desire to foster controversy. For him, the less eventful the campaign, the better. He had sought and won the endorsement of the liberal groups by appealing to their sense of pragmatism without issuing any public promises. Now, he hoped to avoid a full-blown discussion of the issues for the same reason; the polls showed it was Dukakis, the paradigm of virtue and efficiency, not his deeply held beliefs, that had given him the lead.

Interrupting the quietude of the campaign, an embarrassment at the end of May created a minor controversy, precisely what Dukakis had wanted to avoid. Robert Squier, a Washington-based media consultant who was working for Dukakis, created a series of cinema verite television ads. In one ad a supporter is shown shaking hands with Dukakis, urging him on. "You've got to make it. You've got to make it," the supporter said. "We've got to get rid of that son of a bitch." In the ad, the word *bitch* was masked by a "bleep."

Although the campaign said that Dukakis had vetoed using the ad, it aired once, on a Boston TV station on May 27, and created an immediate contretemps. At first, Dukakis staffers blamed the TV station for mistakenly running the ad; then they changed their story and blamed their media buyer. However it occurred, the error ultimately shamed the Dukakis campaign into apologizing to King; the incident called into question the Dukakis campaign's dedication to the high road and suggested that even the Dukakis campaign was subject to episodes of miscommunication or mismanagement. The *Globe* pronounced soberly that it was the "first real blunder" of what until then had been a smooth operation. But rare is the campaign that follows the script; incidents like the airing of the "son of a bitch" ad are inevitable bumps along the campaign trail. Given the intensity and duration of the Dukakis-King rematch, a serene windup would have been surprising.

Responding to polling data showing that many voters who agreed with King on the issues still intended to vote for Dukakis because they did not like Ed King, Reilly, Kaplovitz and Schwartz attempted to try to humanize the clumsy and imperious governor. Schwartz made a series of ads using King family members. In one, King's wife, Jody, talks about the "kind of guy I married." Jody King, a warm, sprightly woman with an easy smile, recalled, "When I had polio and I couldn't move my legs," her husband spent long periods at the hospital learning how to help her with her therapeutic exercises. When Jody became discouraged and wanted to skip her exercises, "He said to me, 'You don't tell an ex-Baltimore Colt you don't want to do anything,' and I did it. That's the guy I married. That's the kind of guy Ed King is."

This ad would kick the King-Dukakis rematch campaign out of its smooth orbit. So extreme would be the distractions that never again would either candidate be able to follow his strategy with consistency. The catalytic agent was not the ad itself, but a parody of it; it became known as the "sex tape." Its effect was not so much to soften King's image as it was to taint Dukakis's.

On June 15 the Jody King ad and two others were sent to twenty-five radio stations across Massachusetts. With the ads went an order that they were not to be used until June 18. On June 16 the ads arrived at radio station WARE, which was located in the central Massachusetts town of Ware; WARE was owned by a member of the Dukakis finance committee. On June 17, a full day before the ads were to begin running, John Sasso played a parody of the Jody King spot over the telephone for *Boston Globe* reporter Charles Kenny. The parody, combining parts of the original with new material, turned the monologue into a spoof of the Kings' sex life. Kenny was laughing so hard that two other members of the State House bureau, Ben Bradlee, Jr., and Chris Black, wanted to know what was so funny. Kenny described the parody tape to them.

Later that day, Bradlee went to Dukakis headquarters on another matter and asked Sasso to play him the tape, which Sasso did. Black mentioned the tape's existence to her friend, King advisor Barry Kaplovitz. In a simple exercise in casual gossip, the enemy had information that could be used to good effect to damage and embarrass the Dukakis campaign.

Reilly and Kaplovitz were in no hurry to strike with the so-called "sex tape." They waited a month, until July 15, to make use of their potentially scandalous insider information. On Thursday, the fifteenth, King released a letter to Dukakis, blowing the whistle on the incident. Ignoring with monumental cynicism the possibility of resolving the insult privately with Dukakis—after all, however demeaning the tape was, it had only been played privately and had not been made or commissioned by Sasso—King said in the publicly released letter that the tape "parodies my relationship with my wife and demeans my wife's struggle with polio."

After King released his letter to the press, complaining incorrectly that Robert Squier, the campaign's media consultant, had made the parody tape that had been played to reporters, Sasso and Dukakis's press secretary, Gerry Fitzgerald, spent several hours denying the charge. Splitting hairs, they were correct, but at least one reporter asked if any tape matching King's description had ever existed, and Fitzgerald answered no. Five hours later, around 10:00 p.m., the Dukakis campaign began acknowledging that, yes, "a tape unflattering to King, one of three sent unsolicited to the campaign, had existed," and that "it had been destroyed a day after its receipt a month ago."

The next day the *Globe* acknowledged that Sasso had played the tape to reporters Kenney and Bradlee "on an off-the-record basis that prevented them from publishing the information." The *Herald* got into the act with a front-page headline: "Duke Trips on Sex Tape." Inside, the *Herald* featured an exclusive interview with *Globe* reporter Chris Black, who had told Kaplovitz about the tape.

Television reporters spent the weekend badgering the campaigning Dukakis for his explanation for the fiasco. "Tapegate," the new consensus title for the episode, had become the most publicized event of the campaign since Dukakis's coronation at the convention in May. Sasso offered to resign; Dukakis refused to accept his resignation. The King campaign, which saw the *Globe* in a liberal alliance with Dukakis, believed that Sasso had played the tape to the *Globe* reporters to strengthen a bond, one that, in the view of the King campaign, had already produced biased reporting in Dukakis's favor. "When we play our own ads for reporters in advance, we're trying to influence them," a King aide said in an interview at the time. "They were trying to do the same thing."

If the Dukakis campaign was not careening out of control, it certainly had lost the initiative to King over the mishandling of the sex tape. Twice during the summer—first with the "son of a bitch" ad and now with the sex tape—the supposedly pristine campaign of the righteous good-government reformer had acted in a questionable, if not tawdry, manner. The events and how they were handled raised doubts about the integrity of the campaign, if not about the candidate himself; and if his integrity had not been damaged, his reputation for running a tight ship had been.

The Dukakis campaign never issed an apology, which might have minimized the damage to some degree. In fact, Sasso, in a television interview explaining why he would not apologize, attempted to turn the tables on King by blaming him for turning the private matter into a public one at the expense of his wife. He then asked for King to apologize.

For two weeks after King brought the sex tape story into the public arena, Dukakis was on the defensive. Then, on July 29, with forty-nine days to go before the primary election, the momentum of the campaign shifted once again. The hard-fought, even dirty, campaign turned tragic. A dead body was discovered hanging from the rafters of a fashionable home in the town of Andover, forty-five minutes north of Boston. The body was that of John Coady, the deputy commissioner of the Department of Revenue, an agency that had been scandalized in June when Stanley Barczak, a low-level department official, was arrested at the Parker House Hotel in the process of accepting a bribe.

Barczak's arrest on June 24 would have been a good story at any time. For years, the Department of Revenue had been a patronage haven with a reputation for crooked deals. In his first term, Dukakis began a house-cleaning, but over the years, every important pol seemed to have placed one of his people "up at Revenue." The old guard was deeply entrenched so the going was slow. By the time the 1978 campaign rolled around, the reform of the department had not gotten very far. The House Republican floor leader embarrassed Dukakis during the 1978 campaign by releasing to the public the names of thousands of citizens and corporations, some of them prominent, who were tax delinquents. The state's revenue collection effort was a joke—and in his first term, the joke had been on Dukakis.

Now, the department's reputation for corruption was haunting King. Within days of Barczak's arrest, the press reported that he had been convicted on a fraud charge in the late fifties and had served time in a Pennsylvania prison, and that he had apparently been sponsored for his job in the Department of Revenue by King himself. Dave Farrell, a politically well-connected *Globe* columnist with close ties to the attorney general's office, on the Sunday after Barczak's arrest, predicted that the small-timer would lead to bigger fish. The Revenue scandal was going to grow to Watergate-like proportions, wrote Farrell, who had once been close to and supportive of Ed King. Farrell, like King, was a conservative on most issues, especially on the issue of abortion, but they had had a falling out at the start of King's term. Since then, Farrell had regularly blasted King.

In the context of the Barczak arrest and the press predictions of a huge scandal in the Revenue Department, the death of John Coady, which was ruled a probable suicide, was a crushing blow to King. For one thing, it meant an end to the sex tape story. With a high-level official of an agency under criminal investigation a victim of suicide, the importance of an audiotape parody of a political ad fell into perspective. Additionally, the taint of corruption that had dogged Ed King from his first week in office at the critical moment for the campaign had turned into a tragic reality.

Worse still for King, the *Globe* reported that Coady and King were friends, and that, at the time of his death, Coady had been a subject of the criminal investigation by the office of state Attorney General Francis X. Bellotti that began after Barczak's arrest. Bellotti, who won the 1966 Democratic party endorsement over Mike Dukakis, had come to like Dukakis very much, and he had no use for King.

Stories that leaked from Bellotti's office to friendly columnists, like Farrell and the *Herald*'s Peter Lucas, who had once served as a press aide to Bellotti, made it seem that Barczak's arrest would lead to major prosecutions. Even worse for King, additional published reports quoting unnamed sources obviously from the attorney general's office said that King had been told that Coady had been a target of the investigation before the deputy revenue commissioner had taken his life, raising the possibility that the governor might have been involved in Coady's learning that he was a target of the probe.

The news of John Coady's death and the follow-up stories of the tragedy put the hard-charging King campaign in a tailspin. Polls conducted by Kaplovitz's firm showed King trailing Dukakis by eight points on the day before the suicide; by the fourth of August, King had fallen thirty points behind. "The Coady incident was like a truck that overturned in the road," a King campaign official said. "Once we got it off the highway, we were rolling again. But how many more of these do we have to handle? How many more of these can we handle?"

By the time John Coady hanged himself, the Dukakis-King rematch had the air of myth about it. Understandably, between the sex tape and the suicide, the public was mesmerized—appalled, but mesmerized. The rematch had come to resemble a real-life soap opera: "Dallas" in Boston. In early August the *Wall Street Journal* complained in a front-page story that the Dukakis-King campaign had degenerated into a mudslinging contest. By that time, however, the nature of the campaign was firmly established and immutable. It would be hardball until the end.

At the end of August, in an effort to highlight the corrupt side of the King record, Dukakis organized a "Stand Up For Integrity" day event. Three thousand Dukakis workers held placards at busy intersections all over the state. The next day, Dukakis held a press conference in front of the State House and in front of a collage of newspaper headlines dramatizing the scandals of Ed King's term.

At about that time, in a clumsy effort to draw Dukakis into the muck, the King campaign charged that William Masiello, the master-fixer whose testimony in 1980 before the Ward Commission put a spit-polish on Dukakis's image for rectitude, had benefited from contract work given him by the Dukakis administration. The Dukakis campaign easily deflected the charge, reminding voters that Dukakis had ordered Masiello's contracts terminated. Launching a counter-attack, Masiello came forward to claim that on four occasions he had met with King to discuss ways in which he could raise money for the incumbent governor.

King denied the charge, but Marty Burke, his former press secretary, said that Masiello was telling the truth, that he had been with King and Masiello at the meetings in question. The *Herald* challenged all three disputants to take lie detector tests. When King refused, the tabloid proclaimed his reponse with a large-type headline which read, "KING TO HERALD: DROP DEAD." Burke, who had been a press spokesman for Attorney General Robert Quinn in the early seventies, agreed to take the test, and so did Masiello. It hardly mattered that Masiello, an admitted perjurer, failed the test, or that Burke's results were inconclusive. Into the final weeks of the campaign, the governor was reported to have repeatedly been in the company of admitted fixer Billy Masiello.

Remarkably resilient, King was still standing, advancing in the polls once again as he and Dukakis headed toward the finish line. "It was the potency of the tax argument," said Kaplovitz, explaining King's resurgence. Kaplovitz knew how to use the argument, how it resonated with voters, ever since he had worked as a consultant for the tax-cutters on the Proposition 2½ campaign in 1980. King had gained considerable momentum around Labor Day with a series of ads that reminded voters of unpopular aspects of the Dukakis years. Would Dukakis raise taxes again, expand the welfare rolls and oppose mandatory jail sentences for drug dealers? the ad wanted to know. "When he did it the first time, it was his fault. If we let him do it again, it'll be ours" read the tag line.

Five days before the September 14 primary, the *Globe* reported on a poll, commissioned by State Treasurer Robert Crane, that showed the election to be "whisker close." When those leaning one way or the other were counted in, King even ran slightly ahead. Barry Kaplovitz, King's strategist, said the "news" about the poll affected the electorate "in a funny kind of way," making voters ask themselves if they really wanted another four years of Ed King. The poll comported with no other polling data. According to Dukakis's most conservative polling, King had never pulled closer than six points. The best explanation for the discrepancy of the Crane poll from all the others was that Crane's pollster undersampled independent voters in a serious miscalculation of the interest that this very expensive and very controversial election had for voters, whether they were registered Democrats or not.

The publication of the Crane poll had the effect of mobilizing the Dukakis field operation in frenzied effort as the threat of Ed King loomed ever larger. Sasso felt that speculation in the press that King might carry the election "created the right touch of nervous tension" among Dukakis supporters. Thanks to the campaign strategy created by Sasso, one that stressed a short list of Dukakis pledges, the candidate had avoided the association with "liberal" issues that would have hurt him among the more conservative residents of the state's older cities.

There would be no eye-squinting newspaper ad this time, as there had been in 1978, listing each and every position Dukakis had taken. In fact, a major responsibility of the campaign's issues director, Tom Glynn, was to stifle the urge of the two thousand past and present—and hopefully, future—government policy-makers and issues experts who had signed on to work up policy papers for Dukakis. "We wanted to avoid the perception that Michael was a smart-ass with an answer for every problem," said a campaign staffer with Dukakis's old image in mind.

As a result of Jack Corrigan's superb field organization—the campaign's "safety net," as described by Sasso—urban voters who were disgusted by the perceived incompetence and corruption of the King administration, were ID'd with a sophistication never before witnessed in Massachusetts.

Primary day voters were blessed with warm and sunny skies; it was a day reminiscent of the balmy September day four years before when the Dukakis reform experiment was shattered. This time, the Dukakis campaign, unwilling to permit an upset again, was ready for a superhuman effort. According to one poll, six out of ten voters who supported Dukakis had been contacted by the campaign. The same poll found that only three out of twenty King voters had been contacted by his campaign.

At the start of the evening rush hour on primary day, Jack Corrigan put the word out that the early Dukakis lead was down to two points and slipping. "He said we could lose," said Barbara Opacki, the field coordinator for Essex County, on the North Shore. The truer statement would have been that King had made a race out of it, but that he most likely would not win—but Corrigan and his field operatives were taking no chances.

Opacki and other regional coordinators passed down orders that a final push was to begin. When Paul Lanzikos, the coordinator for the city of Peabody, finished speaking to Opacki, he ordered calls made to all the definite Dukakis voters. They were told that, while they had already voted, they should go out and find more Dukakis voters. "Call your relatives. Look through your personal phonebook for anyone you think may not have voted and who you could get to the polls. We need it."

Opacki figured that the "recall effort" was worth "a couple of thousand votes just on the North Shore." In Lanzikos's Peabody, one of the twenty-five old urban centers that had supported Dukakis in 1974 only to abandon him in 1978 despite his efforts at urban revitalization, King's 1978 margin of 805 votes was converted to a 1,138 bulge for Dukakis. Dukakis's total vote in Peabody went from 5,430 to 7,036. Results from Peabody mirrored the the statewide trend.

The two "bangers" had their rematch, and the final tallies only served to confirm what everyone had known all along, that this was the most intently followed race in modern Massachusetts history. The turnout was up, way up, over 1978. Ed King received 107,161 more votes in a losing cause than he had when he had beaten Dukakis four years earlier, a pickup of 24 percent. All Michael Dukakis did was garner 266,574 additional votes over his 1978 total, an increase of 72 percent.

Michael Dukakis's vote total was 631,911, or 53.4 percent, to Ed King's 549,335, or 46.5 percent. He had put all the good government types in his pot and let it simmer until it was just done. In the western city of Pittsfield, so much on the mind of Michael Dukakis on primary day in 1978, Democratic primary voters gave the former governor a belated message of thanks for his efforts during the midseventies to revitalize their abandoned downtown; voters who had narrowly favored King in 1978 went for Dukakis this time, 6,498 to 3,802.

It was in no way ironic, although it seemed so at the time, that Mike Dukakis, the new-model Democrat, won the rematch the old-fashioned way, by creating a formidable statewide organization, one that in the hands of a less rectitudinous candidate would surely be deemed a "machine." Hadn't he demonstrated, from his first successful door-to-door campaign in Brookline back in 1960, that he knew the value of organizing and the way to go about it? Dukakis spent one million dollars on the field effort to identify his likely voters. It was ironic, however, that King, the throwback candidate of 1950s values and sensibilities, almost won with modern media technology. King spent two million dollars on media during the campaign, two-thirds of his total contributions; Dukakis spent $800,000 on media, one-third of his total budget.

In acknowledging his victory to the celebrants at the Park Plaza Hotel, at the moment of his greatest triumph and celebration, the culmination of a four-year comeback, Mike Dukakis was gracious, modest and full of thanks. "You've given me something that one rarely gets in American politics: a second chance," he told the throng. "And I'm very grateful."

Chapter 20
The Reformer Reformed

After Ed King had beaten him in 1978, Dukakis refused to support his conqueror. But on the day after the 1982 primary, there were Ed and Jody King at the Democratic party's unity news conference, lending their presence—and words—to the sense of a united ticket. Though the primary campaign was unusually bitter, the forces behind Ed King responded to their candidate's loss with resignation rather than resolve. "Ed King was a hard product to sell," shrugged one cabinet member on primary night. Most of the elected leaders of the party, though they had worked for King's victory, threw in with Dukakis, but the regulars who came aboard the Dukakis bandwagon were bowing to the inevitable rather than applauding it. They were, however, most appreciative of the good will receptions Dukakis hosted for the House and Senate; the affairs were a far cry from the bring-your-own lunches Dukakis had "hosted" for the liberals in the Democratic Study Group in the first term. Held at great expense at the Parker House Hotel, the receptions typically featured open bars and oysters Rockefeller. The Republicans put up a candidate, but hardly a fight, unable to prevent the unrivaled master of the majority Democratic party from reclaiming the title to the government he had lost once before.

After the election, the regulars took advantage of King's seven weeks as a lame-duck governor to get the dirty work done before Mr. Clean returned. Every kind of pork barrel, back scratching, special interest and patronage boondoggle that could be imagined made its way through the legislative pipeline. For Christmas 1982 Ed King, almost spitefully, was playing Santa Claus, and the elves were working overtime.

In an act that would have made the late shadow governor Bill Callahan proud, the legislature enacted and King signed a bill creating a convention center authority charged with the job of building a new municipal auditorium for the city of Boston. One provision of the bill specified that the director of the authority, once appointed, had life tenure. To the surprise of no one, the top aide to senate president William Bulger of South Boston, the sponsor of the bill, ended up with the job.

In King's final days as governor, the denizens of the House and Senate fell into what became known as a "feeding frenzy" of odious lawmaking. Until the very end, King was obsessed with the effort of trying to regain political control of his

beloved Massachusetts Port Authority. Because the seven board members were appointed in staggered terms, a device inserted in the enabling legislation to insulate
Massport from politicization, it was not until the last year of his administration
that King finally got a working majority at Massport. When he did, the board fired
the director appointed by Dukakis loyalists, the very same individual who had succeeded King in the post. Despite delaying tactics by Dukakis's minority of three,
the board near the end of the term finally named King's choice, and the choice
of House Speaker Tom McGee, to take over as director of Massport; the new director was Louis Nickinello, a state representative and a chairman of the transportation committee.

What made the move controversial was that a non-political search process, conducted for Massport by a private firm, had concluded that a number of applicants
were well qualified to be director—and Nickinello was *not* one of them. Asked
about the selection of Nickinello, Dukakis disdainfully observed that "The charade
is complete."

Perhaps, but the farce was just beginning. Two days before King was to leave
office, two of King's appointees to the board stepped down and were replaced on
King's last full day in office. Unfortunately for him, in making the hasty appointments, King violated the Massport statute prohibiting more than five members
of the same party from sitting on the board. With the new members, the board
had six Democrats. After the blunder was revealed, a mad scramble ensued to create
a legal King majority and save Nickinello's job.

Less than four hours before King was to turn over the leather Bible and ceremonial
keys to the Commonwealth to Dukakis on January 6, 1983, the board members
he had appointed the previous day resigned. Another board member changed his
party registration to Republican overnight, but it was doubtful that this gesture
would satisfy the statute. King reappointed one of the men who had just resigned—
after less than a day on the board—and named a seventh, presumably legal,
member. The final appointee, King's naval-uniformed military advisor, was a
legitimate long-time Republican. He had come to work thinking his job would
be to escort King from power and the State House. When he learned he had been
appointed to the Massport board, he raced to call his mother. "She'll have a heart
attack if she hears this on the radio," Massport's newest board member said.

Actually, a collective case of nausea was a more likely reaction to the performance
of the outgoing administration. As Bill Geary, Dukakis's trusted long-time aide
who was coordinating the transition, entered King's appointments office to take
control of public documents on the thousands of appointive positions in the government, he found a fire raging in the fireplace. "They were burning files," said Geary.
"It was out of a Fellini movie." On the floor in the middle of the room were mounds
of shredded documents. Geary called the Capitol Police to secure the evidence and
prevent further destruction of public documents.

King had given the people of Massachusetts a final dramatic reminder of why
they had so ardently chosen the reformer Mike Dukakis to return as governor. The
epitaph for the King administration was a front-page photo of a mound of shredded
paper.

In his second inaugural address, Dukakis reiterated that the good government reform impulse of his first term would remain. "Nothing, nothing can destroy our people's faith in the government faster or more effectively than a sense, whether real or imagined, that corruption or contract rigging and influence peddling are synonymous with government in Massachusetts.

"And it is the governor, above all, who must set the tone, who must send out the message that corruption and dishonesty will not be condoned nor tolerated any time, any place, by any one." Yet the new reformed reformer would be much more than a good-government zealot. Along with the good hands of an honest manager, the new Dukakis would show the doubters that, while out of office, he had developed a big heart. Dukakis wanted to underscore the themes of compassion, partnership and community, concepts that he and his friendly rival, New York governor Mario Cuomo, had been developing over the past two years; they were traditional Democratic party themes that had not played well with voters in recent years.

In the days leading up to his inaugural, Dukakis and his long-time confidant, Dan Taylor, a partner at Dukakis's former law firm of Hill and Barlow and his chief counsel in the first term, found a way: the homeless. In Massachusetts, the idea of removing from the state's mental-health hospitals those patients who, with trained help, could safely live outside of confinement was one of the grand reform hopes of the early seventies. It was a belief that Dukakis shared with former governor Frank Sargent, although it was Dukakis, in the 1974 campaign, who warned that the state did not have the money to support the community-based mental-health system the deinstitutionalization required.

Dukakis's warnings were prescient. The professionally trained help and the community-based homes that were conceived of as critical parts of the deinstitutionalization plan had not been put in place in sufficient numbers. Exacerbating the problem of too many people and too few beds and services was the inability of the state to require the former hospital patients to remain in their community residences and skyrocketing rental-housing monthly payments that effectively denied shelter to these and other disadvantaged people. Nonetheless, thousands of patients had been released, and in the early eighties the state found itself with sad and unsettling living legacies to a noble impulse as yet unfulfilled.

Although Dukakis had only mentioned the homeless once during the 1982 campaign, in a talk on housing issues, by Christmas, he and Taylor had decided that it should be the top priority of the new administration. Homelessness worked as an inaugural centerpiece for Dukakis for many reasons. First of all, obviously, it was a heart-rending problem, one that had not been addressed systematically. Second, "Dukakis was looking for an issue that would speak to the human services community," observed his close advisor, Ed Lashman. After his ruptured relations with the human services community and social liberals during the first term, Dukakis determined to send a clear and immediate message that he had changed. Third, from John Sasso's perspective, Dukakis could make important progress in reducing the plight of the homeless by leading a full-scale effort; in the process he would advance his reputation and garner much good press. When Dukakis met with Phil Johnston on December 27 to offer him the job of chief human services policy advisor, Dukakis told him that homelessness was to be his initial assignment.

Dukakis announced in his inaugural address, ''Tomorrow morning in my office I will convene an emergency meeting of the new Cabinet, the Senate President, and Speaker of the House, nonprofit organizations, civic and religious leaders, and representatives of the Coalition for the Homeless. We will begin immediately to put together a statewide effort which will provide the necessitites of life to those in desperate need. . . .[T]he pain and suffering of those who are barely getting by from day to day and from hand to mouth requires more than planning and good intentions. And so we will act now.''

Dukakis also called upon all the citizens of Massachusetts to join in volunteer efforts in local communities to become part of the program that he had launched that night. To underscore his commitment to combating homelessness on every front, on the morning of his address Dukakis called upon Cardinal Humberto Medeiros of the Roman Catholic Archdiocese of Boston to enlist the support of the church.

In his bold homelessness initiative, there was no mistaking a Dukakis who was markedly different from the elite and cerebral reformer of the first term. He was not merely talking about taking bold action; he was scheduling it for the very next day—and in his office. He would provide leadership in partnership with the legislative leadership and other key constituencies dedicated to helping the homeless. No longer, as he had in the first term, would Dukakis stand diffidently above the fray, assuming and expecting the various component parts of society to act in a way he deemed responsible. ''You can expect a strong executive branch that will set the tone...and that will work hard to exercise strong and effective leadership,'' Dukakis said. ''My administration will listen, we will be responsive to legislative initiative. And we will welcome the advice of legislators who bring a wealth of knowledge and experience to the formulation of public policy.''

When he finished his address, Dukakis turned and hugged the senate president, William Bulger. Cool and aloof, a product of the old politics, the intellectually gifted Bulger had been a rival of Dukakis's when they had served in the House together. Spontaneous or not, Dukakis's hug of Bulger was an act of warmth and affection, an expression of the commitment Dukakis made on the night he launched his rematch campaign, when he told his followers that ''this time we're going to do the politics right.''

On January 7, his first full day back in office, Dukakis arrived at work by car— his dedication to riding the subway all the time was a thing of the past—ready to take decisive action. Massport required immediate attention. The port authority was in chaos. Business leaders, as well as Dukakis, were deeply troubled at how King had left matters. The business community was less concerned with the politics of Massport, as the King-Dukakis fight continued to play itself out on a small scale, as it was that the high quality of management at Logan International Airport and related transportation facilities would continue. The airport was a key to Boston's emergence as a center of international commerce and finance, and the political hijinks of the King administration had done nothing to assuage concerns that the agency would forever bounce along as a political football.

The Dukakis organization—most notably Fred Salvucci, who had been reappointed secretary of transportation and construction—was desperate to reclaim Massport. A visionary thinker and long-term planner as well as a shrewd politician, Salvucci was determined to take down Boston's elevated Central Artery and replace it with a tunnel. The Central Artery, which had opened in the early fifties, was the ugliest and most hated remaining element of the late William Callahan's Highway Masterplan. Winding its way north and south through Boston near the waterfront, the Central Artery was almost always clogged; during rush hours, traffic could barely move. Single breakdowns in the wrong place had the capacity to create gridlock throughout the city's roads system. Nothing built by man was more hated in all of Boston.

Salvucci had been trying for years to put together the local coalition required to make such a gargantuan project politically viable. Now, as Dukakis regained office, Salvucci came to the realization that his only hope for forming that coalition was to embrace the top priority of the business community, a proposal that Dukakis and Salvucci had opposed for years: construction of a third tunnel under Boston Harbor to the airport. The entire effort would cost more than two billion dollars, largely funded by Washington, and take more than a decade to complete. Such a project would have to be sensitive to neighborhood concerns; it would be hopeless to start such an endeavor with Massport under Ed King's influence.

What Dukakis brought to work with him that first day was a long forgotten legal tool that his chief counsel, Steve Rosenfeld, had had presented to him the night before by a career bureaucrat whose personal interest was the arcana of the Massachusetts general laws. For years, it had gathered dust; so far as anyone could remember, it had never been used. Evincing three traits he did not have in his first term—decisiveness, resourcefulness and a willingness to play political hardball—Dukakis announced that, under a 1964 law that allowed a governor fifteen days to rescind major appointments, he had decided to nullify the two appointments to the Massport board that King had made on the day he left office. Before he acted, Dukakis placed courtesy calls to the Senate president and to the speaker to let them know what he was going to do—a gesture he would not have thought to make in his first term.

Although Dukakis insisted that the new appointees would have to make up their own mind about Nickinello's fate, even while repeating his objections to the way in which the selection process was corrupted in the effort to hire Nickinello in the first place, it was clear that Nickinello was not long for his directorship of Massport. To avoid an immediate rift with Speaker McGee, Nickinello's loyal supporter, Dukakis assured McGee that Nickinello could have some other job in the administration if he wanted it.

Dukakis had won the battle for Massport, and this time, in contrast to the first time he was governor, he was winning the war as well. For the first time since

Massport was created, it was under the control of a newly elected governor, and this had been accomplished at minimal cost. Of course, such an achievement would not have been possible without a bow to the one-time Dukakis bogeyman: patronage. To avoid paying a dear political price, Dukakis traded a job for present good will and future favors. In the first term Dukakis would never have considered such a trade, but he had since changed his thinking, and a fundamental precept of his reform philosophy was abandoned. Once a rigid absolutist, Dukakis had become a relativist. In his first term Dukakis had squandered his political capital as if he were a drunken sailor. Given a second chance, he was going to spend as little as possible; the job offer to Lou Nickinello, which must have seemed strange to his workers from the 1974 campaign who could not beg a job then, was the first sign of the change in philosophy.

Not long after the Massport brouhaha, Michael Dukakis shocked a group of housing activists by scrapping their moderate proposal to impose restrictions on developers who were converting rental apartment units into condominiums at an ever-escalating pace throughout Massachusetts. Dukakis proposed a more radical alternative, one his pro-tenant allies thought had no chance of passage in the legislature. What they knew was that Dukakis had become angry because investors not only were depleting the number of affordable rental units in communities like Brookline, but, they also were driving up the costs of condominiums as well; this was not what he had had in mind when, in 1963, he wrote the state's first condo conversion law to provide affordable homes for first-time buyers. What they did not know was that Dukakis had a new, important ally, Louis Nickinello's friend, House Speaker Tom McGee. Dukakis's bill prevailed.

Over the course of the long 1982 campaign, Dukakis and John Sasso had grown close. Each had the rare knack for treating the other as equals. Despite the sex tape imbroglio, Dukakis had total faith in Sasso's judgment and respect for his opinion. For his part, Sasso had totally dedicated himself to Dukakis's election. His interests devolved to his boss's.

After his graduation from Boston University in 1970, Sasso discovered he had a knack for management. One of his first jobs was managing the real estate holdings of a successful developer in Boston, and he became known for his no-nonsense style. In 1972 he volunteered to work in the political campaign of Gerry Studds, an exceptionally bright former prep school teacher. Sasso had been involved with anti-war activities at Boston University and Studds had emerged as a leading anti-war candidate. Studds won that year, and Sasso left the real estate business to become Studds's field organizer for the successful 1974 reelection; after the election he stayed on as director of the congressman's district office. He later managed Studds's reelection campaign in 1976, which Studds also won.

In the 1982 Dukakis campaign, Sasso impressed his dedication to Dukakis and his hardball approach to politics. He was tough-minded, working every angle and nuance, yet at the same time honest; his word was good. And he was obsessed with getting the advantage. When Tom O'Neill announced for governor in cities across the state, Sasso had a friend videotape the announcements; if O'Neill said contradictory things in different places, Sasso wanted to have the evidence on tape. Sasso, a poker player, was looking for an edge.

He was there to see that his candidate won. Sasso was not associated with any particular issue; his agenda was the Democratic party's agenda. His job was not to mold the Democratic philosophy, it was to elect progressive Democrats. Issues, to Sasso, were political opportunities and political problems. He welcomed their arrival on his desk so that he could assess the possibilities. As Dukakis's chief secretary, his first responsibility was to see to it that Dukakis remained on the political track. And that track led straight toward reelection in 1986.

What good are reforms if the reformer does not last? was a question that haunted Dukakis during his years out of office. Gordon Chase had hammered the message home to Dukakis in many private conversations as they developed the state and local executives program at the Kennedy School. As the new governor began creating his administration in 1983, he was taking a two-term perspective, and so was John Sasso. In addition, there was another incentive to winning in 1986: only reelection to a second consecutive term could wipe away the stain of having been beaten by Ed King in 1978. Michael Dukakis wanted nothing more than to be chosen by the people of Massachusetts not as the lesser of evils but for himself, for what he stood for and for who he was. There was an emotional need to do now what he had failed to do in 1978: win on the basis of his own incumbent record. And in John Sasso the presiding officer of the Commonwealth of Massachusetts had found the general manager for his four-year plan to preside in harmony over the political landscape.

To Dukakis's great pleasure, Sasso made himself an alter ego; when he looked, he looked through Dukakis's eyes. But he was an alter ego of a different sort than was Fran Meaney, the man who had played the similar role earlier in Dukakis's career. The architect of all of Michael Dukakis's statewide races from 1966 through 1974, Meaney was the missing half of his friend, Michael Dukakis. Dukakis carried the political message; Meaney said the thank you's, asked for the support, and opened the doors barred to Dukakis by political regulars. The two men were inseparable, yet different. In the Sasso era, there was no mistaking who was the candidate. In the Meaney years, "you could look at the two of them standing in a room together," said one friend of both, "and wonder why Fran wasn't the candidate."

Sasso's position was at the top of a triangular structure in which the agencies and departments executed the policies enunciated by the cabinet secretaries, who in turn got their marching orders from the senior staff; the senior staff worked out the public policy agenda with Sasso and Dukakis. This structure could not have been more different from the approach Dukakis took in his first administration: then, an emasculated senior staff was ordered to serve the needs of a cabinet that was empowered to make policy for the governor.

Repeatedly in the first term, senior staff members had complained to Dukakis about the uncontrolled behavior of the cabinet secretaries. "It was ridiculous," his communications director, Mike Widmer, had told him. "The cabinet announces the good news, and you get to announce the bad news." This was literally true. Just before the start of the ill-fated reelection campaign in 1977, when the struggling administration had finally produced its first budget surplus, the best news of the term was announced by Jack Buckley, the secretary of administration and finance—to the fury of the senior staff, who had not even been told by Buckley that he had a surplus to announce.

Dukakis had miscalculated, and he kept this in mind as he set up his second administration. He had delegated authority to the cabinet officers in a misguided belief that they, somehow, would be immune from the political pressures that distort the finding of theoretically "correct" positions. The cabinet officials were no more capable of working in an antiseptic bubble, immune from political influence, than anyone else involved in the political process. Rather than being free from politics, they simply responded to their own political values and the pressures the political process brought to bear on them. The most basic change in approach from the first term was the recognition that policy, politics and people were inseparable. It was a simple but necessary lesson Dukakis was taught by his late friend Gordon Chase and others at the Kennedy School.

From that conclusion came the determination that it would be *his* politics, not the sum total of all his top subordinates' politics, that should guide the administration. From that decision logically followed the establishment of a political manager to advance the governor's political interests and public policy goals. John Sasso was given the responsibility for achieving the governor's public policy and legislative goals, devising strategies, negotiating with legislative leaders, and marketing Dukakis and his programs through seemingly endless conversations with reporters and editors as he strived to shed the most flattering light on each story, column, article and TV news bit. After denying for so many years the legitimate role of politics in the making of public policy, Dukakis walked enthusiastically out of sanctity and into political reality with his new close friend, advisor and manager, John Sasso.

If Sasso and Dukakis were to effectively manage the administration, they would also need the kind or resources and top-flight advisors that Dukakis had denied himself in his first term. Yet, the model for what Dukakis was striving for had already been created. The Office of State Planning, which Frank Keefe and Alden Raine used in the first term to encourage economic redevelopment of the old cities and mill towns, had been quite successful. In his new administration, Dukakis simply brought the same structure into his own office and added to it. Dukakis appointed Raine to be director of what was designated the Office of Economic Development and gave him authority to manage and coordinate the activities of roughly half the cabinet: the Executive Offices of Communities and Development, Economic Affairs, Transportation and Construction, and Environmental Affairs.

It was Fred Salvucci's idea to create an analogous senior staff position to manage and coordinate the giant human services secretariat; he had seen how well the OSP had functioned in the first term and thought that better coordination of human services policy-making could be achieved under a similar arrangement. Dukakis gave this assignment to Phil Johnston. Chief counsel Steve Rosenfeld was given added responsibility for developing and responding to public safety issues.

From the Kennedy School Dukakis brought into his new administration three important people. Ira Jackson, an administrative dean who had long been a close friend and advisor to Dukakis—his mother had been a Dukakis loyalist in the early 1960s, and he often babysat for the Dukakis children—was made commissioner of the long-troubled Revenue Department. Jackson brought impressive political and administrative skills to the new state administration; he had followed Barney Frank as "deputy mayor" of Boston under Kevin White and was a highly regarded speechwriter.

Dukakis had grown close to Nick Mitropoulos at the Kennedy School, where Mitropoulos managed its public forums and recruited top political and governmental figures to appear. In addition, Mitropoulos had been a veteran of a number of presidential campaigns and was well-liked by members of the national press corps. But mostly, he was an earthy, easygoing political animal, much like the late Allan Sidd, whom Dukakis valued as a confidant; Mitropoulos was put in charge of the sensitive area of appointments, as the administration endeavored this time to do right by Dukakis's political organization.

The third major figure of the new administration to come from the Kennedy School was Manny Carballo, who became secretary of human services. Carballo, along with Dukakis and Gordon Chase, had formed a bond at the Kennedy School; the three were the faculty members most oriented to the practical application of classroom learning. Carballo was a logical choice for the cabinet post that Dukakis had induced Chase to take, if all too briefly, at the end of the first term. The 41-year-old Carballo had begun his public-sector career in New Jersey serving in a variety of mid-level community affairs and legal services positions before being appointed as assistant counsel to the governor. He later became secretary of Wisconsin's Department of Health and Social Services. At Harvard, he taught courses in public management and chaired a faculty group that examined the relationship of government and poverty. There would be no League of Women Voters generalist or investment banker overseeing Dukakis's human services empire this time around.

Sasso convened senior staff meetings twice a week. Dukakis convened the cabinet—now, to everyone's relief, in private—roughly every six weeks. Unlike the first term, when Dukakis freed his top subordinates to pursue their own agendas, Sasso imposed a tight political discipline on the administration. Each agency head was trained; before any public announcements were made, they had first to be reported to Sasso for an analysis of their value to Dukakis's public image.

The performance of the cabinet and the agencies of government were carefully monitored by the senior staff. As he had done in the first term, Dukakis took about six inches' worth of paperwork home each night. When finished with his "homework," he would often change into workout clothes and take a brisk walk around his neighborhood clutching hand weights to keep in shape; the former marathon runner found "power walking" to be less taxing on his body. It was largely through briefing papers that Dukakis maintained his detailed knowledge of the progress of the government. The cabinet was under some pressure to match Dukakis's performance. The governor's correspondence secretary scored each cabinet secretary on the speed with which he or she responded to written communications.

The logical extension of Dukakis's new philosophy was to transplant the various interests from the coalition that helped elect him into the government itself; the coalition that had elected him was the one he had told Sasso in 1980 that he had wanted to reconstruct. It got him back into government, and now it would serve to keep him there. Michael Dukakis institutionalized listening. This time around, he would bring his campaign into his government in order never again to alienate his source of ultimate strength, and he would recruit from the ranks of the interest groups to avoid being caught short by them.

The campaign's top education advisor, with close ties to the Massachusetts Teachers Association, joined the senior staff, on a par with Raine and Johnston, as the governor's education advisor. The campaign's advisor on housing, a consultant to housing groups and authorities, became secretary of communities and development. The vice-president of both the International Association of Machinists and Aerospace Workers and the State Labor Council, a key labor organizer in the campaign, became the secretary of labor. Richard Rowland, the political director of a prominent elderly rights group, and a Dukakis critic in 1975 in his capacity as a welfare rights activist, became secretary of elder affairs.

Many of the same advocates who had marched outside the State House in protest during the first administration were brought inside in the second to fill key staff positions. In the process, the reach of the administration broadened to subsume interests that had been shut out of the power structure since Frank Sargent left office eight years before. The spokeswoman for the group that had formed to oppose Dukakis's first-term workfare program was recruited to work on job training programs for welfare recipients. A prominent legal services attorney and lobbyist became a health policy analyst for Carballo. The director of a coalition of human services groups became chief policy analyst to Johnston. A full-time consultant to the High Technology Council was brought on as an aide to Frank Keefe, whom Dukakis had named as his secretary of administration and finance.

Dukakis's intent was the same as it had been in the first administration: the creation of a reform government that fairly brokered the competing legitimate needs, requirements and demands of the people. This time, however, the debate about what that fair balance was would take place within the administration, among advocates closely associated with the various interests, and in private—not on the floor of the House or Senate, or on the nightly news broadcasts and in the next day's newspapers.

In the first term, in his misguided idealism, Dukakis voluntarily surrendered political control so that the unfettered reform impulses of an inspired body politic could work freely. In his second term, Dukakis was still the reformer, but he wanted to be the reformer in control of the government. John Sasso spent his every waking hour trying to bring the government under Dukakis's control.

Chapter 21
The Most Effective Governor in America

Soon after settling into the corner office once again, Michael Dukakis was jolted with bad news, news with a sickening sense of deja vu about it: Administration and Finance Secretary Frank Keefe was having trouble keeping the current budget, the one inherited from Ed King, in balance. Worse still, he was not going to be able to submit a balanced budget for the next fiscal year, which was to begin on the first of July. The budgetary crisis put Dukakis back on the horns of the same dilemma he had encountered in 1975.

Although the Massachusetts constitution requires a governor to submit a balanced budget, as Frank Sargent proved, there are numerous ways to make theoretical figures balance when actual numbers will not. In January of 1983, it quickly became obvious to Keefe that the current fiscal year budget was about $75 million in the red; through various administrative cost savings measures, that initial mini-crisis was temporarily put to rest. By February Keefe realized that the next year's budget, initially developed by Ed King's staff, was $300 million in the red when he added in some spending that Dukakis had promised during the campaign.

The budget crisis soon became public. First Senate Ways and Means Chairman Chester Atkins, then Senate President William Bulger, and finally House Speaker Tom McGee predicted the state would need to raise taxes if the budgetary gap were to be closed. The *Boston Globe* warned that "a major tax boost is inevitable." Everyone was propounding the same choices: cut the budget and raise taxes. With the first-term Dukakis doppelganger hovering nearby, Dukakis's top advisors considered both paths closed to the governor. To solve the problem solely by spending cuts would almost inevitably mean reducing spending on human service programs, and such a move, conjuring up memories of the 1975 "meatcleaver," would have split apart the coalition that Dukakis, Sasso and Johnston had so painfully assembled. Yet the governor could not simply call for new or higher taxes, either. Ed King had spent two million dollars on media portraying Dukakis as the candidate of higher taxes; raising taxes would only confirm that impression. "If he had raised taxes the first year back, he'd have been all done politically," said one cabinet member. "We might as well have just packed up and gone home."

Dukakis realized as much. In February he called Keefe and Sasso to his office and told them that he was not going to propose an increase in taxes and he was not going to cut spending; the Revenue Department, headed by Ira Jackson, who reported to Keefe, would have to make up the shortfall by stepped up collection from tax evaders and delinquents. "Why can't we enforce the tax laws better?" Dukakis asked. Keefe and Jackson had seventy-two hours to come up with a plan if Dukakis had any hope of getting parts of it into the next year's budget.

Seventy-two hours later, the two top fiscal and revenue aides came back with a 101-section reform measure in the form of a bill based on a lot of old revenue reform ideas that had been lingering around their respective offices for years. Jackson, one of the unquestioned marketing masters of the Dukakis entourage, labeled the proposed program as REAP, the Revenue Enforcement and Protection Act. REAP was essentially an administrative remedy designed to plug the many leaks in tax collection. In it, Keefe and Jackson proposed additional auditors for the Revenue Department, making tax evasion a felony offense, and higher fines and stiffer prison terms for tax evaders. Upping interest on delinquent accounts to 18 percent a year, the package gave the state the power to use private-sector agencies to collect delinquent accounts, to require tax compliance as a condition of any state or local license, and to terminate contracts with companies that were delinquent.

Dukakis, the master reformer, saw the potential in Keefe's and Jackson's work-up. Jackson was confident that increased enforcement and compliance with the state tax code could get the state out of its latest fiscal crisis, but Keefe had some doubts. A frontal attack on scofflaws, he thought, was risky business at best, and he doubted Jackson's estimates of how much new revenue could be raised to put the budget into balance. Besides, he had already heard that House leaders, who would have first crack at the proposal as it worked its way through the legislature, were not impressed with this latest Michael Dukakis "reform." "You won't get a dime from this stuff," the House Ways and Means Committee chairman told Keefe.

Dukakis eventually agreed with Keefe that a few new taxes and higher fees should be slipped into the bill to bring in some quick money in case Jackson could not obtain compliance from the tax cheats. The version of REAP that was eventually filed with the legislature hiked the state's cigarette tax and effectively raised the gasoline tax as well, points the administration left unmentioned whenever possible.

At a meeting with key House leaders to explain their complex proposal, Keefe and Jackson encountered some opposition. The stiffer fines and prison terms outlined in REAP were harsh, said one committee chairman. Couldn't the administration give delinquent taxpayers a grace period, some added time to make restitution without having to face court appearances and possibly worse? Since that idea had been proposed by Jackson earlier and rejected in the governor's office, an amnesty period, during which non-taxpayers could admit their guilt and pay only interest and penalties without further legal action, was added to the bill.

Jackson was one of the few people who believed in the potential of increased compliance with the state tax code. In the spring of 1983 he estimated that as much as $640 million a year in owed taxes was going uncollected. At the time, tax enforcement ranged between weak and nonexistent. Fewer than one-tenth of 1 percent of Massachusetts tax returns were audited. Penalties for evasion were notoriously lax; restaurant owners, for example, evading full payment of the state's meal taxes, were charged with only a misdemeanor.

The "new" Michael Dukakis played an active role in lobbying for passage of his bill. This time around he took the initiative, as he had not done in 1975 when faced with a similar deficit problem. Prior to the official release of the budget and tax package on March 2, he made first-ever appearances before both branches of the state legislature to press his case for REAP. Between March 3 and March 7, Dukakis made six appearances at different locations around the state to build public support for his spending and revenue programs; four thousand postcards were mailed to local officials and interest-group leaders, plus members of the Dukakis political operation, to encourage their attendance. Cabinet secretaries were given copies of a slide show prepared by Keefe's office, which Dukakis also used at his public appearances, to elicit the support of "their" people, the constituency groups that fell under their jurisdictions. Sasso and his staff brought in the leaders of eight groups singled out for special lobbying attention—spokespeople for minority, women's, labor, business, finance, elderly, multi-issue liberal and human service organizations. Dukakis was the featured speaker at annual conventions of the labor-backed Solidarity Coalition, a group that was promoting a hazardous material worker right-to-know law, and the state chapter of the National Association of Social Workers.

To one and all the message was the same: if the legislature refuses to pass REAP, they will cut programs before they will pass a tax hike. It is in your interest, the governor and his people kept saying, to help us pass the REAP legislation. Endorsements of the new revenue bill poured in from social welfare, citizen action and other groups.

At the end of June, on the day when the House was scheduled to vote on REAP, Dukakis met with House members, two at a time in his office, from eight in the morning until eight at night to explain the need for his program. Later that night, the House voted its approval of REAP, and the bill went to the less conservative and more reform-oriented state Senate, where it received quick passage. Discretion would be the better part of valor for this reform with the petty tax hikes melded in; there would be no elaborate bill-signing ceremony for REAP. In order to minimize the opportunity for his foes in the tax-limiting referendum movement to characterize REAP as an elaborate disguise for a tax increase, the governor affixed his name to the document on 4:30 p.m. on the Friday before the Fourth of July weekend. The press was not invited.

In the autumn, in preparation for a tax-amnesty period the following year, the Department of Revenue aimed at closing two delinquent businesses a day. The DOR made a point of seizing tax-delinquent property in highly visible ways, concentrating on restaurants, yachts and small planes. One of the first restaurants to be shut down for non-payment was the Aegean Fair. What the public knew was that the restaurant offered a predominantly Greek menu; what the public did not know was that the owners of the establishment had once retained a young Hill and Barlow attorney, Michael Dukakis. Ira Jackson never asked the governor if he had any problems with the singling out of a Greek restaurant, and Dukakis never complained about Aegean Fair's being made an example of. The department also began to disclose the names of major tax delinquents.

REAP worked. In its first two years, it produced a total of $292.8 million in direct new revenues, including $85 million that came in during the amnesty period, according to Revenue Department figures. On the last day of the amnesty period, more than ten thousand people lined up at the department's Boston headquarters to square things with the state and their consciences. After that, the noncompliance rate dropped dramatically. The number of people filing state tax returns increased 8 percent in the first two years after REAP. Jackson's Revenue Department attributed an additional $564 million in tax collections during fiscal years 1984 and 1985 to the program.

Effective, technocratic and non-ideological, REAP was a classic second-term solution. Best of all, it closed the budgetary gap and widened the tax base in a way in which everyone could agree. In a poll commissioned by John Sasso, 93 percent of those surveyed had a favorable view of the REAP tax collection law. In the first real test since his exile, Michael Dukakis had avoided the politically charged choices of budget cuts or tax increases through superior know-how, effective use of his political operation, and his new-found sense for communication.

After 1983, revenues would no longer be a problem. The Massachusetts economy was beginning to shift into high gear. Unemployment, which had been at 7 percent when Dukakis took office, declined steadily to just under 3.5 percent by the end of 1986. The first three years of Dukakis's second term would see annual job growth as high as 6 percent a year before dropping to 2 percent in 1986. With the economy roaring, the state was soon awash in tax receipts. In fiscal year 1984, revenues shot up $664.3 million, or 13.4 percent over the previous year. Fiscal year 1985 yielded a $759 million, or 13.5 percent, increase over 1984, the largest in the history of the Commonwealth. By 1985 the government was running regular surpluses, even though the rate of government spending increased an average of almost 11 percent a year. The economy added its own heady dose of feel-good tonic to Massachusetts politics. Governor Dukakis's chief political problem was the enviable job of allocating the riches among competing constituencies and needs.

While Frank Keefe and Ira Jackson were crafting the REAP program, Human Services Secretary Manny Carballo set about implementing a new work and welfare program. Perhaps no other public policy issue more intrigued Michael Dukakis than this. His own first-term experimentation with a workfare program for AFDC fathers had helped galvanize liberal sentiment against him, and he had grappled with the issue while out of office during private briefing sessions at his Perry Street home. Now, it was up to Carballo and Welfare Commissioner Chuck Atkins to deliver on the promise Dukakis had made to Phil Johnston and others years earlier that any work program for welfare recipients would not be coercive.

What would take the place of Ed King's more punitive workfare plan? Carballo did not have the answer when he called a group of legal services attorneys and social-service advocates, the very people Dukakis never consulted in his first term and who opposed him bitterly then, to his office to discuss alternatives. "We were all very nervous," recalled Dale Mitchell, a long-time advocate for the poor who attended the session. "We walked in and Carballo said, 'You don't have to say a word. [King's workfare] program is based on all the wrong principles. Let me tell you my basic operating assumption: women have the right to stay at home.' All of us believed that, but we were afraid to mention it because we thought it was too radical."

Carballo issued a challenge to the group: design something new that could operate within federal guidelines requiring states to have some sort of job-finding plan and that would actually help welfare recipients get off and stay off the welfare rolls— and do it within three weeks. Drawing upon their experiences as opponents of earlier Dukakis and King plans and incorporating the suggestions of Welfare Commissioner Atkins, who, as undersecretary of human services at the tail end of Dukakis's first term, had begun developing a non-punitive work program, the advocates were convinced that this time they could do business with the governor and they made their pitch. On May 17, they submitted a forty-page draft proposal to Carballo.

The result was the Employment and Training program, ET for short. The plan eliminated the coercive and make-work job aspects of previous workfare programs and offered real job opportunities to the AFDC recipients who volunteered to participate. The state's job placement and training functions were given a high administration priority, and to induce AFDC mothers to participate, Dukakis offered them money for transportation and child care. For those whose new jobs did not include health benefits, Medicaid coverage was extended for up to one year. To underscore his commitment to the Carballo-Atkins-advocates proposal, Dukakis invited the welfare commissioner to make an unusual presentation on ET to his cabinet; when the cabinet received a briefing in Dukakis's second term, it was typically made by other secretaries or by members of the senior staff, almost never by an agency commissioner.

With the help of welfare rights advocates, Manny Carballo and Chuck Atkins were able to fashion a welfare reform plan that was very much in keeping with Michael Dukakis's basic philosophy regarding the role of the state in matters of poverty. Throughout his political career, Dukakis has rejected New Deal and Great Society notions of entitlements; he never saw cash assistance payments to the poor as a solution to their most basic of needs, or, for that matter, society's needs. All Dukakis had ever needed was the opportunity to prove himself, and here he was— "the son of Greek immigrants who arrived in this country with no knowledge of English and who went to Harvard Medical School and graduated from Bates College as a member of Phi Beta Kappa," as he liked to say—the governor of Massachusetts. The Dukakises never borrowed money nor needed help. They pulled themselves up by themselves and made it in "the land of opportunity"—another popular Dukakis aphorism—by dint of effort. Through this lens Dukakis has always seen and analyzed poverty.

The Dukakis philosophy on welfare programs could have been stated as: "If you show me your desire to get to your knees, I'll help you to your feet." It was there in his first term when, as part of an undeveloped philosophy and political approach, Dukakis summarily declared that half the recipients of the state's general relief program were "employable" and therefore unworthy of receiving benefits at a time of acute unemployment, when even the most job-ready of the unemployed were finding it difficult to find work. And it was there in his failed workfare plan when he decided that male heads of households on AFDC should either get a job or be denied welfare. The sentiment led liberals to conclude that he was heartless.

ET was officially launched on October 1, 1983, but the public heard little of the program for eight months. Michael Dukakis had been embarrassed once before with his workfare plan, and Ed King's contribution to getting people off welfare and into jobs was an even greater failure. Dukakis told Atkins and Carballo at an earlier cabinet meeting that he did not want any claims to be made for ET until there were some successes to which he could point. That day came in June 1984 at the American Optical Corporation plant in the suburban town of Framingham; the firm produced contact lenses and had hired some ET program graduates. Dukakis announced that the state had exceeded its initial goal of placing five thousand welfare mothers in full- or part-time jobs by one thousand placements.

It was to be Manny Carballo's greatest accomplishment as Massachusetts human services secretary, but he was not present when the announcement was made. On January 27, 1984, at the age of forty-two, Carballo died of the disease lupus after a long illness that had kept him away from his office for half of the time he occupied it. As a memorial to his friend from their days at the Kennedy School, Michael Dukakis established an annual awards program named after Carballo to honor meritorious public servants, state agency divisions and programs.

To Michael Dukakis, poverty has always been a state from which people can climb if they have the desire, if they will assume a personal responsibility for themselves, and if government can provide the ladder. With ET, the governor finally had the ladder that he had been seeking for many years. But he did not find peace with his historic adversaries on the political left despite the rave reviews he received for switching gears and backing a program as innovative and as progressive ET. Dukakis was made to seem cheap and unsympathetic early in his second term when he fought off a judge's order requiring that the administration propose enough money for welfare programs to close the so-called poverty gap—the difference between what an AFDC family received in benefits and what the federal government says it costs to live in Massachusetts. The estimated cost for closing the gap was put at $500 million, half of which was the responsibility of the state and half the responsibility of the federal government. Though Dukakis asked for and got less for AFDC recipients than the human services community would have liked, benefit levels went up by 32 percent over the four years of his second term.

Meanwhile, a combination of administrative and legislative initiatives added monthly clothing allowances and rent supplements for those recipients not living in subsidized housing to the benefit package. Infusions of new money made available nutritional and medical-service programs for pregnant women. In the second budget of his second term, Dukakis restored medical coverage to the general relief population, a benefit that he and the legislature terminated in 1975 at great political cost to Dukakis.

Not all of Michael Dukakis's attempts at consensus-building proved as successful and as free of controversy as REAP and ET. The administration's posture on a worker protection bill made critics question Dukakis's willingness to risk controversy or disagreement for the sake of principle in the name of his new-found fondness for consensus-building, partnerships and coalitions.

To cement the support of organized labor for the 1986 election, Dukakis promised to produce a right-to-know law, one that would let workers and community residents discover what chemicals a company was using. Organized labor, Mass Fair Share, a citizen action group, and MassPIRG, the state chapter of the Ralph Nader student organization; and other health organizations favored a comprehensive law that would require firms to keep on file safety data sheets on any one of a hundred thousand chemicals and compounds if those were used at their plants. These sheets would be available for inspection by workers and community residents. The business lobby, on the other hand, favored no bill at all, though they would later submit a proposal to list only about five hundred chemicals.

In June 1983 industry spokespeople called the initially proposed right-to-know bill "totally unacceptable"; labor and community activists countered that the industry alternative was tantamount to a "right to know nothing." This dispute, with a Dukakis promise the imperative behind it, was a classic test of consensus government. The two sides were nowhere near achieving a compromise on the issue, and the labor-backed bill was stuck in the House. Al Raine served as Dukakis's shuttle diplomat on the negotiations, while Evelyn Murphy, the secretary of economic affairs, worked with business, and Paul Eustace, the secretary of labor, worked with the other side. The negotiations were conducted in Dukakis's name, never in his presence, until his negotiators were close to finding a middle ground that was acceptable to both sides.

At Murphy's suggestion, Dukakis called business and labor leaders to arrange two meetings at Dukakis's house on Perry Street. On the first night, three business leaders, representing high tech, defense contractors and the manufacturing industries' lobbying group, sat down with Dukakis in his living room. "Here is the principle you've stood for: that your employees ought to be protected from harmful chemicals, right?" was how Dukakis posed the question. "Can we all agree on the principle?" he wanted to know. The businessmen could hardly have disagreed. "Good," the governor said, "let's let the staffs work out the details." Nothing of substance had occurred except that one side in the negotiations had given tacit approval to a yet-to-be finalized compromise.

The next night Dukakis had a similar meeting with the leaders of organized labor, Arthur Osborne, the state president of the AFL-CIO, and his first assistant, along with Labor Secretary Eustace. Changing the titles and names, Dukakis used the same successful script he had employed the previous night, this time adding a flourish. During the talk Dukakis asked, "Can I get you guys a beer?"

When his appreciative guests said yes, Dukakis adjourned to the kitchén, whence he returned moments later with a single can of beer and two glasses, which the laborites nursed until the meeting broke up. The beer story, reiterating Dukakis's sober and catchpenny image, laughingly made the rounds among union members in the days that followed. But Dukakis produced on his campaign promise to create a right-to-know law.

When final details were worked out in October, the bill required 2,500 substances to be be listed, with the possibility of more being added at the decision of the state commissioner of public health. Access, however, was strictly limited. A worker could demand to know the chemicals around which he was working, but requests from community residents would first have to be ruled on by the state Department of Environmental Quality Engineering. Anyone disclosing to "unauthorized parties" information gleaned through the right-to-know process would be open to prosecution and as much as a five-thousand-dollar fine.

Critics argued that the law was such a watered-down compromise that it provided no real protection to workers or neighbors, but Dukakis's defenders countered that the law was a good deal more than an abstract commitment and, in any event, was as much as the disputants and the political climate would have allowed.

No one disputed that Dukakis had ushered in a new era of political management on Beacon Hill; after ten months in office, the Dukakis model of government by consensus had become a fixture. Of the right-to-know law, the *Boston Phoenix* wrote: "[T]he compromise bill...represents a victory for Michael Dukakis, and for the way he believes government should operate in matters of high controversy. This is especially true given the governor's interest in applying these tactics to future issues, where the success of the technique in one case strengthens his hand in the next." The confrontation style of the first term was clearly a thing of the past.

At the end of his first year in office, in mid-December, with REAP and ET rolling along, with the right-to-know bill signed into law, Michael Dukakis granted a series of interviews with the print and broadcast media to assess his first year back in office. When asked by a reporter to choose the top headline of 1983, Dukakis became thoughtful, as was his new-found wont. "Well," the governor answered, "I'd have to say it's that people are working together and getting things done without a lot of bitterness."

Reporters winced, hoping for something more dramatic as they considered the leads for their reports, but Dukakis was not in office to entertain the scribblers from the fourth estate. He was in office to make government work, and a sign of his success was the dearth of screaming headlines emanating from Bulfinch's Golden Dome. At the start of the term, John Sasso had said that, after a term of the earlier Mike Dukakis and one of Ed King, the next governor would have to bring stability with him. Measured against his goal, the reworked reform government of Mike Dukakis was an unqualified success. Gordon Chase and Manny Carballo would have been proud.

Chapter 22
Going National

The stability and calm that Michael Dukakis had brought to his new, improved reform government bathed the normally warring factions on Beacon Hill in luxuriant good will. "He's grown incredibly as a person," observed a longtime legislator who, at times, had thought of Dukakis as a bit of a jerk. "He's come to appreciate that while he's bright, there are other people just as bright, and that while he's honest, he certainly hasn't cornered the market on integrity."

Dukakis's new amiability did not come naturally. He had always been impatient with small talk, what Fran Meaney had been so good at in the early years as Dukakis groped his way to the top. He worked at it as part of the job he had chosen for himself, and he got the act down convincingly. At political gatherings, wrote a columnist, "he still looks like nothing so much as a statue of Calvin (or perhaps Coolidge) with a Cheshire Cat grin grafted on. But he's trying, and that isn't lost on the legislature."

"We all have our egos in this business," said House Majority Leader Charles Flaherty, "and I don't care who you are, when the governor calls you up to thank you, you've got to feel a little bit of self-importance." Since he had come back to office, the governor had been making a lot of calls to say thanks. When the House Education Committee chairman rewrote an elementary education reform bill in 1984, Dukakis said thanks and adopted the measure as his own. When, as a result of the booming economy and the success of REAP, Dukakis proposed a tax cut only to have the House Ways and Means Committee make it more progressive, Dukakis said thanks for the improvement.

The rigid and uncompromising performance of his first term in a way became the standard by which King's four years of profligacy and incompetence were judged. The two terms marked the extremes of political behavior that the people had rejected. Between those extremes lay a broad range of reasonable political behavior, and, in his second term, Dukakis settled in to govern reasonably, with broad public support.

Michael Dukakis had learned how to be governor; he created and staffed a government that worked. He and John Sasso had built a management structure for the government that effectively and efficiently dealt with the vast majority of problems that emerged. The senior staff had the information it needed and the authority to move the cabinet and the agencies of government to do the will of the governor. Without histrionics, Massachusetts became a one-party state for all intents and purposes, and Dukakis became master of the party, the benign boss of all things political. The government and the party came to include all but the left and right fringes.

So grand was the coalition—ranging from the teachers' unions, which were interested in higher wages and better benefits, to the association of cities and towns, which was interested in keeping personnel costs down—that somehow the component parts had to be convinced they shared common ground. It was Sasso's job to convince them that the success of one group was the success of them all. To accomplish this, the administration maintained a short list of top priorities. New initiatives and projects made it to the list only when those at the top were dispensed with. "If you were a member of the coalition and your priority was number five, it was obviously in your interests to push priorities one through four," said a long-time observer of and advisor to Dukakis. "And John knew he had to move the short list quickly enough so that the line wouldn't grow too long and restless, but slowly enough so that the people understood they were in line waiting for Michael Dukakis—quickly enough for them to have a sense of movement, but slowly enough for them to feel bound and obligated. John knew just how fast to turn the spigot."

The effectiveness of the Dukakis administration seemed all the more remarkable after the dissonance the previous governors—Ed King and a very different Mike Dukakis—had created on taking office. But then, neither of them had had the advantage of four years of practice and four years of review at the Kennedy School.

A moderating calm fell over Massachusetts in 1984, just in time for the presidential election. Although he had been back in office for only a year, already Dukakis was attracting the first stirrings of national attention, thanks to Ira Jackson's REAP. On January 17, 1984—the same day Dukakis delivered his annual address to the legislature—TV viewers of the national network news saw the dramatically successful tax amnesty element of the REAP reform featured.

Over the course of the election campaign, both Dukakis and Sasso insinuated themselves into the center of national Democratic politics. For Dukakis, it was a matter of being in the wrong place for Walter Mondale at just the right time. After initially holding back while waiting for the field to settle out—Ohio senator John Glenn's campaign was financed to a large extent through the efforts of Bob Farmer, who was Glenn's national campaign treasurer—Dukakis endorsed the candidate of the Democratic establishment, former Vice President Mondale. After Gary Hart upset Mondale in the New Hampshire primary, Mondale and his wife Joan were in Boston for a state political party dinner, guests of Michael and Kitty Dukakis, when the news came in that Hart was beating Mondale in the Maine caucuses. This setback had not been expected, and it was another body blow to the Mondale campaign, leaving it gasping for air. In the campaign's darkest hour, the Dukakises and the Mondales sat in a Boston hotel room and commiserated about the depressing turn of events. Northern New England was harsh on Walter Mondale, but Dukakis promised that he would do everything he could to help Mondale bounce back in the March 13 Massachusetts primary.

Dukakis was true to his word. He personally campaigned tirelessly for the former vice president and tried to rally his organization, but the cause was hopeless. Gary Hart's campaign was coming into full flower just as the Massachusetts primary campaign took center stage. His youthful energy and outsider's image appealed to Democratic primary voters, who tended to be suburban, and looking for a way out of the old New Deal arrangements. They wanted nothing to do with the candidate of the Democratic special interests that seemed to be the core of the Mondale coalition.

Nonetheless, when Mondale finally secured his nomination, despite his trouncing in Massachusetts, out of respect, affection and appreciation for Dukakis and his effort on his behalf, Mondale put Dukakis on his short list of candidates for the vice presidential nomination. Dukakis was Mondale's insurance policy against the possibility that his first-tier choices—New York congresswoman Geraldine Ferraro, San Francisco mayor Dianne Feinstein and San Antonio mayor Henry Cisneros—would self-destruct during the background and security checks. When Ferraro passed muster and was anointed, she gave up her position as the chairperson of the party's platform committee; Dukakis moved in to present the platform to the convention. The transition was made easy by the presence of a key Dukakis operative, Susan Estrich, who had served as Ferraro's top aide during the actual platform-writing months.

John Sasso, whose reputation had been growing, especially with New York governor Mario Cuomo, was drafted by the Mondale braintrust to manage the Ferraro campaign. With Dukakis's approval, he took a leave of absence in July and spent the summer and fall traveling the country with Ferraro. The Ferraro campaign was buffeted, seemingly from beginning to end, with charges and allegations about her husband, John Zacarro, and his business dealings; at the end of the rocky road for the Mondale-Ferraro campaign, Sasso had an appreciation of the difficulties of running a national campaign.

He also had the opinion that his real boss, Mike Dukakis, had what it took to run for president. "Dukakis was what the party needed," said Sasso. Voters "didn't trust us Democrats on fiscal and economic issues to run the country. We were all heart and no hands. [Gary] Hart was intriguing, but he had no hands. He'd never run anything."

Sasso wanted to begin thinking about the 1988 presidential campaign, but Dukakis would not hear of it. Quite literally, Dukakis refused to countenance even the most casual conversation about presidential politics: not from Sasso, not from Kitty, who, like Sasso, saw no reason why Dukakis could not become a viable presidential candidate in four years, and not from Bob Farmer, who was excited at the thought of raising millions for a Dukakis campaign.

Since the day he returned to office in 1983, Dukakis had his eye focused on the 1986 gubernatorial election. In his victory over Ed King he had been vindicated, but he had not had his performance as governor validated. For that, he needed to be reelected as an incumbent governor. He would never forget how Ed King had snuck up on him back in 1978, while memories of the blizzard danced in the heads of his supporters. The last thing he wanted was to be thinking beyond 1986.

Nonetheless, if Dukakis was to have the option of thinking about a presidential run after the 1986 gubernatorial election, planning had to begin immediately. For this, Sasso turned to a group of his close friends and advisors, with whom he had been meeting regularly on Thursday nights in his office over pizza or Chinese food. The members of the Thursday night group included Assistant Welfare Commissioner and longtime aide Tom Glynn, the issues director of the 1982 campaign and a designer and marketer of the successful ET welfare reform; media specialist Dan Payne, who had worked on the 1982 campaign; Professor Ralph Whitehead of the University of Massachusetts, a political demographer who was developing a model of a ''new collar'' voter who was politically independent and economically cautious, but dedicated to personal freedom; and Revenue Commissioner and chief speechwriter Ira Jackson. Pollster Irwin ''Tubby'' Harrison would attend from time to time, as would other members of the governor's staff. With this group, Sasso began plotting ways to get Dukakis's name and his accomplishments before a national audience. ''We talked about how to avoid screwing up the possibility of Michael's becoming a presidential figure,'' said Dan Payne. ''We never talked about how to actively pursue the presidency.''

It was the Thursday night group that came up with the term ''The Miracle of Massachusetts'' to describe the state's economic turnaround, and it was the group that decided that Dukakis ought to become intimately associated with the complexities of the economy so that he could convincingly assert some ownership of it. Dukakis understood what Sasso was trying to do and endorsed the idea. Even though Sasso thought of his effort as having a political purpose, Dukakis saw it as consistent with his role as an innovator and leader of the Democratic party; by the end of 1984, he had come to view his state as a laboratory for progressive policies, as a model of reform government for other states to follow. The more the country knew of REAP, the tax revenue collection plan, and ET, the welfare reform, the more other states might consider adopting them. He voiced no objection to Sasso's attempts to market his accomplishments.

It was a perfect marriage: Sasso's desire to position Dukakis as a potential 1988 presidential candidate and Dukakis's desire to market his successes. As Sasso was planting the seeds of a national campaign in New York and Washington, back home Dukakis was immersing himself in the complexities of Massachusetts' booming economy. Knowing that Dukakis preferred to learn from experience, rather than from briefing papers, John DeVillars, the chief of operations in the governor's office, came up with the idea of a ''Creating the Future'' project, in which Dukakis would spend long periods of time at companies renowned for their innovative and entrepreneurial spirit. ''The goal was for Michael to go out and learn about the Massachusetts economy, what was making it tick, and what the state could do to sustain it,'' said DeVillars. Politically, the goal was to further identify Dukakis with ''The Miracle of Massachusetts.''

In all, Dukakis visited thirty-six different companies, from the nationally known Ocean Spray Cranberries, which produces cranberry and other juices and cranberry products, to small firms working with advanced technology in fields such as photovoltaics. The naturally upbeat Dukakis returned from these trips ebullient about entrepreneurial spirit around the state and more than a bit pleased when he learned that the chiefs of these firms, unlike their counterparts during the late seventies, appreciated his efforts to stimulate the state economy.

In mid-1985 Dukakis was named by Paul Kirk, the chairman of the Democratic National Committee, to chair the party's Committee on the Industrial and Entrepreneurial Economy, which had been created to help develop a policy agenda for the party. For his work on the committee, which included Missouri congressman Richard Gephardt, as well as more than two dozen municipal, state and national party leaders, Dukakis pulled together a group of local academics and economists to discuss national issues. The group included Thomas Axworthy, the chief of staff of former Canadian prime minister Pierre Trudeau, who was associated with the Center for International Affairs at Harvard; Rosabeth Moss Kanter of the Harvard Business School, a specialist in entrepreneurialism; William Spring of the Federal Reserve Bank of Boston, a longtime Dukakis and former Jimmy Carter advisor; Kennedy School economists Dutch Leonard and Robert Reich; David Birch of MIT, an economist and consultant specializing in small business developments; and Ezra Vogel of Harvard, an East Asian economic development scholar.

By the end of 1985, the Pax Dukakis had existed for two full years. Dukakis's hegemony over the Democratic party was so complete that Ed King had given up hope and joined the Republicans. As the stability continued, Dukakis, if anything, was becoming even more popular. Acting on another idea conceived by the Thursday night group, he introduced a proposal for a one-time $64 million tax rebate, and by the time Barbara Anderson and the Citizens for Limited Taxation had had their say, Dukakis happily signed the largest state tax cut ever that included the repeal of what Ed King had insisted on calling the "Dukakis surtax."

Over the course of the term, Dukakis fought drug abuse, making ads with Bernard Cardinal Law of the Roman Catholic Archdiocese of Boston, and worked hard on a similar issue that cut across ideological lines: drunk driving. Dukakis ordered weekend roadblocks to get drunks off the highways, instituted "Operation Last Call," a sting operation which targeted bars serving intoxicated patrons, and put a stop to "happy hours," when bars discounted drinks to bring in business.

It was obvious to most observers that, barring a miracle, Dukakis would stroll to his reelection. At the end of 1985 he had no putative opponents in either party, but Dukakis was determined to keep running scared, and Bob Farmer continued to accumulate campaign contributions to discourage the thought of anyone mounting a serious challenge to the incumbent. It was also obvious to Sasso that, if Dukakis was to keep open the option of deciding later to make a run for the presidency, the ground would have to be laid immediately. Campaigns to secure a party nomination had become two-year affairs in recent years, and Sasso did not want lesser candidates to pass by his man.

In January 1986 Sasso began to showcase the incumbent governor seeking reelection who could not talk of the matter himself. Taking advantage of contacts he had made while managing Geraldine Ferraro's campaign in 1984, Sasso began to interest the national press corps in ET and REAP: creative, non-ideological reforms that were transferable from the state to the federal level. After so many years of personal hype from presidential contenders selling character, vision and honesty, Sasso was selling substance. And Washington was buying.

On February 6, 1986, two days after President Reagan suggested an overhaul of the federal welfare system in his State of the Union address, Dukakis was in Washington as the kickoff presenter of the Democratic National Committee's new "Spotlight" series, DNC chairman Paul Kirk's program to show the nation that state and local Democrats had plenty of "new ideas" to offer the nation. After Reagan's speech, a reporter at a news conference, the *Boston Globe*'s Walter Robinson, asked the president why, if he was interested in getting people off welfare, was he proposing the elimination of the work incentive program that was helping finance Dukakis's ET program, "which has taken twenty-three thousand people, trained them in jobs and taken them off welfare." Reagan answered with a misstatement of fact; he said that "what Governor Dukakis is doing in his state is what we did in California."

Dukakis jumped at the opportunity to challenge the president's claim as "inaccurate. It reflects a lack of awareness of what's happening [in Massachusetts]," Dukakis said. The dispute was good for a long story in the *Washington Post* by staff writer, Massachusetts native and Sasso confidant Sidney Blumenthal.

To introduce Dukakis to the opinion-makers of Washington, Sasso got House Speaker Tip O'Neill to host a reception for Dukakis in the Speaker's private dining room—something that O'Neill rarely did. Several members of the United States Senate showed up as well as many national news correspondents. From Washington Dukakis and his entourage flew off to promote ET in South Carolina. Along with him, Dukakis brought Ruby Sampson, a former welfare recipient who had gone through a forty-four-week ET training program and was at the time working in a Boston hospital surgery unit as a technician. Sampson, the daughter of a Georgia sharecropper, ate dinner in the governor's mansion in South Carolina to help Sasso promote Dukakis's political future while she and Dukakis were promoting his program.

In early February the *Washington Post*'s influential columnist Mary McGrory wrote a laudatory column on Dukakis's ET program that focused on Ruby Sampson, who was termed "a star graduate" of her state's superb job training program. "She is a living, breathing can't-stop-smiling example of how a person can escape the trap," wrote McGrory. Two days after the McGrory column was published, Dukakis was back in Lowell, a national model for urban renaissance, as the main attraction of the U.S. House budget committee's regional road show. He urged a federal REAP to help close down the federal deficit. The next day, ET and the governor were the stars of an "ABC News Special Report" on welfare programs that work.

Later in the month the national Democratic party's Committee on the Industrial and Entrepreneurial Economy brought 150 Democrats from around the nation to Massachusetts, where chairman and host Michael Dukakis led the interested visitors on a tour of successful examples of economic growth, Massachusetts style, Dukakis style. "The first effort to test the waters," as DeVillars put it, had proved enormously successful. It wasn't just that Sasso knew how to market, or that Dukakis had a couple of creative successes to talk about. The time was right for Dukakis.

"We have a unique situation now," noted Kirk O'Donnell, former staff chief to House Speaker Tip O'Neill. "The Congress is stalemated with the president over budget deficits, while a number of states are running budget surpluses that allow them to promote new programs and new ideas. Democratic governors are showing that in these states, government is part of the solution."

But the sudden interest in Dukakis went beyond the reemergence of state government as a laboratory for democracy. Sasso had been correct: Dukakis did seem to have the heart and the hands. Moreover, as Dukakis had been insisting for years, the left-right, liberal-conservative construct was of little use in explaining him. He was not a liberal, or a conservative, or a moderate, properly speaking. Rather, Michael Dukakis had come to exist almost completely outside of and beyond the New Deal matrix. He had taken a step away from the entire New Deal era which imprisoned the Democratic party through a shopworn vocabulary and a set of arrangements forged in the Depression. Dukakis was next year's model, even as he was promoted and marketed by John Sasso the old-fashioned way.

Back home, the coalition that had elected Dukakis mostly on faith—given the intentionally vague positions of his campaign against Ed King—had reason to believe that their faith had not been misplaced. When Dukakis declared, on a cold day in January of 1983, that helping the thousands of people sleeping on heating grates, in alleys, doorways and subway stations was his very first priority, he had meant what he said. When Dukakis took office, there had been only two state-supported shelters for the homeless. By 1986 there were more than sixty. The state was spending some two hundred million dollars on food, housing and services for homeless people.

Dukakis had set up a homelessness program that was second to none in the nation. In addition, the administration also approved plans to invest hundreds of millions of dollars in modernizing the state's mental health facilities and programs. All told, over the four years of his second term, appropriations for human service programs increased 31.5 percent.

The second term would also bring on an aggressive implementation of the governor's core beliefs in growth policy. Eight state-funded urban-heritage parks, aimed at enhancing city centers, were completed, and another five were funded and planned. The administration pressed ahead, over Reagan administration opposition, to win upwards of $2.5 billion to build a third tunnel to connect the Massachusetts Turnpike with Logan Airport, and to sink and widen—and thus alleviate the quotidian clogging of—the Central Artery through Boston. A quarter of a billion dollars were sunk into modernizing port facilities in and around Boston

Harbor. A major prong of the metro-Boston subway was rerouted to improve public transportation and promote development in Boston's economically depressed minority neighborhoods, and another prong was extended north through Cambridge to increase public access and reduce traffic into and out of Boston; both projects had been initiated during Dukakis's first term and completed in his second.

Older and emerging businesses received considerable attention as Dukakis refined his thinking on economic development matters. The Mature Industries Act of 1984 created an Industrial Services Program to provide services to older firms, and an Economic Stabilization Trust Fund to help ailing companies and their workers reorganize and refinance their operations.

The state's Centers of Excellence Program, while minimally funded, nonetheless committed the state to backing and promoting emerging technologies in areas such as photovoltaics, polymer plastics and applied technology. Michael Dukakis had clearly failed to heed the earlier warnings of state high-technology executives who had wanted, in his first term, nothing more than tax cuts from their governor. By the end of his second term, Dukakis's favorite word had become "innovation," the topic of speech after speech.

Al Raine's Economic Development office became a combination welcome-wagon and one-stop-shopping agency for new businesses; it identified needs, helped arrange financing and discussed potential environmental problems. Most importantly, Raine tried to match companies with regions, pushing new development toward depressed areas of the state.

Dukakis, with his elaborate system of reform government by consensus, had fashioned a record that won praise in most quarters. Often elements in the grand coalition felt frustrated that they had only gotten half of the pie and complained that they should have gotten more, but it was hard to find an element in the Democratic coalition that felt mistreated or betrayed—hard, but not impossible. In 1985 the gay community became outraged after Dukakis ordered two happily adjusted foster children removed from the care of a couple of gay men following a *Boston Globe* article revealing the placement and claiming neighborhood opposition to the practice.

Despite the protests of social workers and leading clinical psychologists, along with those of the gay community, Dukakis refused to budge. Even as he ordered increased lobbying pressure on the legislature to pass a gay rights bill that would prohibit discrimination against gays, the protests continued. But the bitter disagreement with the gay community, his ongoing struggle with welfare rights advocates who wanted higher benefit levels to close the poverty gap for AFDC mothers, and the opposition, led by a radio talk-show host, to Dukakis's proposal to mandate automobile seatbelt use, were the only significant failures in the politics of consensus Dukakis practiced through the flush economic years of his second term, which, as voters in Massachusetts had come to expect of Dukakis, was scandal-free.

The best expression of the fondness Democrats had for Dukakis came during the Democratic party state convention in June. This was the forum Dukakis had divined as the best expression of democracy, where citizen-activists came together to choose party leaders and express themselves on the issues of the day. Dukakis had used the newly restored caucus-convention system to begin his rematch comeback against Ed King in 1982. Now, four years later, the convention of delegates in Springfield was ready for something of a coronation.

There were no Barbara Ackermanns or Tom O'Neills challenging him from the left, no Bob Quinns or Ed Kings standing in his way to the right. For the first time in his life, Michael Dukakis was unopposed within his party for a statewide election. For delegates at the convention held four years earlier, the tribal war between incumbent governor Edward King and former governor Michael Dukakis meant fratricide. But when Dukakis, triumphant that November and now transcendent, strode to the microphone at the Springfield Civic Center to accept the endorsement by acclamation of the nearly five thousand delegates, his demeanor—confident, relaxed and unthreatened—suggested the totality of his triumph. The composition of the convention reflected how completely he had consolidated his control. The road to Springfield Friday afternoon was rife with cars affixed with D'Amico, DeNucci, Murphy, Shannon, Myerson, Spiegel and AFL-CIO bumper stickers, but, almost without exception, the cars also proclaimed: "I'm With The Duke."

As be began his acceptance speech, Dukakis was playful. "Those of you who have been up to my office in the State House know that I've got a portrait of Sam Adams hanging over my mantlepiece. He was a great revolutionary, a great governor, and he was from a family of great political leaders who achieved great things; first here in Massachusetts, and then in the highest office in the land, the presidency. Often I look at the portrait for inspiration. Sometimes I can almost hear old Sam Adams's voice. I can hear him saying, 'Dukakis, if you play your cards right, maybe someday, just someday...they'll name a beer after you.' "

The normally businesslike Dukakis had begun to joke about "the presidency," but he still would not talk about it. Not to his chief of staff and campaign manager John Sasso, and not to his wife. "I couldn't talk with Michael about it," said Kitty Dukakis, "because it takes two to have a conversation."

But she spoke of it with others. On an evening early in the summer, Chuck Atkins, the enormously successful welfare commissioner who had not only crafted the ET program but also managed to restore the confidence of a wary public in his agency, went to the Dukakis home in Brookline to tell the governor something of a personal nature. After a long and enjoyable eight and a half years with Dukakis, dating back to the first term, when Atkins came along with Gordon Chase to serve as Dukakis's undersecretary of human services, Atkins had decided to leave state government for a private sector job.

Dukakis would not hear of it, and he proceded to explain all the benefits, of both a personal and professional nature, that might accrue to his talented commissioner if he would just stick it out a big longer. When Kitty Dukakis pulled up to the rear of the house in her car, Dukakis called it a night and ushered Atkins out the front door. Kitty ran through the house to give her friend a warm embrace.

The following morning, Atkins received a call from Kitty Dukakis, "How'd it go?'' she asked, foregoing any small talk. "Great," responded Atkins, "I never had a better talk with Michael and I've decided to stay."

"No, not that," she interrupted. "What'd he have to say about the presidency?" The subject had never come up, Atkins reported, to the dismay of the governor's wife.

Dukakis persisted in his determination to run a full-throttle campaign for reelection, as if he were haunted by the ghost of Ed King, circa 1978, even though the Republicans, less than four months from the primaries, still did not have a serious candidate. During the spring and early summer, the GOP actually had two candidates at one time or another, but they were decidedly not serious. One, Greg Hyatt, the New Right populist who, as director of Citizens for Limited Taxation, ran the Proposition 2½ in 1980, was ready to run at the state convention in April until a former employer held a news conference to charge that Hyatt had been guilty of "bizzare behavior." A secretary, among other accusations, said she saw him standing naked in his office, and that he sometimes spoke into his telephone with no one on the other end of the line.

In light of the Hyatt stories, the Republican conventioneers picked a bombastic state representative from the wealthy, western suburban town of Wellesley, Royall Switzler, to be their sacrificial lamb. For a month and a half after getting the convention nod, Switzler did nothing. Then, on June 3, he revealed that he had lied about his military record on previous campaign brochures where he had called himself a captain and a member of an army Special Forces unit who had seen action in Vietnam; in fact, he had only been an army sergeant, had not served in the Special Forces unit (though he had undergone some Special Forces training), and had been to Vietnam only once, while on a short leave from Korea, where he was serving non-combat duty. When his Democratic colleagues in the House publicly recalled his references in debate to having seen people die on the battlefield in Vietnam, Switzler responded, "I've seen people die in Vietnam on TV."

Switzler withdrew after his admission, but Hyatt returned to the battle. The end of his star-crossed campaign came after a *Boston Herald* article in mid-July reported that a law-enforcement wiretap had recorded Hyatt, about a week after the Republican state convention, soliciting campaign contributions from an accused extortionist and possible gunrunner whom federal law enforcement officials suspected of having ties to organized crime.

The Republican state committee empaneled a blue-ribbon commission, headed by former governor John Volpe, to find a candidate qualified to run. They ended up with another Greek-American: George Kariotis, the founder of Alpha Industries, a Route 128 high-tech company, who volunteered to take on Dukakis. Although Kariotis had served in Ed King's cabinet, he had never run for office before, but he was wealthy and willing to underwrite much of his own campaign, an important criterion since GOP leaders could not look forward to anything resembling a successful campaign finance operation by that time. On July 22 the party gave its nod to Kariotis, and the race for governor finally began.

Ironically, the Republican Kariotis was one of the first businessmen to raise significant money in 1970 for Democrat Mike Dukakis when the young state representative ran for lieutenant governor. Earlier, in 1963, after Kariotis had founded Alpha Industries, he retained Dukakis, then a young Boston lawyer, to draw up new wills for him and his wife. Kariotis called an end to his financial support for his fellow Greek-American in 1974, when he came to believe that Dukakis was too liberal for his tastes.

Kariotis was smart, blunt and inexperienced, and he had an impossible time getting his campaign off the ground. As he had known, he had to answer questions about his company's guilty plea to a federal kickback charge in 1985. Alpha executives had paid $57,000 to a Raytheon Company executive for a pledge that Raytheon would help Alpha land a sizeable radar-jamming equipment subcontract for the Air Force's EF-111 fighter jet. Kariotis, who was not involved with the company's day-to-day operations at the time, although he had retained his position as chairman of Alpha's board of directors, said he had no knowledge of the matter beforehand, as did the federal prosecutor of the case. Nonetheless, the story was damaging.

What Kariotis did not expect was the deluge of other accusations that followed. The very day he announced, a former assistant attorney general with close ties to the Dukakis camp, reminded the press that in 1985 Alpha had paid a sixty-thousand-dollar civil fine to settle a suit that the state had brought charging Alpha with violating the state's water-pollution laws. Later, he had to answer charges that the Revenue Department had assessed him a penalty for the late payment of the state's sales tax for a yacht he had briefly moored in Massachusetts after his Delaware charter-boat service had gone out of business.

Kariotis's one hope of salvaging something from the campaign was the single debate which had been scheduled for October 27. Obviously, it was not meant to be his or anyone else's year besides Mike Dukakis's. As things turned out, the debaters came to the podium at the same time as the Boston Red Sox were taking the field to start game seven of the 1986 World Series against the New York Mets. The moderator of the debate introduced the non-event to "whoever is out there."

A week later, Michael Dukakis stood on the stage of the grand ballroom of the Park Plaza Hotel in Boston, where a happy but proper crowd—a Dukakis crowd—celebrated his 69-31 percent record victory. Finally, Michael Dukakis had achieved ratification. His victory in 1974 was mostly a vote against the status quo. In 1982 again, while vindication was sweet, the most Dukakis could distill from his victory was that the voters preferred him to Ed King. But in 1986, his reelection to a third term was achieved on the basis of how he and his government had performed. It was an affirmation of the course on which he had been all along in redefining political values and expectations in Massachusetts.

Recalling some of the many fights and the many victories of his long career, Dukakis smiled happily. "Friends," he said, "this is the sweetest one of all." Now, maybe, he would be willing to talk about the presidency, Sasso thought. So did Bob Farmer, who had amassed a $400,000 campaign surplus. It was money that could be rolled over into a federal election fund so that a presidential campaign would not be strapped at its start. But Dukakis put off presidential talk until he and Kitty could get away for a vacation.

Chapter 23
A "New Path" to the White House

Michael Dukakis's third inaugural address, which he delivered on January 8, 1987, was not a typical full-of-thanks, full-of-promises speech. The rhetoric was there, prepared by John DeVillars after a month-long process that included many hours of consultations with senior staff and cabinet members. The agenda for 1987, according to Michael Dukakis, the bootstrapper who believed that the role of government was to help those who would help themselves, would be a frontal attack on some of the root causes of poverty that a state government could mitigate. The speech was labeled "Bringing Down the Barriers," a reference to the barriers to opportunity that have meant "generational poverty and dependency for too many." Michael Dukakis's remedies for these problems were: stricter enforcement of child support laws; enhanced efforts against drug and alcohol abuse, leading to "drug-free schools by 1990"; a major assault on adult illiteracy, including the establishment of a volunteer-based Citizens' Literacy Corps; and programs to reverse the alarming upward trends of teen pregnancy and school dropout rates.

But this ambitious plan, and the rhetoric that went with it, was not what the speech was remembered for. On the morning of his inaugural, Michael Dukakis called John Sasso and DeVillars into his office and handed them a page of type-written notes which he had prepared at home, additional comments that he wanted appended to his speech. The two aides, who had spent a good part of the last two years marketing Michael Dukakis and his "new ideas," doing so to position their boss for a presidential bid, read the sheet, looked up at one another and smiled.

Michael Dukakis was finally going public; he would take the opportunity of the inaugural to inform the people of Massachusetts of what many had wanted to hear all along, that he was thinking of running for president. Without ever mentioning the office, Dukakis added a page of remarks to his prepared speech that included a reference to "some awesome decisions" that he had to make "in the next few months." In words that suggested that his mind was made up, Dukakis added, "And whatever decision I make, I want you to know that being governor of Massachusetts has been the richest, the most fulfilling and the most enjoyable experience anyone in public life could possibly ask for."

There had been hints for weeks that an announcement of some sort was coming.

Bob Farmer, Dukakis's chief fundraiser, had told inquiring reporters how much he thought a presidential race would cost and how much he thought he could raise. Dukakis himself had indicated that something was in the works when, on election night in November, he quoted a lyric from a hit song by the rock group, Timbuk3: "The future's so bright, I gotta wear shades." Coming, as it did, from the mouth of the jazz-loving son-in-law of a violinist with the Boston Symphony Orchestra, the quote, so out of character, only served to fuel speculation.

But Dukakis had not given the idea of running for president much thought. In November, one week after defeating George Kariotis, Sasso asked Dukakis if he would now, finally, like to focus on the presidency. Dukakis told him that he wanted to enjoy the victory, take a vacation, and relax over the Thanksgiving holiday with his family. He did, however, agree to take a memo along with him on his holiday, prepared by Sasso and reviewed by members of his Thursday night group, which detailed the steps he could take as he prepared to make his decision.

Dukakis also agreed to let Sasso set up a series of out-of-state speeches and meetings with local officials from around the country, and phone conversations with prominent Democrats, so that he could assess his chances and get a feel for what it would take to run a national campaign. "We did a mini-campaign for ten weeks," said Sasso, "so that Dukakis could answer the questions he had about running." Uppermost on Dukakis's mind were: Could he be prepared to decide the issues a president had to deal with—very non-gubernatorial issues such as defense policy and arms control? Could he win given the field he would be up against? Could he run and still govern Massachusetts? And what would it all mean for him and his family? Sasso was never certain that his man would take the plunge. "He's one of the few people I know who could look around with so much going for him and say no," the staff chief said.

Sasso was not the only one with a vested interest in Dukakis who was looking for a sign that the just-elected three-term governor would go national. The Boston media was nearing a frenzy in response to the rumors that Dukakis might run. So extensive was the coverage of Dukakis that a National Governors Association (NGA) hearing in Iowa on February 5, attended by Dukakis, became better known for the large size of the Massachusetts media delegation hovering around Dukakis than for anything the governor said or did. When a reporter leaned over to Boston television correspondent Andy Hiller and asked, rhetorically, why they were all there, he answered his own question by saying, "I guess we're all waiting for a wink." Hiller followed up the remark with a story broadcast back to Boston which dubbed Sasso's mini-campaign as the "wink-watch." The name stuck.

The "wink-watch" kicked off in Washington, D.C., where, on the third of February, Dukakis testified before a Senate committee hearing on welfare reform; the Massachusetts governor once again held up his enormously successful ET program as a model. The next three days were spent in Iowa, the home of the first-in-the-nation Democratic party delegate selection caucuses. In addition to co-chairing the NGA hearing (on the subject of jobs, growth and competitiveness), Dukakis attended a benefit for the Iowa Democratic party. On the eleventh, he flew to North

Carolina, where he participated in a forum on "Emerging Issues" hosted by former governor James Hunt.

During the late winter, as he was agonizing over his decision, Dukakis asked for advice from close friends and party elders. One of these was Jerome Grossman, a "father" of the peace movement whom Dukakis had known for years. It was Grossman who helped talk Eugene McCarthy into running for president in 1968, and who was a key financial backer of George McGovern four years later; he also served on the Democratic National Committee from 1972 to 1980. In Massachusetts, he organized Father Robert Drinan's anti-war Congressional campaign in 1970.

"He asked me to come over to Perry Street to talk to him and some of his fundraisers about whether he should run," said Grossman. He had prepared a paper on running for president, one that listed the "eight paths" Grossman believed could lead to the White House, and he gave Dukakis a copy of his paper to read. The eight paths to presidential nomination included: controlling the party apparatus, as Mondale had done in 1984; gaining the allegiance of a personal constituency, as Reagan had done in 1980; riding the crest of an overwelming issue, as McGovern had done in 1972; engaging in a permanent campaign, as Carter had done from 1974 to 1976; campaigning as a national hero, as Dwight Eisenhower had done in 1952; and proving one's self a charismatic orator, as William Jennings Bryan had done three times around the turn of the century.

Grossman said Michael and Kitty "fought with me" over whether there were any other ways to run. "Mike said, 'Hey, I don't fit any of the eight paths. Are you trying to tell me something?' I said, 'No, it's you're choice; if you don't fit, it's up to you.' He said, 'What do you think?' 'No,' I said, 'you don't fit any of the eight paths.' " The meeting ended with Dukakis acknowledging that he had a lot to think about.

After taking a few weeks off the mini-campaign trail, Dukakis picked up his schedule again early in March. On the sixth, he delivered what his aides viewed as the most important speech he would make during this period. It was the keynote address at the annual dinner of the New Hampshire Democratic party. Dukakis enjoyed considerable popularity in neighboring New Hampshire, the site of the first-in-the-nation presidential primary election; that much was known. What Dukakis himself did not know was whether he could deliver a rousing speech, the kind he would have to make if he had any chance of moving a nation of activists and voters in the months ahead.

Dukakis worked harder in preparation for this speech than he had for any other in his life, and so did his staff. Ira Jackson was brought in to work up the themes and the actual text; a speech coach was recruited to help Dukakis with his always slightly preachy and usually low-keyed delivery; and Jack Corrigan made certain that the Sheraton Wayfarer in Bedford was jammed with Dukakis partisans to make the governor feel welcome and comfortable. The New Hampshire speech was going to be the final-threshhold test of the mini-campaign, and John Sasso was taking no chances.

Dukakis was introduced by Paul McEachern, who had lost a bid to become governor the previous November in a general election contest against the Republican incumbent, John Sununu. During that campaign, Dukakis had hosted a fundraiser for McEachern at the Brookline home of Bob Farmer, at which fifty thousand dollars was pledged for the Democratic challenger in the final weeks. In his opening, Dukakis quipped that he and his family had talked "about whether this spring wouldn't be a good time to climb the presidential range" of New Hampshire mountains.

Dukakis spoke about what his state and New Hampshire shared—the Red Sox, the Celtics, the New England Patriots—and their "common history" when New Hampshire volunteers fought side by side with brethren from Massachusetts as the battles for the independence of a new nation were fought, and of the rivers they shared that powered the early mills as the region entered the industrial age. The Massachusetts governor closed his remarks by telling, for the first time in any detail, of the odyssey of his immigrant parents, who had touched down in America on both sides of the Massachusetts-New Hampshire border seventy-five years earlier, with little but a "burning desire" for a better future.

In between, Dukakis referred back to many of the themes that had worked so well for him as governor over the past four years: creating economic futures, community, opportunity for all, and the tearing down of barriers. For a man not known for his rhetorical inspiration, the speech was considered his very best. He was enjoying the mini-campaign, and it showed; he had passed the final test. The New Hampshire speech was tantamount to an announcement, although a formal declaration would not come for another ten days.

Five days after the New Hampshire speech, Dukakis was back in Washington, to testify on housing issues before a Congressional sub-committee during the day, and later that evening to deliver the keynote speech to the Children's Defense Fund, a liberal advocacy group. The following day, March 12, Dukakis headed south one more time, to Baton Rouge, where he was the main speaker at the annual dinner of *Louisiana Business Reports*, a regional business magazine. In the heart of oil-producing America, Dukakis reiterated his opposition to oil import fees, a position that was anathema to hard-pressed domestic oil producers.

During these days, John Dukakis, who was working for U.S. Senator John Kerry and living in Washington, D.C., was calling Perry Street constantly, wanting to know if his stepfather had revealed what his decision would be. Back home in Brookline, on Saturday morning, March 14, Dukakis calmly announced to Kitty that he had made up his mind. All the recent travel experiences, all the many phone calls—to every Democrat who had run in the last three elections, many of the managers of those campaigns, twelve governors and fifteen senators—had convinced him, as John Sasso believed, that he could run and that he could win.

Sasso got the call to come over to Perry Street, the scene of many political campaign planning sessions over the years, on Sunday. The answer was yes; he would announce on Monday. Sasso assembled his Thursday-night group for a meeting that very night.

Dukakis would not actually announce, Sasso told the group; that occasion would be held for later. Instead, he would hold a press conference the next day to announce the formation of a presidential campaign committee. To the surprise of no one, Sasso, seemingly always one step ahead of events, produced a draft of a statement that had been prepared by Marty Kaplan, a vice president of Walt Disney Studios of Los Angeles.

Kaplan, an acclaimed speechwriter for 1984 Democratic presidential nominee Walter Mondale, was the husband of Susan Estrich, a professor at Harvard Law School and a veteran political operative and confidante of Sasso's. Early the previous week, just days after Dukakis's impressive New Hampshire appearance, Sasso had his assistant, Jack Corrigan, contact Kaplan and ask if he would be willing to prepare a statement. Kaplan agreed; he wrote the draft on Thursday and telexed it to Boston the following day. On Sunday, Kaplan joined his wife in San Francisco, where she was assisting Geraldine Ferraro at a conference at which the main speaker was Walter Mondale. Only then, when they called Sasso to find out what, if anything, Dukakis was going to do with the statement, did they learn that Dukakis would use it the following day.

On Sunday evening, Tom Glynn and Jack Corrigan reworked the Kaplan draft. John DeVillars prepared a list of questions that reporters might be expected to ask at the following day's press conference and answers Dukakis might want to give. Nick Mitropoulos put together the list of people to be called, including family members and local and national party figures. One of the calls the candidate made went out to anti-war leader Jerome Grossman. "Jerry, it's Mike Dukakis," he said. "I know I don't fit any of the eight paths. But I'm going to create a ninth path— and I want your help."

At his press conference on Monday, Michael Dukakis expressed the rationale for his campaign. As he had done throughout his political life—from his first successful campaign in 1959 when he engineered the takeover of the Brookline Democratic town committee, through his 1966 bid to become state attorney general and his attempt to become lieutenant governor in 1970, to his fourth campaign for governor in 1986—he placed the emphasis on issues of personal character. And why not? Hadn't he been the catalyst for the transformation of politics and government in Massachusetts? Hadn't he systematically replaced the grafters with the whiz kids, inspired by his presence to try their hand at public service? A state that once was a political embarrassment, encouraging national magazine features on corrupt politics, had become a model of probity, effeciency and creativity. Wasn't this the Dukakis legacy: a political system reformed from within and solidly in place? "[A]t the end of this campaign" Dukakis stated in his prepared remarks, "in the privacy of the voting booth, I believe the American people will ultimately entrust the presidency to one of us on the basis of who we are.

"I welcome the test. Americans ought to measure our integrity. They have a right to know our values. The next president of the United States will face challenges that no campaign position paper can possibly anticipate. But what can be measured in advance is the character of the person who will confront those challenges."

Dukakis asked a series of questions that he assumed were on the minds of voters, the kinds of questions that he hoped would be asked because they so neatly dovetailed with his themes of integrity, values and character. ''I can imagine Americans trying to picture each of us in the White House. They'll ask themselves: ''What kind of people will he surround himself with? Will he really be in charge? Will he tell us the truth?''

Six months later, after Dukakis had emerged as one of the leading Democratic candidates, those questions, when restated, took on a cruel irony. On Wednesday, September 30, Dukakis stunned his local supporters and the press by revealing that his campaign manager, John Sasso, and his campaign political director, Paul Tully, a veteran of many presidential campaigns—two of the most important people surrounding him in his quest for the presidency—had supplied videotapes to three news organizations, tapes which, when used by two of them, helped derail the presidential candidacy of Delaware senator Joseph Biden.

The content of the tapes was hardly sinister: footage of Biden, speaking during a recent televised candidate debate in Iowa, talking about his family roots and the inspirations that had lead him to a career in politics; and footage, from a paid TV advertisement, of Britain's Labor Party candidate, Neil Kinnock, saying almost precisely what Biden had said—only months earlier. Unfortunately for him, at the Iowa debate, Biden had failed to credit Kinnock with the rhetorical flourish he had used.

The *New York Times* and the *Des Moines Register* reported on Biden's apparent plagerism, in itself hardly a crime, but the video inspired new stories. Out of the woodwork came other examples of political plagiarism, and a story that Biden had been forced to repeat a law school course after he had been called up on charges of plagiarism on a paper that he had written.

All of a sudden, the nudge Sasso had meant to set Biden back on his heels helped push him over a cliff—just as Biden was preparing to preside over a U.S. Senate confirmation hearing on President Reagan's nomination of Appeals Court Justice Robert Bork to the Supreme Court. When Biden folded his campaign, the press took an interest in who had deep-sixed him. The *Des Moines Register* reported that the Biden-Kinnock story had been captured in an ''attack'' tape provided by a rival camp.

Time magazine attempted to determine who put out the Biden-Kinnock story. Unnamed sources at the *Des Moines Register* fingered the Dukakis campaign. News reports on Sunday, September 27, reported that the next issue of *Time* would claim that the Dukakis campaign had helped do in Biden. The story was a problem for Dukakis; of all the candidates in the Democratic field, he had gone out of his way to claim the moral high ground for himself.

In a brief telephone conversation on Sunday night, Sasso told Dukakis about the upcoming *Time* article, although he did not hint at its accuracy or his own role in distributing the tapes, and he told Dukakis he did not know what *Time* was going to say. Dukakis did not seem particularly concerned. He did not ask

Sasso directly if the campaign had been involved in the Biden tape affair, but he told Sasso to look into the matter.

On Monday Dukakis, off the campaign trail, met with the Boston press in his role as governor. Asked about the *Time* article, Dukakis came as close as possible to issuing a categorical denial that his campaign had a hand in the Biden-Kinnock matter. He said if a campaign staffer had been involved, he would very likely fire the person. Dukakis had come back to Boston to prepare for a gala fundraising event Tuesday night at the World Trade Center on the waterfront, a sparkling monument to Boston's rebirth as an international port of call for the computer age. As many as ten thousand supporters were scheduled to attend; Bob Farmer expected to bank close to one million dollars, adding more luster to the best-financed and most far-flung Democratic campaign in the land.

When he learned what Dukakis had said at the news conference, Sasso knew that Dukakis's virtual denial had forced his hand. At 4:00 p.m., as Dukakis was getting ready for the gala party where he was to play the trumpet during the finale, Sasso told his boss and close friend the truth: *Time*'s story was correct. He, in fact, had sent out the tapes.

Dukakis was shocked. He had to think this through—and he had ten thousand guests to entertain in just a couple of hours. Concerned that Kitty would not be able to suppress her fury at the fundraiser, Michael did not tell his wife until later. He conjured up his best "the show must go on" facade and played the happy host as he shook hundreds of hands and made small talk with friends and supporters; Dukakis had always been able to compartmentalize problems while dealing with other requirements and responsibilities. But he could not keep his mind from the revelation. Not until their driver let them off at 85 Perry Street did Michael tell Kitty what he knew. They stayed up all night agonizing over the devastating news.

On Wednesday morning Dukakis met with Sasso to discuss what was to be done. Sasso said that he had to resign, but Dukakis could not bring himself to accept that reality. His responsibility to his campaign was in conflict with his instinct to support Sasso, whom he described as "like a brother" to him.

Fourteen years before, Dukakis had lost his real brother, Stelian. Riding his bicycle in Brookline, Stelian was struck in a hit-and-run accident and suffered irreversible brain damage. While he was in the early stage of his first campaign for governor, Michael visited the hospital daily to sit with his comatose big brother, who finally died four months later, in July. Though the emotionally troubled Stelian had been a burden and an aggravation for Michael, trying at one time to undo his political career, Dukakis remained loyal to and supportive of Stelian to the very end. Now it was his impulse to be true to Sasso. At a hastily called news conference, at 11:00 a.m., Dukakis announced the bitter news but said Sasso would remain with the campaign after taking a two-week leave of absence. However, Sasso was not looking at the problem in familial terms. He knew he had to go.

From Washington and elsewhere, calls flooded in to Dukakis's campaign and State House offices from supporters—including both Massachusetts senators, Ted

Kennedy and John Kerry—and the advice was overwhelming. Sasso had to go. At 3:00 p.m., an emotional John Sasso came out from the background to hold a news conference of his own. He announced that Dukakis had accepted his resignation and that of political director Paul Tully. Sasso's thirty-three month effort to manage Michael Dukakis's political fortunes to the White House was over. Throughout the day, Dukakis and Sasso called one another a number of times, but they never had a complete conversation; each attempt was cut short as one or the other, or both, broke down in tears.

As he often had done in times of trouble, Michael Dukakis turned to his trusted friend, Paul Brountas, his law school classmate at Harvard and the chairman of his recent campaign committees, to help him sort out the choices before him. In addition, Dukakis instructed his campaign's legal counsel, Dan Taylor, a partner at his former law firm and a confidant, to conduct an internal investigation to ascertain the extent to which other members of the campaign staff might have been involved with Sasso in the making and distribution of the Biden-Kinnock tape.

Dazed but not overwhelmed, Dukakis stuck to his prearranged campaign schedule. On the day following the Dukakis and Sasso news conferences, Dukakis flew to Hartford, Connecticut, to pick up the endorsements of the Connecticut House speaker and the Senate president, plus fifteen of their colleagues. On the flight, Brountas presented Dukakis with a preliminary list of candidates for campaign manager. Dukakis asked him to continue to make his calls and to conduct his interviews. There were many people who needed an explanation from someone close to Dukakis and who had suggestions to offer. Dukakis also told Brountas to add the name of Susan Estrich to the list.

Later that day Dukakis attended a fundraiser in Massachusetts, followed by a speech at the annual Manny Carballo awards dinner, and then he flew off for a three-day, seven-hundred-mile campaign swing through Iowa. The trip returned memories of 1981 when the out-of-office Dukakis traveled Massachusetts from one border to its opposite, issuing apologies for the many mistakes he had made during his first term in office. But this was not 1981; likely Iowa Democratic party caucus-voters who came out to meet the Massachusetts governor were not as concerned with the tape story as Dukakis and his entourage had expected them to be. His mea culpas, nineteen delivered at as many stops, were, for the most part, accepted and brushed aside.

Six days after his dramatic Wednesday press conference, Governor Dukakis appeared before a rare, closed-door session of the Massachusetts House of Representatives; the galleries were emptied of spectators and the media. He was there at the invitation of the House Speaker, to personally lobby on behalf of the most complex piece of legislation that had been introduced in decades. It was Dukakis's ultimate reform effort.

One month before Dukakis had filed a bill to require all Massachusetts employers to provide health insurance to each of their employees; the unemployed who were not eligible for the federal Medicaid medical benefits program would be covered by a new state health insurance agency. In addition to the ''universal health-care coverage'' provision, the bill would totally revamp the state's health-care system by, among other things, changing how much and the way by which hospitals are paid for their services; establish a large state agency combining the health-care and regulatory functions of others to purchase insurance on behalf of the uninsured and those employed by small businesses; and overhaul the health-insurance industry by beginning the process of taking away the non-profit status of the giant Blue Cross-Blue Shield insurer. The health insurance reform bill threatened hospitals, insurers, health mantainance organizations, big businesses and small businesses—all these groups worked determinedly against the Dukakis initiative.

Within a matter of hours after the governor had made his private pitch for his bill, the House voted overwhelmingly against him on a preliminary amendment, and further action on the bill was tabled. In the climactic reform effort since his return to office—a reform that was far more encompassing than his no-fault auto insurance success of 1970 or his court reform achievement of 1977, efforts that stretched over two years each—Michael Dukakis had suffered his second setback in a week.

But this was a preliminary bump in the road. He vowed to return to the House with a revamped bill. The next day, one week after accepting John Sasso's resignation, Dukakis picked Susan Estrich to be his new campaign manager.

With his reformer's zeal still undaunted and his campaign back on track, Michael Dukakis continued his quest.